Dear George,

One of the best things about writing this is how many times I get to mention Inc in a McGraw Hill book! Hope we can work on a book one day...

CUSTOMER CHEMISTRY

soon?

Sincerely,

Susan

CUSTOMER CHEMISTRY

How to Keep the Customers You Want—and Say "Good-bye" to the Ones You Don't

MARY NAYLOR and **SUSAN GRECO**

McGraw-Hill

Chicago New York San Francisco Lisbon London Madrid Mexico City
Milan New Delhi San Juan Seoul Singapore Sydney Toronto

Library of Congress Cataloging-in-Publication Data

Naylor, Mary.
    Customer chemistry : how to keep the customers you want—and say "good-bye"
to the ones you don't / Mary Naylor and Susan Greco.
        p.   cm.
    Includes bibliographical references and index.
    ISBN 0-658-00144-2
    1. Consumer satisfaction.   2. Marketing.   I. Greco, Susan.   II. Title.

    HF5415.335 .N39   2002
    658.8'12—dc21   2001052133

McGraw-Hill

*A Division of The **McGraw·Hill** Companies*

1 2 3 4 5 6 7 8 9 0   LBM/LBM   1 0 9 8 7 6 5 4 3 2

ISBN 0-658-00144-2

This book was set in Janson Text
Printed and bound by Lake Book Manufacturing

McGraw-Hill books are available at special quantity discounts to use as premiums and sales
promotions, or for use in corporate training programs. For more information, please write to
the Director of Special Sales, Professional Publishing, McGraw-Hill, Two Penn Plaza, New
York, NY 10121-2298. Or contact your local bookstore.

This book is printed on acid-free paper.

To my mother, Karen, who believed in my entrepreneurial dream when no one else did. Here's to the wonderful mom who truly made her child's dream come true. Thanks for always being there.

To my father, Frank, whose love and encouragement always kept me going.

To my brother, Wes, whose friendship and caring kept a smile on my face and in my heart.

To Marc, whose unconditional love and support has kept me going through the toughest times and has made the good times even better.

To my first customer, The John Akridge Company, who took a big chance on a small upstart. You made it all possible.

—MARY NAYLOR

To my parents, Joan and Eric, and in memory of Bob Rockwell, who inspired everyone he knew to read great books.

—SUSAN GRECO

CONTENTS

Preface   xi

Acknowledgments   xv

Introduction   1

CHAPTER 1 THE CUSTOMER DATING GAME
RULE 1: KNOW YOUR CUSTOMERS   11

Attention All Companies at the Crossroads:
  Are You Making Money Yet?   12
Can You Really Know Customers?   13
Start with the Most Promising   16
Six Stumbling Blocks   16
Overcoming the Obstacles   19
The Quest for Customer Chemistry   19

CHAPTER 2 THE CUSTOMER RATING GAME
RULE 2: RANK YOUR CUSTOMERS   23

Much More Than a Feeling   24
Eight Ways to Rank Customers   27
And the Winners Are . . .   33
Let Your *Best* Customer Pick Your *Next* Customer   35
How Start-Ups Can Rank Customers Before They
  Have Any   36
Ranking Pays Off   39

CHAPTER 3   EMPLOYEES ENTER THE CUSTOMER-
CHEMISTRY EQUATION
RULE 3: TEACH EMPLOYEES TO FOCUS ON
BEST CUSTOMERS AND PROSPECTS   43

Build a Workplace Where Chemistry Can Grow   45
Find Employees Who Care   46
Train Employees to "Get It"   48
Share Your Best-Customer Profile with Employees   52
Teach Employees to Be Detectives   56
Help Employees Stay Focused   60
The Customer-Chemistry Team   62
Capitol Concierge Best Practices   63

CHAPTER 4   ENGAGING CUSTOMERS IN A
CONTINUAL CONVERSATION
RULE 4: NEVER STOP LEARNING
ABOUT YOUR CUSTOMERS   75

Make Every Customer Contact Count   77
Opportunities for Customer Contact   82
The Role of Technology   88
The Mechanics of Customer Contact   93
The Customer Database   99
The Web Difference   104

CHAPTER 5   HOW TO REACH YOUR BEST CUSTOMERS
RULE 5: CREATE TOP-OF-MIND
MARKETING CAMPAIGNS   107

Top-of-Mind Marketing Is a Mind-Set   109
Top-of-Mind Marketing Is Personal   110
Top-of-Mind Marketing Is Timely   111
Capitol Concierge Best Practices: The Top-of-Mind
   Marketing Campaign   113
Top-of-Mind Marketing Online   115
Top-of-Mind Marketing Is Value Added   121
The Top-of-Mind Marketing Budget   123

CHAPTER 6   HOW TO ENHANCE THE CHEMISTRY
RULE 6: TREAT YOUR BEST CUSTOMERS LIKE
YOUR BEST EMPLOYEES—RECOGNIZE AND
REWARD THEM   127

Customers Need Recognition   129
Customer Loyalty Programs   131
Designing a Loyalty Program for Service Firms   135
Operational Rewards   137
Capitol Concierge Best Practices: Saying Thanks   139
Doing Something Special—Customer Events and More   141

CHAPTER 7   WHEN THE RELATIONSHIP
DOESN'T WORK
RULE 7: SAY GOOD-BYE TO BAD CUSTOMERS
AND DYSFUNCTIONAL RELATIONSHIPS   147

Dealing with Dysfunction   149
Circumstances for Saying Good-Bye   152
The Customer Life Cycle   157

CHAPTER 8   THE CUSTOMER-CHEMISTRY CHECKUP
RULE 8: TAKE THE PULSE OF
YOUR RELATIONSHIPS   159

Taking the Pulse in a Changing Economy   162
The Five Ws (Who, What, Where, When, and Why)
    of Staying in Touch   163
Seven Proven Pulse-Taking Methods   166
Creating Your Own Economic Indicators   179

CHAPTER 9   CONCLUSIONS, PREDICTIONS, AND
CHEMISTRY CHECKUP QUIZ   183

The Making of a Marriage   186
Review of the Rules   187
Beginning the Journey   188
Farther Down the Road   189

Customer Chemistry and the New Economy: Our Predictions   191
Customer-Chemistry Checkup   195

References   199
Suggested Readings and Resources   205
Index   223

PREFACE

When I stumbled into the entrepreneurial world, I was an optimistic and somewhat naïve twenty-four-year-old who had no formal business training. I founded Capitol Concierge with the goal of placing a concierge in the lobby of every office building in Washington, D.C., and I got off to a quick start, making the *Inc* 500 list of America's fastest-growing private companies in 1994. By then I had placed concierges in eighty-five office buildings, housing seventeen hundred companies and close to fifty thousand people in our nation's capital. But, as entrepreneurs know all too well, building a company can be a roller coaster ride of highs and lows and unexpected twists and turns. I fought just to hold on. As I struggled to find the right success formula, my company's mistakes outweighed its successes three to one. But it was through this long discovery process that my most valuable business lesson of all emerged, which we will share with you in the pages to come.

When all is said and done, a successful business is about building sustainable customer relationships. I believe all great relationships start with great chemistry, which I define as mutual interests that can be nurtured over time. Wouldn't it be great if life equipped us with a road map for building successful relationships? The reality is that we learn by trial and error.

I was fortunate enough to have my trials and errors featured in the October 1995 *Inc* magazine cover story written by Susan Greco. The process of working with Susan to chronicle my company's journey enabled me to step back and formally document our road map for successful customer relationships. Since the article appeared, I have received thousands of phone calls, letters, and e-mail messages from other business owners and managers. Many are eager to learn about the evolution of Capitol's strategies for getting closer to customers. What's surprised me is that just as many want to know how I got started in business. When I speak at conferences, I hear the same questions: "How did you get the idea for your company?" "How did you make your first sale?"

The short answer is that the concept for the company came pretty easy—it was pure serendipity—but the first sale was very hard to make. I conceived the idea for Capitol Concierge in midair. During a cross-country flight, I read about this little California company offering a hotel-style concierge service for corporate clients in commercial office buildings. With a little imagination I was able to envision this working in D.C., my hometown. Thus the name Capitol Concierge.

But my catchy name wasn't much help when it came to selling the idea. I had no sales experience and no contacts in the real estate community I hoped to crack. One door after another shut in my face. No one wanted to take a chance on a brand-new entrepreneur until I had a few feathers in my cap. Everyone said, "This is a great idea, but I don't want to be your guinea pig. Come back when you've done it." It was a classic catch-22. The banks wouldn't talk to me either, but I didn't lose hope. After my parents gave up on the dream of their daughter becoming a lawyer, they supported me all the way. My mother lent me $2,000—with interest—to start. I marched down to Mail Boxes Etc. and rented an address. My mom dusted off an old lawyer's desk in the basement for me. Finally, eight long months later, I had one. A real live customer!

But almost as soon as I was in business, I had four competitors undercutting my fees. My profit model flew out the window. The good news was that when some of my rivals folded, I picked up accounts. The bad news was that to make payroll, I had to race from bank to bank (they were talking to me by then). I called it "lifestyles of the poor and pitiful." I knew then something was fundamentally wrong.

In my fourteen years as CEO of Capitol Concierge, I have experienced a number of turning points along the way to building a lasting and profitable $5 million business. At the start of each chapter in this book, I give you my recollection of a crucial moment in the company's start-up history. I tell each story to let you know it wasn't easy. Building customer relationships takes time. The chemistry isn't always instant. It's something I work on cultivating with customers every day.

—Mary Naylor

When I first met Mary in May of 1995, it was one of those happy accidents. I was in search of a good story, and Mary appeared at my lunch table. And not just any lunch table: it was the annual gathering of the fastest-growing privately held companies in America. Mary was, as we say in journalism, a "hot lead." To my delight and to the delight of my editor, her experiences at Capitol Concierge provided an excellent case study of a cutting-edge approach to business known as one-to-one marketing. I wrote the story. But as I listened to her then, I knew there was more to the story. I also figured it would take time to unfold.

Over the last decade, Capitol Concierge has experimented with relationship marketing, database marketing, as well as one-to-one marketing—better known today as CRM, or customer relationship management. But Mary found no one strategy did the trick. How could it? What she's discovered transcends all the marketing initiatives. She's mastered more than techniques. Mary has experienced firsthand what it means to develop a bond with customers, what we call "chemistry"— the kind that makes customers say, "I love that company!"

What I loved about working on this book was the chance to present the viewpoint of real businesspeople at growing companies just like yours. We did not turn to consultants for their solutions to tricky dilemmas like how to rank customers or how to say good-bye to customers who don't fit your company's mission. Instead we talked to company owners and managers—in short, the people who know the score.

—Susan Greco

ACKNOWLEDGMENTS

I would like to express my heartfelt thanks and gratitude to my fellow team members, past and present, at Capitol Concierge, Inc. and VIPdesk, Inc. Over the years, each of you has contributed invaluable lessons to my own entrepreneurial journey.

I wish to give special thanks to a few individuals. Thank you Sally Hurley for your unwavering support, dedication, commitment, and friendship. Special appreciation to my mentors, Mark Teitelbaum and Cal Simmons, for your wisdom and guidance. I could never have made it without the core Capitol Concierge team: Bridget Barrett, Helena Durant, Lynda Ellis, Ingram Link, Chris MacBride, Lori Naylor, Andrea Wade, and Dana Wright. My gratitude to my fellow entrepreneurs for your ears throughout the years, Mark Morris and Diane Beecher, and my YEO and YPO forums.

Finally, to those of you who made this book possible. Thank you, Gina Martin. Your tenacity, diligence, and positive attitude truly pulled us through. You are one in a million. To our editor, Danielle Egan-Miller. I can't thank you enough for your guidance, insights, patience, and encouragement. And last but certainly not least, my coauthor, Susan Greco. You saw something in our little start-up company years ago. It has been a pleasure and privilege to share our adventure with you.

—Mary Naylor

This book culminates several years of reflection and research. I want to thank my husband, Douglas Dalke, for being my cheerleader throughout; my four sisters, Loretta, Nancy, Peggy, and Janet, for their can-do attitude; and my children, Casey and Christopher, who spurred me on with questions like, "Is the book almost done?"

I want to thank *Inc* magazine, which has provided me with an incredible perch for the last 12 years from which to observe and write about how smart entrepreneurs build successful businesses. I've had a chance to learn from the best, including the CEOs of the fastest-growing companies in America. I also gleaned a great deal from the example of *Inc* founder Bernie Goldhirsh, who knew how to connect with his customers in a big way. Many *Inc* staffers past and present have helped shape my ideas about business, which in turn informed this book. I want to thank the editors I've worked with over the years. The "short list" includes Nancy Lyons, Karen Dillon, George Gendron, Josh Hyatt, Elyse Friedman, Tom Richman, Jeff Seglin, and Michael Warshaw.

In particular, Michael Hopkins, *Inc* executive editor, showed me how to take hot concepts like one-to-one marketing and make them relevant to an audience of growing companies. *Customer Chemistry* reflects my continuing quest to bring compelling business trends into focus for entrepreneurs in a way that's immediate and dramatic. I am indebted to all the company owners who so agreeably shared their stories and advice. My gratitude also goes out to my team of talented young reporters: Maria DiMento, Rebecca Dorr, Libby Ellis, Andrea Forker, and David Weliver. They brought Chapter 8 to life with a variety of thought-provoking and unusual company examples.

In my personal life, many at Faith Lutheran Church in Andover, Massachusetts, have been wonderful mentors and friends, especially Wilma Breiland, a longtime manager at Lucent, who shared her business wisdom and inspired me to believe I could complete such a large project; Catherine Lowery, Sue Morin, Chris Hayward, and Pastor Jon also offered moral support.

Author and guerilla-marketing guru Jay Conrad Levinson stressed to me the importance of writing a detailed outline—you were right, Jay. But no good book is ever completed without the help of a watchful editor. Danielle Egan-Miller possesses an unwavering eye for what's missing and helped guide this book to reaching its full potential. Finally, I want to thank Mary, who opened a new door when she invited me to write this book with her.

—Susan Greco

CUSTOMER CHEMISTRY

INTRODUCTION

In human relationships chemistry has been described in various terms. It's that indescribable *something* that makes two people fall for each other. It's animal attraction. A physical sensation. Although falling madly in love hardly feels logical, researchers tell us that what we feel is actually a chemical reaction that begins in the brain. That's an interesting distinction for business relationships as well. In the rush of making the sale and signing the deal, we fall head over heels for the client. It's the infatuation phase of romantic love. Like any crush, our customer relationships can end in a hasty breakup or go on to bloom into a deeper professional friendship rooted in respect and shared interests.

If the deal we've done is a smart one, there's reason to truly care for the customer. It's not capricious. One measure of any business relationship is reflected in the courtship period. Was getting that first sale a very rocky road? How about the next sale? Your financial numbers often tell the story—of healthy margins that kept your business alive, or hoped-for profits that never materialized. And the numbers don't lie. Chemistry is, by definition, a synthesis or analysis of the facts.

What Is Customer Chemistry?

Chemistry is one of those things shared by two. When it's not, you can't fake it. Customer chemistry is not serendipitous; it does not happen by chance; you must discover it and cultivate it. We define customer chemistry as all the tangible and intangible factors that lead you to believe there's a future with a customer. At its heart, customer chemistry is a mind-set that demands complete and brutal honesty. Where is the business really making money? No assumptions, just reality. Take a hard look at each customer relationship and face the facts. Which customers have yielded the most repeat business? Greatest margins? Most referrals? New product ideas? And which customer relationships have not really "clicked" after years of high hopes? Our heartfelt advice: take emotion out of the equation and get down to business. Since you can't focus on all customers equally, you naturally start with customers at the top of your list today. At the same time, you need a model for new customers, a way of rating your prospects so you don't spend time on those who are less likely to be worthwhile.

By focusing your energies on a select universe of customers, you can devote more time to each, learning about their individual needs. What information is most important to know and how should it be gathered? We consider the advantages of various methods from on-site visits to website surveys. Once a company understands what makes each VIP customer tick, the next level of customer chemistry begins. This level calls for not one marketing plan, but one for each customer. You can create individualized plans for pursuing key sales prospects as well.

When customer chemistry reaches its peak, nearly everything about the relationship is tailored and individualized. When this plays out in the business-to-business (B2B) world, for example, employees spend more time at customer sites than at their own offices. When this occurs, you're no longer estimating when customers *might* buy—you're part of the buying process. Clients are no longer paying for your products, they're paying for your intelligence. It's the best business model there is. Finally, when you enjoy real customer chemistry, it's a lot easier to turn away the wrong kind of business. You don't need it.

We have endeavored to break down what we've learned about customer chemistry into a few essential principles, the eight rules listed below. Each chapter of this book is devoted to one of these rules. Reflecting on our list, we realized our eight rules are a pretty good prescription for how to run a company in these fast-changing times. We live in an age of Internet anonymity, and yet more than ever people want to be recognized as individuals. This holds true for customers as well.

The Eight Rules for Building Customer Chemistry

1. Know your customers.
2. Rank your customers by being brutally honest.
3. Teach employees to focus on best customers and prospects.
4. Never stop learning about customers.
5. Create top-of-mind marketing campaigns.
6. Treat your best customers like your best employees: recognize and reward them.
7. Say good-bye to bad customers and dysfunctional relationships.
8. Take the pulse of your relationships.

The Insider's Guide to Creating Customer Chemistry

Rule 1: Know Your Customers

If you're too busy putting out fires, you can't focus on what really matters. In Chapter 1 you'll learn that the stumbling blocks to knowing customers are many, but they can be cleared. For consumer companies it's tough to even identify customers by name. In the B2B world there are other barriers like getting stuck in the infatuation stage of a customer relationship. The quest for customer chemistry begins with a resolution to know which customers value you as much as you value them.

Rule 2: Rank Your Customers by Being Brutally Honest

Chapter 2 presents eight ways to rank your customers so you can concentrate on the winners. You'll learn how to let your *best* customer pick your *next* customer as well as how start-ups can rank customers *before* they have any.

Rule 3: Teach Employees to Focus on Best Customers and Prospects

In Chapter 3 you'll find out how to learn more about ideal clients by training employees to be detectives. The process starts by finding employees your customers will love and mentoring them well.

Rule 4: Never Stop Learning About Your Customers

Chapter 4 tells you to make every contact count by techniques such as starting conversations and getting customers to reveal themselves as well as twenty-five other ways to learn more about customers. We discuss technology: tracking your customers by database, making use of the Web, and avoiding technology pitfalls.

Rule 5: Create Top-of-Mind Marketing Campaigns

You'll find out in Chapter 5 why it's crucial to put the smallest part of your customer universe at the top of your marketing plan and how the customer chemistry marketing campaign is timed to the customer's calendar, not yours.

Rule 6: Treat Your Best Customers Like Your Best Employees—Recognize and Reward Them

Find out how you can enhance customer chemistry in Chapter 6. There's no lack of ways to surprise, delight, and otherwise reward customers for their loyalty.

Rule 7: Say Good-bye to Bad Customers and Dysfunctional Relationships

In Chapter 7 you'll learn how to end customer relationships that don't work. It's not easy but sometimes it's the only way. There are gentle ways to turn away customers that just don't fit. Sometimes you don't even have to say it.

Rule 8: Take the Pulse of Your Relationships

Once a customer, always a customer? Don't count on it. Customer chemistry is fluid. The key is to review and renew. In Chapter 8 you'll learn how to monitor the status of your best customer relationships.

How to Get the Most from This Book Individually

How well do you and your customers really get along? To help you get a handle on your relationships, we wrote a quiz that was inspired at least in part by the quiz formats you see in popular women's magazines. This is our version of a *Cosmo* quiz for business. Of course, our quiz has a serious intent as well: you can use it as an audit or snapshot of your customer relationships today. We also wrote the quiz to suggest the many ways you can improve your customer chemistry. Let's see how you score.

Quiz: A Customer Match Made in Heaven or Hell?

1. I met my first customer
   a. in a bar (0 points)
   b. on a blind date (cold call) (5 points)
   c. through a mutual friend we both trusted (10 points)
2. I met my most recent new customer
   a. in a bar (minus 5 points)
   b. on a blind date (cold call) (0 points)
   c. through a targeted marketing campaign (5 points)
   d. through a referral from a current customer (10 points)
3. I accepted my most recent customer because
   a. I needed the cash to make payroll (0 points)
   b. it represented a very large sale (5 points)
   c. it was a great fit and offered numerous growth opportunities (10 points)

4. Negotiating the terms of a sale
   a. is pure hell (0 points)
   b. is tough at times but fair (5 points)
   c. is fast and straightforward because I know my customers so well (10 points)

5. My customers and I have a mutual interest in
   a. making a buck (0 points)
   b. our marketplace (5 points)
   c. our companies and our community (10 points)

6. Do my employees like and respect our customers?
   a. No—they wouldn't be caught dead with customers outside work. (minus 5 points)
   b. Yes, they have a cordial relationship. (0 points)
   c. Yes, they have a real passion for some customers. (5 points)
   d. Yes, they consider customers to be true colleagues and friends. (10 points)

7. My employees can name our top customers
   a. on a good day (0 points)
   b. by revenue (5 points)
   c. by revenue and profit (10 points)

8. My customers' last-minute and special requests are
   a. a pain in the you-know-what (minus 5 points)
   b. great—if there's time to research the request (0 points)
   c. an opportunity for new sales or products (5 points)
   d. the lifeblood of my company (10 points)

9. I can count the number of new product ideas from customers
   a. on one hand (0 points)
   b. by revenue growth last year (5 points)
   c. by revenue and profit growth over several years (10 points)

10. Most of my new business comes by way of
    a. heavy sales and advertising efforts (0 points)
    b. referrals, word-of-mouth, and some advertising (5 points)
    c. previous customers and referrals (10 points)

11. My budget for sales and marketing
    a. has increased but sales have not (0 points)
    b. has stayed constant and sales are up (5 points)
    c. has increased for my best customers and prospects
       (10 points)
12. In recent years our new customers
    a. have been equal to the number of our lost customers
       (0 points)
    b. have been enough to meet our sales projections
       (5 points)
    c. have decreased while repeat business has increased
       (10 points)
13. I know what my customers are worth over a lifetime of
    business.
    a. No, it's impossible to say—I don't have enough information.
       (0 points)
    b. I know it's a nice sum if I can keep them for more than a
       year. (5 points)
    c. Yes, and so do my employees because we talk about it.
       (10 points)
14. Customers respond to my surveys
    a. once in a while (5 points)
    b. on a regular basis (10 points)
15. My customers call me personally
    a. once in a blue moon (minus 5 points)
    b. if I call them first (0 points)
    c. when they're angry (5 points)
    d. for any reason (10 points)
    e. less often these days because they communicate with my
       employees (15 points)
16. I have to call customers about a late bill
    a. at least once a week (minus 5 points)
    b. once a month (0 points)
    c. once a quarter (5 points)
    d. very rarely (10 points)

17. My customers generally pay in 30 to 60 days
   a. when they feel like it (0 points)
   b. some of the time (5 points)
   c. all or most of the time (10 points)
18. I could imagine starting a company with one of my customers
   a. when hell freezes over (0 points)
   b. or perhaps two (5 points)
   c. since, in fact, I have strategic alliances with several now
      (10 points)
19. I could recite five personal details about my top customers
   a. if this were a quiz show for money (0 points)
   b. if I had access to my customer database (5 points)
   c. off the top of my head (10 points)

Scoring

- *Zero points—Headed for Divorce*: You are either extremely new in business or extremely angry toward your customers. (Or else you're cursed with the world's worst customers.) Examine your company's reason for being as well as your own motivation for becoming an entrepreneur, and then proceed to Chapter 7.
- *5–45 points—Beginning the Dance*: You're a relative beginner at this game of customer relationship building. Proceed from the beginning of the book and fill out as many of the worksheets as you can.
- *50–100 points—Getting to Know You*: You've been around the block a few times, been burned once or twice by bad customers, and now you have your priorities straight. See Chapter 2 to review various approaches to rating customers and prospects. Then proceed directly to Chapters 3, 5, and 6 for tips on how to enhance the chemistry. Occasionally, you still need assistance in how to say no to the wrong customers—for tips on this, see Chapter 7.
- *100–150 points—Geared for Growth*: You know your ideal customer and are poised for serious growth, but you need help when it comes to issues like how to get employees in on the act—see Chapter 3. You may also need pointed advice on how to use technology to your best

advantage—proceed to Chapter 4. And you've only just begun to reward your best customers—for more ideas, see Chapter 6.

- *155–185 points—Courtship in Bloom*: You're extremely confident in your customer relationships, but are always searching for ways to fine-tune your skills. For inspiration, see the good forms throughout the book, and go straight to Chapter 6 to pick up several advanced techniques for building customer chemistry.

- *190 points—Customer-Chemistry Master*: Congratulations! A perfect score! Your customers are truly a match made in heaven! But don't get too comfortable unless your profit margins are just as heavenly—and you've tried every technique in this book.

CHAPTER 1

THE CUSTOMER DATING GAME
RULE 1: KNOW YOUR CUSTOMERS

When Capitol Concierge won its first contract, I felt a tremendous feeling of victory and a deep sense of gratitude toward the people who were giving life to my entrepreneurial dream. The John Akridge Company, a well-respected regional real estate company, took a chance on my fledgling company. I celebrated with my mother by going up to the rooftop terrace of my client's building at 1667 K Street. We had a panoramic view of the city and its landmarks. There I was twirling around on the roof and chanting, "One day we'll have concierges in every building in Washington," while my mother smiled and said, "You'll be the queen of K Street."

I have to admit, however, that I sometimes felt more like a pauper than a queen as I confronted the reality of running an extremely demanding business. I was running around town delivering catered lunches, videos, and flowers. I stood in line in the rain at RFK Stadium so I could buy concert tickets for customers too busy to stand in line. I was establishing the service, "the magic wand," that could make things happen.

Even though I was working like a dog, I felt like nothing could compare to this: I was an entrepreneur. I had the life I wanted. Few memories compare to the beauty of the day you receive that first revenue check made out to your very own company. For me that magic day was June 13, 1988. Capitol Concierge was officially in business. Soon after, I hired my first employee.

By the end of my first full year in business we had something to show for all the hard work: concierges in twelve buildings in downtown D.C. All sorts of expansion possibilities beckoned. In one of my wilder fantasies, I imagined my company as the concierge to Capitol Hill.

Despite the company's growing success, we made our share of mistakes. I'll never forget searching frantically for a customer's missing clothes at a dry cleaning plant. Unfortunately, as far as my P&L was concerned, I was losing my shirt there too.

At the end of my fourth year, I had concierges in fifty buildings. The company employed more than fifty-five people. My total sales reached $2.4 million, but the company wasn't yet in the black even though it seemed like we were picking up new customers all the time. Slowly it dawned on me that maybe volume wasn't the answer. We started looking at our numbers a lot more closely. We started to ask questions about our customers. Who were they? And were they the customers we really wanted?

Attention All Companies at the Crossroads: Are You Making Money Yet?

Capitol Concierge was clearly at the first of many entrepreneurial turning points. Perhaps you can relate to the company's predicament. Everyone said your first few years would be grueling, but hey, your company's not brand new anymore and you're no longer a beginner at this game of business. Why aren't your sales growing as expected? You're not as profitable as you'd hoped to be by now. Perhaps you're not bringing anything to the bottom line. Yet you can't figure out where or how things have gone wrong. You know not all customers are equal, but you've got plenty who are loyal and consistently profitable. Don't you?

The truth is many companies—let's venture to say most companies—don't know who their best customers are. They may not have a clue which ones consistently contribute to the company's net profits or which bring the most referral business. Even worse, many companies don't know their customers at all. If you don't know who your customers are, how can you possibly have any kind of relationship with them?

Without a relationship each sale is like a one-night stand. Maybe he'll call tomorrow and maybe he won't. *Customer chemistry thrives above all else upon knowing your customers, really knowing them.*

Can You Really Know Customers?

Why bother to get to know more about customers? Why not just offer a super product and take orders? Anyone can make sales. Not everyone knows how to build chemistry. Done right, it can be a competitive advantage. Harvey Mackay, the bestselling author of *How to Swim with the Sharks Without Being Eaten Alive*, is a classic example. He grew his envelope company by turning his talkative streak and good ear into an art form and one incredible customer database. Years ago, he created a list of questions called the "Mackay 66" that is just as relevant today for building a customer profile. His legendary recall of the important details of customers' corporate and personal lives paid big dividends.

Chris Zane has done something similar in the competitive world of bicycle shops. For more than a decade the owner of Zane's Cycles in Branford, Connecticut, has been collecting little details about twenty-seven thousand customers. He doesn't forget and neither do his customers, who have rewarded him with a high level of repeat sales.

There's a more basic reason for making the effort to know customers: you learn which customers want you to know them. It is the customer, after all, who makes the choice of who to do business with—and doesn't do so blithely. Customers who want you to know them are often the very same customers who give you more of their business. The way in which you try to get to know customers will also say a lot about you as a businessperson. Know customers and they will know you. It's got to be reciprocal to work.

Yet how do you start the conversation? For some business owners it is difficult if not impossible even to learn customers' names. Consider the case of a retail store where customers pay with cash and not a credit card with name imprinted for all to see. Meet Mark Zimmerman, who quit his advertising job several years ago to run his own bakery in Chapel Hill, North Carolina.

"Getting to know customers is hard at the start," says Zimmerman, "and doesn't get any easier." The use of frequent-buyer cards helps to identify some customers if they write in their name on the card, but it doesn't go far enough for the nearsighted, name-challenged, and harried sales clerk. "We do try to get names on the frequency cards, but that doesn't help people like me who can never seem to put a face with a name because we don't see the card until the transaction is under way." Here's how he solves the problem when he's the one waiting on customers. "I often find it easier to remember something about someone— like if they've been sick or that their kids are into sports—than their names. I can strike up a conversation about that subject, and they feel like I know them personally."

RULE 1: KNOW YOUR CUSTOMERS

This is the first step to building customer chemistry. Identify customers, interact with them, and use every chance to be personal. As you know your customers, so they will know you.

Why does the bakery shop owner bother to remember if someone's kid plays soccer or just got over the chicken pox? It's simple. Stores, at least the best ones, still play a vital role in the lives of the people who live and shop in the store's neighborhood. A good hometown store provides community and a connection. That connection can happen instantly or it can take more time.

How do you get closer to close-to-the-vest government clients? Frank Dominguez, CEO of Imperial Construction Group in Elizabeth, New Jersey, eats a lot of lunches out. He believes you have to get to know clients on a personal level and talk to them about their interests both on and off the job. "It's harder with the government people. You can't even buy them a cup of coffee—they are so worried about regulations," he says. But he's persevered in his quest to better know his customers, along the way landing on the *Hispanic Business Journal*'s list of the five hundred fastest-growing companies.

Andrea Keating's challenge is that she works with many of her customers sight unseen. Despite the huge phone bills and the stumbling blocks of maintaining long-distance relationships, Keating has built a successful business providing production crews to the audiovisual and marketing departments of large corporations, many of whom grace the Fortune 500. She works with some of her customers on an almost daily basis. "Our relationships with our top clients do become personal because of the nature of our business."

Perhaps no one has it tougher than an entrepreneur running an amusement park—talk about anonymous customer masses. Yet Ken Cormier, the owner of Funtown Splashtown USA in Saco, Maine, has managed to make himself known to his guests, and they have revealed a few things to him about their fantasies for new rides they'd like to see, park pet peeves, and opinions on pricing.

Luke Chung competes in a very different arena, yet shares the same qualms and concerns about getting to know customers as the amusement park operator and corner retailer. Chung sells software tools to buyers at Fortune 500 companies, government agencies, financial institutions, and other businesses. His Virginia-based company, FMS, is fifteen years old. While it might seem easier to acquaint yourself with other professionals than to cozy up to an anonymous public, Chung knows otherwise. He says: "We try to get to know our customers only when the situations present themselves and the customer is comfortable with the relationship. It's very difficult to turn a business relationship into 'part personal' unless you're sure it won't be problematic." Yet he too has found ways to get around the "problematic."

For the businessperson to develop a relationship the customer must be open to it. Opt-in e-mail programs—aptly named *permission marketing*—capture that principle online. It's certainly an accomplishment when customers don't view your marketing messages as *spam* (electronic junk mail) and openly elect to receive them. But in truth, opt-in e-mail efforts are just one possible tactic in the larger goal of creating a relationship. E-mail, however personal or selective, is not the relationship.

It's just one means to starting the engine. What it really takes to ignite customer relationships is *your* personal time and attention. Of course, as the owner or manager of a growing company, time is exactly what you don't have.

Start with the Most Promising

In an ideal world, you would invest the time to learn a great deal about each and every customer as well as every serious potential customer. That is the ultimate goal. Some company owners purposely keep their businesses small for that very reason—so that they know a handful of customers so well they are more like old friends. For most companies, getting to know each and every customer and sales prospect just isn't practical—at least not at first.

Because your time and resources are limited—and because everyone knows the cost of acquiring a new customer has steadily risen—it only makes sense to focus on your very best customers and prospects and grow them one by one. It's both practical and proactive to begin this way. So why don't all companies conduct business in this fashion? If they did, they'd surely save a bundle and TV commercials might cease to exist.

Six Stumbling Blocks

So what, exactly, keeps companies from zooming in on their very best customers? There's no shortage of reasons. For one thing, there is the logistical challenge: how do you actually go about selecting one customer over another? We'll get to that in Chapter 2, but there is also a philosophical barrier to overcome: For those who were taught to value sales volume and market share above all else, rejecting any customer seems foolhardy. In fact, many business stumbling blocks are rooted in emotions—the emotions of the entrepreneur who has shed blood, sweat, and tears trying to make the dream come true.

1. You're Still in the "Honeymoon Phase" of Business

"I made a sale!" This is a personal moment of triumph. Taking a closer look at customers can lead to a fear of rejection. The fear is twofold: fear of rejecting customers you have come to rely on, as well as fear that your best customers will reject your overture to get closer.

2. You're Too Busy Putting Out Fires

If you're managing a young company, you're probably caught up in the frenzy of creating a product or service that didn't previously exist. Who has time for analysis? For Capitol Concierge, the business was as demanding as it was different every day. There was no telling what customers might ask for next, and the company frantically tried to fulfill every conceivable request. In the start-up years there's a new fire to put out every hour. Watch out; the role of firefighter is habit forming for some entrepreneurs who don't feel right unless they are wielding a fire extinguisher or an axe. To get out of continual crisis mode, you've got to put down the sword and pick up the pen.

3. You're Blinded by Love

Falling in love with the product prevents many from seeing who the real customer is. Caught up in perfecting products, these entrepreneurs can't see beyond their creations. Owners of technical companies frequently fall prey to this trap, but they're not alone.

If *you* fit the description of "blinded by love," your first job is to analyze the profitability of each of your product lines, an exercise that will force you to look at your customers in a new light.

4. You Suffer from a Lack of Information

Oftentimes the raw data is there to make judgments about customers. At least, the information is there somewhere, but you haven't had time to locate the numbers you need, never mind make sense of them. Try this remedy: put away the spreadsheets and start tracking crucial customer data by hand. Norm Brodsky, a popular columnist for *Inc* and owner of several fast-growing companies, is a big fan of pencil and paper. He urges entrepreneurs to track monthly sales and gross margins by customer. Write the numbers out by hand and calculate the percentages yourself, he counsels entrepreneurs. You lose something when you let a computer do the math for you.

5. You've Forgotten Your Focus

Many companies lose their focus as they grow. Sometimes, success is the enemy of focus, notes Al Ries, marketing veteran and author of the book *Focus*. Companies who depart from their areas of expertise risk losing their hard-core fans, who are often the biggest consumers of the product.

One company famous for its focus is Starbucks, which put thousands of little diners out of business by doing one thing: making a better cup of joe. In recent years Starbucks has expanded into supermarkets (ice cream, bottled coffee drinks, and now the beans themselves), as well as the office food-service market (small businesses and even home businesses). Only time will tell if all this expansion is true to its focus and loyal customer base.

Knowing who you are as a company—and sticking to that focus—makes it easier to do everything: to advertise, to hire and train staff, and, of course, to win customers. You can't begin to improve your customer relationships until you understand who your customer is. And you can't begin to improve your marketing success before you understand who your best customer is. Some of this seems so obvious, it's almost trite, sort of like the self-help books and pop songs that preach "before you can love someone else, you've gotta love yourself." And yet, lack of focus on the right customers is the reason so many companies go out of business.

6. You're Stuck in Status Quo Mode

You've been doing things the same way for so long it feels impossible to change. It's like being stuck in a dead-end marriage. It happens to the best of companies. As dangerous as it is to expand beyond your specialty, it's equally dangerous to do nothing.

Consider the example of Custom Research Inc., an award-winning marketing research firm in Minneapolis that was once a little stuck in its ways. Stagnating sales and profits moved the company owners to take a cold hard look at their customer list. What the owners saw wasn't pleasant, but they made the necessary changes to help the company thrive again. Getting unstuck is worth the effort, however gut-wrenching.

Overcoming the Obstacles

As you've probably surmised by now, each stumbling block can spell disaster if left unresolved. Any one of the six can kill a business as surely as running out of cash can. Some stumbling blocks are the emotional baggage people carry into business. If you find it overwhelming to confront your business demons, that's understandable. (One business owner was reduced to tears during a conversation about the issues raised above.)

Often company owners ask the hard questions only when forced to confront a grim reality. "I'm losing more money every month." "I can't make payroll." "My bank note is due." When you're fighting for your company's very survival, panic has a way of creeping in uninvited. Yet in the midst of a crisis is exactly the time you need to step back and take stock. The only way to move on is to confront the issue head on. Lighten your load. Get rid of the baggage and move on to the real reason for being in business: relationships—strong, healthy customer relationships. You'll be glad you did.

The Quest for Customer Chemistry

For many entrepreneurs the real thrill of owning a company is not sitting behind a desk in some ivory tower but getting out there and talking up customers. Conversations with clients remind us of our core mission and reinforce the feeling that you can make a difference in the world. If your customers feel just as passionately about the difference your company makes, you've got chemistry.

Customer chemistry takes business to another level that is at once more personal and satisfying. Customer chemistry means never taking another customer relationship for granted. It means being dedicated to continual learning so that you are able to make distinctions among customers. You are prepared to devote even higher levels of service to your very best customers.

As you get to know customers, they get to know you. The wall between customer and supplier comes down.

Some companies are using the Internet to strengthen customer bonds. For example, Bob Carbonell, the owner of a $12-million move management firm, maintains a richly detailed customer database that he allows his customers to dial into any time of the day or night. Cheap? No. But after steadily growing his best customers for five years, Carbonell's company, Relocation Management Resources (RMR), could afford the technology.

The quest for customer chemistry can take many paths. Some companies are going "back to the future" by writing handwritten notes to clients and throwing dinner parties that bring groups of customers together. And here's another way to get personal: Susan Ascher, who owns a successful recruiting firm in Roseland, New Jersey, took a chance and asked one of her leading customers to be her golf partner in a charity tournament (he said yes). Ascher figured the social event beat the pants off a face-to-face sales call. And with the cost of a sales call now in the $300 to $500 range, who can argue that it isn't better to meet outside the office?

While such examples of customer intimacy inspire, admittedly they're not going to happen with every customer. Even the best customer relationships don't always stay that way. You may be in search of a more perfect union, but no customer relationship is ever perfect, just as no marriage can be. While chemistry can fade just as it can be renewed, the only way to have customer chemistry at all is to seek it out. Resolve to make daily contact with customers—whether by phoning, by serving in the field, or by answering customer e-mail with personally written responses.

The quest for customer chemistry begins by looking in the mirror, overcoming your business demons (being stuck, losing focus, fearing rejection, etc.), and moving on to more meaningful relationships.

Chemistry Checklist

1. *Make a list of your five most pressing business problems.* Are your margins shrinking? Is there a new competitor on the horizon? Or consider the following: Few or no repeat sales? Lack of referrals? Expensive marketing campaigns are not yielding strong results? Difficulty automating your systems and customer contact data? Poor customer service? Low staff morale?

2. *Consider which customers are contributing to the problems and how others could alleviate them.* Once you have completed the list of your top five problems, pull out your customer list. Under each problem, note the names of those customers who contribute to each problem and of those who could be part of a solution.

3. *List (from memory) your best and worst customers.* Check to see if the ones you list from memory are the same culprits or helpers identified within your top-five business problems list. This process will serve as the starting point of customers that require attention.

4. *Ask yourself who your dream customers are and why your goal is to work to enhance your best customer relationships.* Chemistry can be developed more easily with customers that fill your dream-customer criteria. Each business will have unique dream attributes. Several to ponder include your product or service is critical to the customer's operation; the customer pays their bills on time; the customer readily and eagerly provides valuable feedback; your company's culture and values match the customer's.

CHAPTER 2

THE CUSTOMER RATING GAME
RULE 2: RANK YOUR CUSTOMERS

I remember the summer of 1992 clearly because it was truly the best and worst of times. I knew I had to find a new way to attract customers. As a small company in our fourth year of business, Capitol Concierge didn't have the money to engage in traditional mass marketing campaigns. Around this time, my staff and I got lucky. A group of MBA students asked to study our business. We said, "Come on in!" Over several weeks, the students pored over all the customer data we could wring from our accounting system. Finally the day of reckoning arrived: we learned which clients were using our services, and which they were using most frequently. What might have been obvious wasn't because by then our list of clients had grown to three thousand.

What the students found was really eye-popping. We all know the "80-20" rule of sales (that 80 percent of a company's sales usually come from 20 percent of its customers), but it really hits home when you stare down at the cold hard numbers. My managers and I saw clearly how a few customers accounted for the majority of our sales. At that point I made the decision to radically refocus our marketing efforts. That's how it all started—that was the epiphany that led us to change our business model.

Though we didn't know it at the time, this was the beginning of all our efforts to get to know customers individually. Back then, there really was no name that summed up all we were trying to do. But I can say now it's a lot like trying to find a potential husband or wife without having to suffer through blind dates and disastrous courtships. In our personal lives we all keep a mental checklist of who is right for us as a partner—the ideal match. Our list evolves over time. In business, however, you don't have the luxury to take your time. When we zoomed in on my company's best customers it was like short-circuiting a lifetime process of looking for the right one to come along.

Much More Than a Feeling

Customer chemistry may start with a feeling, a gut instinct about a customer's importance. That's the "dating game" stage of the relationship. Many successful entrepreneurs listen to what their bellies tell them. But if the customer courtship is to continue and the chemistry to grow, you can't rely on first impressions and intuition alone. Sooner or later you need evidence that this customer is a good match. In short, you need to move beyond the dating game and on to the "rating game."

In business, as in life, no one wants to spend sixty hours a week on dead-end relationships. In our personal lives we may no longer have to; according to recent research, scientists have observed how the brain "looks" when someone is truly head over heels. Not only is there a chemical reaction in the brain, but it can be seen. This finding leads one to speculate that brain scan images will one day be required as part of the prenup agreement. If only we had such indisputable evidence in our business relationships. Think of all the bad deals and ill-fated partnerships that could be averted!

Of course, avoiding heartache is what ranking customers is all about. For now the closest anyone has to a customer brain scan is the picture that emerges when you look at customer purchases over time. On a most basic level any company can focus on the customers at the very top—the 10 percent or 30 percent who generate the majority of sales. However, customer ranking is not a cookie-cutter kind of process. How you approach it is going to vary a lot depending on the type of business you're in. Retailers, for example, have special issues. They don't have the ability to pick their customers per se since stores are open to anyone who can physically get there. Of course, in cyberspace even the physical barrier is removed. Still, even if retailers and e-merchants can't control which customers wander in, they can and should decide which customers they are going to reward and pursue going forward.

In the business-to-business (B2B) world the issues are quite different. Companies that sell to other companies can select their customers. In addition the universe of potential clients may be limited. The tighter the niche, the smaller the field. In some cases, you could be talking about how to rank just a handful of customers. (If you sell to both consumers and businesses, as in the case of Capitol Concierge, you will need to approach customer ranking in several ways.) In the end, though, the number of customers may not matter as much as the thought process that goes into the ranking.

If you have two customers, you still have to decide which is first and which second. One client may be worth so much to you that you want to devote half your week to that customer, while the other client may be worth just 25 percent of your time. With the rest of your hours perhaps you should be hitting the pavement in search of new clients. How about when you have five customers? With five "contestants" the rating game suddenly gets trickier. With five clients this may be the crucial point where you need to hire an employee and seek out a bank line of credit. Obviously before you take on a payroll and debt, you need to ask, "Are these five customers the right five?" How you answer that question will largely determine whether you focus your time growing those accounts or looking for new customers.

RULE 2: RANK YOUR CUSTOMERS BY BEING BRUTALLY HONEST

Not all customers are created equal. This is the starting point that will shed light on which customers are contributing to your company's long-term growth and which customers could potentially stunt your growth. By ranking customers by profitability, you will be able to allocate your customer-chemistry building resources accordingly.

Moreover, how you rank your *current* customers will most certainly affect how you rate *prospective* customers. Betsy W., the owner of an events-marketing company in the Southwest, is one company owner who took a hard look at the business coming in her door. After growing her company quickly for a few years, she realized that when she accepted too many assignments from nonprofit and government agencies, profits really suffered. Though Betsy loved working for high-profile clients such as the mayor's office, certain projects were all-consuming. So Betsy made a conscious effort to track staff time spent on each client and to think carefully before taking on new work.

It's easy to understand why many entrepreneurs become slaves to their businesses. It can seem so much easier to let the company lead you rather than you lead the company—that is, until all the problems of uncontrolled growth rear their ugly head.

Even when a company owner has accepted the fact that not all customers are equal, the act of putting one customer before another can be extremely painful. You might as well ask the owner to rank his siblings or children. But in truth, ranking customers need not be as gut-wrenching as all that. Indeed, you might even find it liberating, and you may also find yourself in the vanguard of forward-thinking companies. Among two hundred global companies surveyed by Arthur Andersen a few years ago, 50 percent said they expect to be organized around customer types (rather than product types) by 2002. In addition nearly 50 percent said customer profitability will be a critical measure by 2002. The survey concludes that as these companies become more sophisticated at tracking customers, they will measure not only customer revenues but how quickly customers pay, what services they require, and whether they generate special handling costs. Any company would be wise to pay attention to those factors.

There's no single right way to rank customers, so you'll want to consider a number of approaches, both formal (by the numbers) and informal. There are a number of less tangible, more subjective ways you can measure a customer's worth: Does the customer actively influence other buyers? Do sparks—and new ideas—fly every time you meet certain customers? Does the client help you be the kind of company you want to be? Do your employees enjoy your customers? After all, customers can have a huge impact on your own corporate culture. Your employees ought to enjoy working with your customers.

Eight Ways to Rank Customers

1. The Cash-Flow Saviors

These customers are good for their word. They not only pay their bills on time, but early. They're willing to pay faster, pay up-front, or put down sizable deposits. Why? These customers want to help you get off the ground or help you stay in business. One or two of these saviors are all you need to get started. They're as good as gold—even if you have to give up some margin at first.

You may even find that some of your corporate customers have special terms for start-ups and other growing companies. Ask and you shall receive, as Bob Carroll did. Carroll is the CEO of TelStrat International, a manufacturer of telecommunications equipment in Plano, Texas. Several years ago when he was completing a crucial sale with Nortel Networks, he discovered that his new customer had a special small business program for suppliers like TelStrat. With less than $3 million in sales at the time, Carroll's company qualified for net-15 terms. The CEO learned of the preferential terms during contract negotiations with a Nortel Networks purchasing agent. The CEO found it easier to give price concessions knowing his company's cash flow would benefit from the improved terms. The special treatment continued until TelStrat's sales reached $10 million. If the companies you are negotiating with don't have such a program, suggest they start one.

On a related note, Capitol Concierge has found that individuals who entrust the company to bill their credit cards tend to be ideal customers in other ways. And of course, getting paid virtually overnight by the credit-card-merchant bank is great for Capitol's cash flow.

2. The "Venture-Capital" Approach

From a portfolio of customers rises a few big winners. For every "prince," you've got to kiss five frogs—or so the thinking goes with this approach to finding your most valuable customers. Not everyone can afford to take this tack, but companies who rely on project work must often experiment with a variety of clients. The key to finding the winners: a religious accounting of all time and resources dedicated to each project. Rainier, a high-tech public relations (PR) firm, subscribes to this approach. The $2-million company based in Princeton, Massachusetts, has discovered that a good project-management program is a must when you're dealing with dozens of clients at once. (Rainier has used a program called Profits and Clients designed for PR agencies, but there are many other off-the-shelf packages as well.) The goal: use your knowledge about each project to zoom in on the stars in your portfolio.

3. Buzz Value

Some companies generate an abundance of positive publicity—or "buzz." And lucky are the entrepreneurs who land a few of these hot companies as customers. Both your sales and your image will get a valuable boost just by your association with news-making clients.

Adjacency, a San Francisco–based website developer, is a good example of how buzz value works. Andrew Sather launched the company in 1995 by targeting brand names he identified with and loved dearly. In fact, he wrote his own version of a "love letter" to ten companies that were legendary for one reason or another. Sather's mailing list included Patagonia, Nordstrom, Apple, Land Rover, and Rollerblade. Although it didn't happen overnight, seven of the ten letter recipients became Adjacency clients. Sather's buzz strategy allowed him to be choosy about his customers. Part of that strategy was to seek out clients who were rated a great place to work by their employees. In other words, potential new customers must have buzz.

Eric Schecter is another entrepreneur who understands the value of buzz. Schecter has built a number of fast-growing companies over the last decade. When he started Great American Marketing and Events (GAME), an events-marketing company in Scottsdale, Arizona, Schecter courted his first clients specifically for their celebrity status. So valuable were they, he was willing to make product and price concessions in exchange for these clients' testimonials. And he wasted no time making his first big-name customers the stars of his marketing campaign. In return for generous terms, the clients agreed to be filmed and photographed and to speak to dozens of prospects who'd see their faces all over Schecter's brochures. The celebrity endorsements helped the company break through what he called the barrier of newness.

Now don't get us wrong; buzz value doesn't mean you have to enlist Martha Stewart to endorse your product or service. Buzz is in the eye of the beholder. You know the movers and shakers in your industry—and their endorsements have the power to put your company on the map and lead you to customers. That's another benefit of the buzz approach; it reduces your selling costs.

4. It's a Matter of Mission

There are advantages to selecting customers that fulfill a larger company mission. For example, Leegin Creative Leather Products, a leading producer of leather belts, handbags, and other accessories in City of Industry, California, believes in helping independent stores and smaller chains compete with the superstores. It's a crucial part of what it means to work at Leegin. As a result, it does not do business with the Targets of the world. Instead, the company has become indispensable to its highly loyal customers.

5. Banking on the Big Spenders

We're talking revenue streams. These customers buy nearly all your lines, not just one or two. That's always a good sign unless they require so much personal hand-holding that you're not making any money at the end of the day. Track these accounts carefully—for overhead expenses.

6. The Loss Leaders

These are marginally profitable accounts or unprofitable accounts worth keeping for some other reason—and it better be good. Just be clear about what these customers are really costing you. A closer look at your gross margins with these customers should speak volumes. Continue to review the status of your loss leaders often.

7. The Lifetime Club

Using what you know about repeat customers, you can calculate or project a customer's *lifetime value*, or LTV. It's a tricky calculation worth attempting. Obviously the job is made easier if your industry keeps benchmarks on average order size, how often customers order, etc. In some industries—fast food and catalogs come to mind—statistics for comparison are more plentiful. If you're in a highly specialized niche business, coming up with a meaningful number for LTV will depend on your own market research. Martha Rogers and Don Peppers— authors of the bestselling *One to One Future*—suggest that you create a "proxy" for LTV that has particular significance to your company. This could be as simple as the total of annual orders plus the value of each referral from each client. Catalog houses do a lifetime P&L on customers. Figure 2.1 illustrates a simple LTV calculation for a direct-mail customer.

The real value of coming up with a lifetime value is that you can more clearly communicate to yourself and your employees what the stakes are, or what it means in hard dollars to gain or lose a customer.

Figure 2.1 Lifetime Value of a Catalog Customer

Buys every twelve months over a six-year customer life

Total purchases	6
× Average order	$100
= Gross contribution	$600
− Cost of goods (50%)	$300
= Gross margin	$300
− Marketing costs (6 years × $10/year)	$60
− Fulfillment costs (6 orders × $7/orders)	$42
= Gross profit	$198

Note: Numbers don't represent industry averages.

These customers may not be your biggest in any given year, but if they are steady buyers that fact alone can make them highly profitable. Recency and frequency of purchasing are everything in direct mail, for example. In truth, every business should review the active status of customers over six to twelve months.

8. The A Team

These are your largest *and* most profitable customers—often the 10 percent or 20 percent of customers who account for 80 percent or 90 percent of your sales and perhaps a good chunk of profits. How do you know? You don't at first, but after a year or so in business, you can start doing the calculations. There are several popular ways to measure customer profitability—by gross margin, for one. And also by contribution margin, which is basically a measure of how much each customer contributes to covering a company's overhead after all direct and indirect expenses have been tallied for that customer. Or think of it this way: what costs would you not incur if a customer went away.

If you're really ambitious, you can take customers down to the bottom line; the ultimate in this approach is called *activity-based accounting*, or ABC for short. The theory behind activity-based accounting is that you shouldn't arbitrarily allocate overhead—or simply split overhead costs among all your customers. Some customers place more demands on your resources than others, and the differences can be dramatic. Some experts argue that for many companies a small percentage of customers account for the bulk of profits because the majority of customers actually cause them to lose money. The profitable accounts are basically underwriting the unprofitable ones.

When you have thousands or even a few dozen customers, endeavoring to rank them all on profitability can be a daunting task to say the least. In some cases it's impossible without making an overall assessment of the company's product lines. Likewise, you may want to start the ranking exercise by looking at groups of customers by product line, industry, geography, or distribution channel. Analyze the sales and profits of this group of customers as a whole before you attempt to gather the transactions of each individual customer.

What's more, in many industries there's a shorthand way of looking at customer profitability. Sometimes there's a simple calculation, a key number or ratio, that says it all. If you don't have the industry experience to know the shorthand, join a trade association or seek out a peer group of indirect competitors to advise you on benchmarks.

IN SEARCH OF THE RIGHT CUSTOMERS: CUSTOM RESEARCH INC.

Problem: After fourteen years and $10 million in sales, Custom Research Inc. (CRI) had stopped growing.

Overview: Judy Corson and Jeff Pope, who had left their positions at Pillsbury to start CRI, had watched their business grow without much difficulty. Many clients were household names. But CRI had too many customers—or too few good ones—and it was hard to tell the good from the bad.

Solution: Corson and Pope decided to rank all of their 157 clients based on sales volume and profitability. CRI calculated the profit for each customer by subtracting all direct costs and selling expenses from the total revenue generated by that customer for the year. Each customer was then placed in one of four categories based on sales volume and profit margin. The best category was "high volume/high margin," followed by "low volume/high margin," "high volume/low margin," and finally "low volume/low margin." The cutoff points for "high" and "low" scores were purely subjective—they corresponded to CRI's goals for profit volume and margin.

Of CRI's 157 existing customers, only 10 fell into the most desirable category of high sales volume/high profit margin. Those 10 accounted for 69 percent of profits and 29 percent of sales. Most of the rest—or 101 customers—contributed very little to the top or bottom line. Many weren't profitable when you factored in the selling costs. The hard reality was that these 101 weren't likely to become more loyal to CRI despite all the company's best efforts to make them so. Based on their findings,

Corson and Pope decided to curtail work for the unprofitable clients and give their full attention to their best customers and most-promising prospects for future growth.

Results: By being more selective, the company more than doubled its sales over the next decade with half as many customers.

TWO CUSTOMERS, ONE SCORECARD

In Table 2.1 we present a mini profit-and-loss statement for two customers. At first blush, Customer A appears to be worth more to the company than Customer B. However, B racked up far lower direct costs and a third of the selling expenses, making it more than twice as profitable as A. In the end, B makes a substantial contribution to overhead.

Table 2.1 Representative Profit-and-Loss Statement

	Customer A	Customer B
$ Volume	$203,320	$156,000
Direct costs	174,856	113,162
Gross margin	28,464	42,838
Selling costs	14,232	3,120
Gross profit	14,232	39,718

And the Winners Are . . .

Once you've arrived at a reasonable way of ranking all your customers, it's time to draw some lines in the sand. When you look at the matches you've made, inevitably you're going to uncover customers who are no longer worth catering to. Are they marginally profitable? Are you losing money? Obviously, the time you invest chasing deadbeat customers takes from the time you have to build relationships with good customers. You end up jeopardizing everything else.

Of course, drawing a line between customers is a highly subjective thing. What one company would consider a top tier or A customer might not make the cut at another company. How you ultimately determine the winners from the losers depends on the company's maturity, industry norms, and the owner's or investors' expectations for sales and profits. Some companies define their A customers as any customer that hits a dollar threshold that allows for a healthy gross profit. In the case of Capitol Concierge and its corporate customers, tier one designates a customer with sales of more than $30,000 per year.

At this point your customer relationships are starting to come into focus. To sharpen the image, you'll want to ask more questions like, "What do my best clients have in common?" It's like that stage in personal relationships where one strives to know a new partner better by getting to know the partner's best friends. In business the idea is to take what you have been able to glean about your best customers and use that to create a more telling profile, a *best-customer profile*. There are no rules about what a best-customer profile must include. You will surely add and subtract details over time. Table 2.2 illustrates one type of profile.

One company chose to define their ideal customers in a different way—by drawing up a list of declarative statements. Fallon McElligott, an award-winning advertising agency in Minneapolis, is perhaps best known for some of its Super Bowl ads, including the "walking" Christopher Reeve spot. Corporate clients have included BMW and Nordstrom among many other household names. Here's how the agency openly defines its best customers:

Table 2.2 Capitol Concierge Best-Customer Profile

Type of customer	Corporate
Geographic location	Downtown, central business district
Key decision maker	Office administrator
Male-female	Female
Average age range of decision maker	35–50
How customer makes purchases	Telephone, online, in person
Length of sales cycle	2–3 weeks
Industry type	Property management and law firms

1. They have a great product.
2. They are passionate about their brand, their customers, and the results of our collective efforts.
3. They expect and receive total candor and bone honesty.
4. They have someone to champion great work.
5. They believe in a streamlined approval process.
6. They are committed to integrated marketing.
7. They encourage us to be profitable and have fun doing it.

Let Your *Best* Customer Pick Your *Next* Customer

Once you know, really know, what your best customers look like, you're in a much better position to define the kind of relationship you're seeking in future customers. This is a very different approach to the conventional notion of sales prospecting that basically says that if you start with a large enough sales field, sooner or later you're bound to strike oil. Though still widely used, that philosophy is about as antiquated as searching for water with a divining rod. The premise of starting out in the dark in a wide-open field is not only expensive but hopelessly outdated in the world of niche marketing and one-to-one electronic communication. But no matter what the marketing medium or distribution channel, getting new customers has never been a cheap endeavor.

Why is prospecting so expensive? Here are a few reasons. For one thing, most sales prospecting starts at the bottom rung of the sales ladder. It's a marketing model we've all internalized by now. The *customer loyalty ladder* starts with strangers on the bottom rung, progresses up to prospects, and from prospects to customers, and from customers to advocates (or raving fans). As you climb, so presumably do your profits (if you don't run out of cash first). If you don't have the means to hire a sales force or engage in mass marketing, it's tough to get a toehold on the traditional prospecting ladder.

But what if you discarded the ladder altogether? What if you adopted a different strategy that relies on cultivating a few key relationships? What if you essentially let your *best* customer pick your *next* customer? When you are pursuing the relationships you want, business life takes on a whole new dimension. There's a rhyme and a reason. You are not simply responding to lead forms filled out at a trade show or accepting the first customer who calls you on Monday. Instead, you are pursuing sales leads that fit a defined notion of who you should be doing business with. Thus, in a very real way, your best customers of today help select your best customers of tomorrow.

How Start-Ups Can Rank Customers Before They Have Any

Clearly, identifying your best sales prospects is challenging for a brand-new venture. For some entrepreneurs, particularly soloists, the very thought of sales prospecting induces great anxiety and nervousness.

Magda, who started a menu planning newsletter from her Manhattan apartment, expressed a fear of showing so much of herself to strangers (particularly online); she found it easier to bury herself in the details of writing her newsletter and developing recipes than to make the effort to attract new customers.

In fact, for any start-up there are endless distractions. Add fear to the equation and it's no wonder entrepreneurs get completely wrapped up in product details and forget about finding customers. Granted, it's tough starting with a blank slate, but even as a start-up you can still go through the process of determining a best guesstimate of your best customer. It's all intuitive in the beginning: what you *think* will be the common characteristics of customers in your chosen market segment. The challenge is to be very selective because it's so easy to let your first customers lead you. Only some are worth following.

And some are worth following everywhere they lead. What every entrepreneur needs is to find his or her own inner circle of industry insiders, people who have the ability to shape trends and influence other buyers. Michele Gerbrandt, founder of *Memory Makers* magazine, found her inner circle and it made all the difference to her young company's success. In many ways having a good inner circle is even more important than having actual customers, although certainly many in your inner circle may become your first customers. More important, a well-cultivated inner circle will lead you to multiple customers and prospects. For Capitol Concierge, the inner circle was a select group of property managers who generated repeat sales and new customers for Capitol on several levels. RightNow Technologies, a Montana software firm, even created a club called the Inner Circle for customers willing to act as references and help publicize the software company's successes.

Developing an inner circle is the fast track to building customer chemistry. It is something you can do even as a start-up with no customers.

REACHING THE INNER CIRCLE: MEMORY MAKERS MAGAZINE

Problem: In the spring of 1996 *Memory Makers* had a circulation of zero.

Overview: Many sales pitches start with a letter to a perfect stranger. Michele Gerbrandt, the founder of *Memory Makers* magazine, knew she wouldn't survive on the kindness of strangers in the cutthroat world of publishing. Launching a magazine usually entails renting mailing lists and sending a special offer to hundreds of thousands (if not millions) of prospects in the hopes of quickly ramping up circulation, which is the key to selling advertising. In Gerbrandt's case there wasn't a mailing list to rent. She was launching the first magazine in an industry so new—scrapbooking—that it didn't exist five years before. She was starting from scratch. That meant Gerbrandt couldn't just "buy" customers with a massive mailing even if she could have afforded that approach (she couldn't). Undaunted, she launched *Memory Makers* magazine with her husband, Ron, from the basement of their Colorado home.

Solution: Out of necessity, Gerbrandt rewrote the rules of sales prospecting: she appealed to a small inner circle of friends and colleagues before attempting to reach out to the wider mass market. Thus she started not with strangers, but with people she knew were devoted to the craft of scrapbooking. The inner circle in turn introduced Gerbrandt to her first customers and prospects.

Though Gerbrandt was new to the world of magazines, she was no stranger to the subject of her magazine. In her previous life she had sold photo album supplies through home parties. To start her campaign for subscribers, Gerbrandt tapped her own homegrown list of some four thousand names collected over the years—friends, colleagues, former customers, and other scrapbooking enthusiasts she'd met along the way. They each received a package: a free sixteen-page sample issue and a half-price subscription offer in exchange for giving Gerbrandt the names of twenty friends. Each of those twenty also got the sample issue and the same half-price offer.

The inspiration for the twenty-friends campaign came from an unlikely source: a bottle of salad dressing. As Gerbrandt tells it, she was sitting at the table with her husband, who is a graphic designer, and their three children over dinner. A bottle of ranch dressing caught her eye. There was an offer on the label soliciting the names of friends also keen on ranch dressing. The offer read something like: "Send in the names of two friends and get a ranch dressing recipe book for free." Gerbrandt knew a good idea when she saw one and decided to steal it for her fledgling magazine.

"I thought a similar offer would work in the scrapbooking community because it's all word of mouth," recalls Gerbrandt. "At the dinner table, we said, 'Well, how many names should we ask for—five, ten, fifteen, twenty? Let's try twenty.'"

Results: The names came pouring in. The postage bill wasn't slight but Gerbrandt paid it, confident she was doing the right thing. "I felt like you can't get a better hit than from this list of people you know." The offer began in May of '96 and by August of that year, "all one hundred thousand copies of the comp issues were gone," says Gerbrandt. The average direct-mail campaign nets a 2 percent response, but Gerbrandt's yielded more than twice that. In just the first few months alone she netted a 5 percent response or approximately five thousand prepaid subscribers. Another two thousand waited patiently for their issues until the company could process credit-card orders. Indeed, the names of thousands of prospective subscribers continued to roll in long after the offer ran out. "I think the scarcity of the issue helped. It was like Beanie Babies."

The Gerbrandts were officially in business. The prepaid subscribers provided enough revenue to officially launch a full issue of the magazine in September 1996. After the debut, subscriptions grew by 50 percent to 100 percent with each new issue. *Memory Makers* has since doubled its frequency, and its circulation was two hundred twenty-five thousand at the time of this writing. Michele Gerbrandt says there's no mystery why her subscriber base expanded so rapidly. "We started with this core, and now we're working out to the edge of the circle. Everyone else works from the outside in."

Ranking Pays Off

By ranking customers we keep our egos in line and the business in perspective. Company owners wise enough to stop and listen to the numbers often reap many rewards. We become better at negotiating, customer service, and sales prospecting. And we might just save our companies from a premature ending or a slow death. How you choose to carry out the ranking process may not matter as much as just doing it. You can always do it again (and should) to continue testing your assumptions. But be forewarned: once the rating game begins, there's no going back. You can't help but act on what you've learned. You will use what you know to develop a deeper relationship with the customer, or else you will eventually break up. Either way, the infatuation stage is over.

When you start ranking customers and prospects, you're making a conscious decision to reject traditional approaches to sales prospecting.

That's not easy. The process affects how you manage sales, who you hire, and even how you compensate them. Customer chemistry is a way of thinking about business that starts with you, but the message needs to radiate throughout your company.

Chemistry Checklist

1. *Consider several ways you could begin ranking customers.* There are numerous ways to evaluate customer rankings. Take a look at annual sales, profitability, number of referrals, long-term contracts, and cost to service the customer. Be sure to consider soft factors, such as ease of doing business with the customer, level of effort to support the customer, customer support of your business, and type of industries that the majority of your customers are in.

2. *Gather the sales data to rank all customers.* Using the sales data, create a list and rank your customers by sales volume for the past month and the past year. For certain types of businesses, it may also make sense to review sales over a longer period of time, for example, three to five years. For certain retailers who may not have sales data for individual customers, analyze how the customer buys from you. Review whether foot traffic, catalog, or online customers generate the most sales.

3. *Attempt to rank customers on their profitability, using the formula that makes the most sense for your industry.* Consider using our sample worksheet (shown in Figure 2.2) to drill down to contribution margin.

4. *Enlist outside help (from a mentor, peer group, business school class, a trusted accountant, or recommended consultant) to help you make sense of the numbers.* Many college business schools and small-business development centers (SBDCs) are eager to work with companies to conduct real-life case studies.

5. *Create a "best-customer profile" based on the results of your customer ranking.* Explore the characteristics of your best customers and what they have in common. Are your best customers all from the same industry or geographic location? Consider demographics such as title of purchaser and age range.

Figure 2.2 Contribution Margin Worksheet

Name of Customer:		The Carr Company
Product Lines Purchased in the Last Year:		Event, Flowers, catering

Total Sales		200,000.00
Variable Manufacturing/Service Costs	Less:	140,000.00
Gross Margin	Equals:	60,000.00
Variable Selling Expenses	Less:	5,000.00
	Equals:	55,000.00
Variable Administrative Expenses	Less:	40,000.00
	Equals:	15,000.00
Contribution Margin*		15,000.00

*The "contribution" that this customer makes toward the fixed costs and profits of the company, or what's left after all of the variable costs associated with the customer have been accounted for. Think of variable expenses as the costs that would "go away" if this customer left.

6. *Use what you know about your best customers to pick new customers.* You can create a profile of your best sales prospects by linking closely to your best-customer profile. Be sure to secure input from your entire staff. Your frontline employees typically can provide invaluable input as to the characteristics of best customers and prospects.

CHAPTER 3

EMPLOYEES ENTER THE CUSTOMER-CHEMISTRY EQUATION
RULE 3: TEACH EMPLOYEES TO FOCUS ON BEST CUSTOMERS AND PROSPECTS

For the first several years in business, the goal at Capitol Concierge was to dominate our market by trying to add as many customers inside each building as we possibly could. We held contests among the concierges for opening up the most new accounts. They were rewarded on transactional volume. Of course, I was sending the wrong message to my concierges about what really mattered. I was putting the numbers before the relationships the concierges needed to develop in order to succeed.

The customer-ranking process provided the push I needed to upset the apple cart. As my managers and I came to an agreement about Capitol's best customers, there was a kind of domino effect. I realized we had been doing so many things all wrong. The way we had been recruiting new concierges was shortsighted. Our training lacked focus. Rewards for good performance—monetary and otherwise—needed to be updated and directed toward the ultimate goal. For Capitol Concierge the ultimate goal was and is to learn more about our best customers' needs and in the process increase service revenue, defined as income generated by all the products and services an individual could request from the concierge desk.

Just as I now had a picture of my ideal customer in mind, so I began to develop a portrait of the ideal employee, based on real concierges who had done an outstanding job of getting to know hundreds of customers. I started to pay a lot more attention to those individual concierges and even mapped out their personality traits. What I really wanted was to clone them. At the very least I could attempt to hire others who shared some of the same personality traits.

At the same time I started to change the way I thought about market research. All of a sudden the market didn't seem to matter so much; individual customers did. Before this breakthrough I thought about market research in a very rose-colored, academic way. You know, you sit in corporate headquarters, or what I call the "ivory tower," saying, "I know what the customer wants." You decide, you push it out there, but you don't really know if customers will be receptive.

I've learned that customer chemistry comes down to aligning your company's agenda with that of your best customers. In aligning Capitol Concierge's agenda, I realized the value of listening to our customers. But it's not enough that I, the CEO, listen to what my customers have to say. I want everyone I hire to care. I want everyone to be an active listener. I want everyone to be like TV's Detective Colombo asking "just one more question," but in a courteous way. I want everyone to really listen because we've got a lot to learn.

A few years ago, Capitol Concierge launched something called the "2 + 10 + PM" campaign wherein every concierge had the same assignment: get to know two corporate customers, ten individuals, and one property manager. My managers and I repeated the message over and over: "Two corporations, ten individuals, and your property manager. That's it. That's all I want you to focus on. We want them, we want you all over them."

I think it helps immensely to have a theme and some kind of goal, even if it's not a traditional sales quota. Otherwise, the process of getting to know customers can be pretty overwhelming. In 2000 our theme was "Back to the Future" because even as the company was leveraging the power of the World Wide Web to build customer relationships, it returned to one of its best and most basic tactics: handwritten notes and personal phone calls. Each concierge was assigned to make five personal contacts a week.

Build a Workplace Where Chemistry Can Grow

Great companies know a thing or two about customer chemistry because they cultivate it actively—from the inside out. They listen to their employees and teach them to listen to customers. There's both an art and a science to this. First you have to hire the kind of people who care. Of course that's easier said than done in an economy where labor shortages (at least at some levels) are expected to persist for years to come. Perhaps that's why college internships and apprentice programs through community colleges are more popular than ever.

RULE 3: TEACH EMPLOYEES TO FOCUS ON BEST CUSTOMERS AND PROSPECTS

Once you have identified your best customers, your team needs to know who they are. Provide your employees with techniques to uncover customer preferences and make every customer interaction count.

Despite the dearth of skilled and unskilled workers, the companies voted the best to work for invariably have a waiting line. Staffing up is not a problem for these companies. Hiring is one part of the equation; creating a winning culture and training employees in the ways of service are equally important. Even in a tight labor market in which you don't have as much control in hiring, you do have total control over how employees are trained and the environment they walk into the first day on the job. Indeed, there are five pillars on which to build a foundation for strong relationships:

1. Find employees who care.
2. Train employees to "get it."
3. Share your best-customer profile with employees.
4. Teach employees to be detectives.
5. Help employees stay focused.

Find Employees Who Care

The process of getting closer to your best customers starts with you—and builds with every employee you bring on, whether it's a sales rep or a part-time person to answer the phones. For example, at Beverly Hall Furniture Galleries, a leading furniture store in Atlanta, owner Jerry Hux makes a priority of recruiting the type of employee "who derives satisfaction from converting an unhappy customer into a fan," he says. The last person Hux wants to hire is someone "who questions the reason the customer has a problem." Beverly Hall Furniture Galleries is known for its superior service—from the store designers to the delivery staff.

Superior service is one path to customer chemistry. But again it comes back to the people you hire. No wonder so many companies use personality testing today as part of the hiring process. There's an imperative to hire the right temperament for the job, for the company culture, and also for the mix of clients.

Match Employees to Customers

Some company owners even ask valued clients to help them interview job candidates. It's all about matching up the right employees with the right customers and the right customers with the right employees.

Claudia Brooks D'Avanzo takes the matchmaking process very seriously. She is the owner of an Atlanta-based marketing and public relations firm called Creative Communications Consultants. Her clients include divisions of large companies. She has succeeded in attracting big-name customers by offering them an irresistible combination: "senior people at small agency rates." Her secret? She maintains a network of soloists and other small company owners she brings together for specific projects. Within her network, she has carefully screened each team member-graphic artist, photographer, speechwriter, or PR/marketing professional. "You have to vet the people you work with" just as you do clients, she says. D'Avanzo has known many in her network for ten years or more. And so she is comfortable introducing her team to her best clients. In fact, she relishes the chance to play professional matchmaker by pairing up network members with particular customers whom she thinks will hit it off. "I love bringing the talent to the client. The client never forgets who brought the talent to the table." Nevertheless, D'Avanzo's reputation is always on the line, and if a combination isn't working out, she doesn't hesitate to step in and make changes. Usually the matches do work precisely because she takes the time to recruit the most suitable people for each project and oversees the work herself. Forging such precise matches among workers and customers was something she didn't have time to do in her previous life as a senior vice president at a prestigious PR agency.

You can also bring about good matches by providing a forum for employees and customers to become mutually acquainted. Special events are one way, but there are other, less expensive means to begin the process. Christopher Schmus, president of ProDriver Leasing Systems in Greenfield, Wisconsin, and winner of a Young Entrepreneur award from the Small Business Administration (SBA), helps his employees get to know his customers through a quarterly newsletter in which customers also get the scoop on the company's drivers. Each installment of "The ProDriver Times" includes a customer spotlight detailing the customer's business, the owner, and more. Driver profiles include career highlights as well as personal information on hobbies. Schmus also gives his drivers awards and writes about that in the newsletter as well. This helps bring the drivers and customers together in a friendly atmosphere, and he believes that it is one of the reasons many of his clients continually request certain drivers.

Rethink Your Recruiting Strategy

The quest to match your staff to your best customers is critical to building customer chemistry. It's not always easy. It may mean revamping your recruiting strategy altogether or at least widening the range of your employee search. Consider the strategy of the SoftAdGroup, a high-tech public relations firm in Mill Valley, California. SoftAdGroup circumvented the recruiting wars in Silicon Valley by helping to create an internship program on the college campus of the CEO's alma mater located across the country. Many interns have become SoftAd employees, who despite their young age have a serious advantage over other job candidates: they already know the company and its clients. The idea was the brainchild of SoftAdGroup's CEO, Paula George Tompkins, who grew up in a small town in West Virginia and attended nearby Marshall University, which now provides interns to SoftAd. The company started as a one-woman, home-based business but grew over sixteen years to a company of 175.

As the labor crunch worsened in the late '90s, Capitol Concierge began recruiting more mature workers, often from the hospitality industry. Reaching out to baby boomers (and older) has meant a big demographic shift in hiring, but the effort has paid off in more reliable workers who are enthusiastic, possess a good work ethic, and want stability. Capitol has also found that recruiting from the hotel and retail fields has an added advantage—it's easier to attract service-minded people who want to transition back to a normal workday.

Get in the habit of giving out business cards to anyone you meet who impresses you with their service. Bob Carbonell, the CEO of Relocation Management Resources (RMR), found one of his best customer service managers during a frustrating experience at the airport. Upon finding out his flight was cancelled, Carbonell called the airline to complain—bitterly. The woman who took the call remained poised despite the CEO's self-described ranting and raving. By the end of the conversation Carbonell had made the woman a job offer, which she later accepted. Today she deals directly with RMR's top clients.

Train Employees to "Get It"

Hiring caring individuals—or building a network of outside talent you can rely on—is a crucial step to building strong customer relationships. But you must also provide staff with the training and support they need to make good decisions, ask good questions, and, most of all, give customers satisfying answers. Whether you have one employee or one hundred, everyone affects the customer chemistry equation. Sometimes it's the lowest-paid person in the company (like the part-time receptionist you thought was a bargain at $8 an hour) who has the greatest effect.

Teach Employees the Art of Active Listening

One of the greatest things you can teach any hire is how to listen. In that regard there are lessons to be learned from the nonprofit world. Consider, for example, the best consumer hotlines. Although the hotlines are often provided by nonprofit operations strapped for cash, they take the time to really train their volunteers before sending them to the phones. One example stands out in Boston: the Parental Stressline spends no less than six weeks training every new volunteer phone counselor. The training focuses on *active listening*, and what that boils down to is this: "listen first, ask questions second." Don't try to solve someone else's problem; help the person arrive at their own solution. That philosophy may not seem to have much in common with the business world where we are relentless in the pursuit of solutions for our customers, but actually it does. Making assumptions about a customer's needs doesn't get you the sale. Listening does.

To paraphrase the title of a bestselling book on parenting, you want to teach employees to listen so customers will talk and talk so customers will listen. Brothers Ned and Dave Nelson decided to do just that. Not long after they started Aims Logistics, they invited their employees to practice public speaking. They even created a nighttime class they called "mock Toastmasters." Why would they go to such lengths to make staffers sound more polished? After all, their $9-million company in Collierville, Tennessee, is in the unglamorous business of processing freight charges for multinational clients. It's meticulous, nose-to-the-grindstone work; too much talking is a drag on productivity. Or at least that's the way the Nelson brothers had always known their industry to be.

When the two set up their own shop in 1994, they were vocal about changing the rules. Every employee, they decided, would talk to customers. Every employee would be responsible for customer service—not a designated department.

As such, they've opted for a tag-team approach to serving customers that avoids the us-versus-them mentality that commonly creeps in when customer service is an isolated entity. Instead, eight teams are each responsible for one, two, or three clients. (In the year 2001 about 135 employees were assigned to 24 clients.) That kind of ratio of employees to clients means each client gets personalized attention from the moment of the sale through billing. That's paramount when your typical client is a big-volume shipper that has chosen to outsource all its freight payables to you. The practice has been to marry old and new employees for each new team—there are usually seven to ten employees per team—and to cross train everyone. Today that training goes well beyond mock toastmasters. Team leaders instruct members on every process of the operation as it pertains to each client.

To measure customer satisfaction, Aims conducts not one survey but fourteen, one for each team. So far the results speak volumes: Aims has lost only two customers in seven years (and one of those to a merger).

Encourage Compassion for Customers

To help build empathy for the customer, flower seller ProFlowers, for example, requires that all staffers get a taste for what it's like to answer the phones during peak hours. ProFlowers sells flowers over the Internet but still makes many sales by phone. Around holidays like Valentine's Day, when the pressure is at a peak, everyone takes customer calls. "It gives you an incredible experience of what the customers are looking for and what's important to them," says CEO Bill Strauss. "When people go back to their own departments, it keeps them from being in a vacuum." (They also walk away with more compassion for customer service reps.)

Make Training Customer Specific

Beyond teaching employees to "feel" for all customers, you want them to be particularly sensitive to the needs of specific customers. Consider the customer service training at ScriptSave, a Tucson company that manages prescription drug programs for insurance companies. ScriptSave employees undergo extensive instruction with pointers on the particular concerns of each insurance firm, which often vary by state. That's just the beginning. Every employee is also taught to be in tune with the needs of the consumers getting prescriptions filled. Consumers call ScriptSave to get started on the program and when problems arise. Many are senior citizens, and some have problems seeing and hearing. The average senior has three to four prescriptions filled a month, so before employees get on the phone with customers, they first complete a senior sensitivity workshop. At ScriptSave the staff is trained to understand the *core customers* as well as the core products.

Broadcast Who the Top Customers Are

There are many, many ways a company can communicate to employees who the core customer is. Here are a few approaches some have used: A manufacturer posts the Top Ten Clients list on the factory floor for all to see. A service firm ensures that anyone who answers the phone is versed in the names of individuals who call from top accounts. Smed International, manufacturer of office furniture, based in Calgary, Canada, publishes detailed customer case studies that spell out the importance of a major new customer or repeat sale. Springfield Remanufacturing Corp., a company well known for its open-book practices, posts a daily sales sheet that includes such facts as who's buying, what they're buying, and how much they're buying. Likewise, you can see at a glance who's who when you visit the front office of the St. Paul Saints, a minor league baseball team in St. Paul, Minnesota. Just peruse the white boards for the names of the corporations who are sponsoring game promotions and have reserved the Saints' premium (and quirky) "luxury" seating.

At Grand Circle Corporation (GCC), a Boston company that arranges travel tours for senior citizens, there are three basic customer designations. Drawing clear and simple distinctions helps the company's telemarketers use their time wisely. Best customers are defined as people who have traveled with GCC in the past two years and have spent $10,000 or more on trips—Grand Circle calls this group the "GCC Inner Circle." The other customer groups are equally straightforward in nature. "Active Travelers" have taken at least one trip with GCC in the past year but have spent less than $10,000. "Inactive Travelers" have taken a GCC trip in the past, but not in the past year.

The workers at Great Harvest certainly know who "butters their bread." Great Harvest Bread Company is a franchise of small bakeries. Like many retailers, Great Harvest stores make use of a frequent-buyer card, which is simply called the bread card. After you buy so many loaves of bread you get one free. Here's the charm: each time a store worker stamps a customer's card, he or she also writes in the date, transforming the bread card into a *smart card*. The next time the customer buys bread, the store worker simply checks the last date of purchase and makes a quick determination of the customer's loyalty.

Janene Centurione, the owner of Great Harvest store in Ann Arbor, Michigan, with sales of about $2 million, has had great success using the bread card to instantly identify the frequent customers. She explains the significance of dating each purchase: she and her staff know that the best customers come into the store at least once a month. So when a best customer returns, the sales clerk offers a point-of-sale perk such as a complimentary muffin. Not only is this a simple way of identifying VIP customers, but it's in real time. Furthermore, a B customer can be upgraded to A status by virtue of his or her most recent purchases. "When someone hands you their card, you have an immediate frequency profile!" And all without the help of technology! Centurione has made the bread card a central element of the customer service training all employees receive. In Centurione's there's a script for how to handle each kind of customer according to where the person fits in the bell curve of all customers. For example, for customers who shop less frequently the store clerk will take the time to explain new products the customer probably doesn't know about.

Share Your Best-Customer Profile with Employees

Your staff should be part of the process of building out your best-customer profile. Even if you're not an open-book company, the customer profile is not something you want to keep secret. It's too important to keep under wraps. Along with you, employees should be actively engaged in exploring the characteristics of top customers. What, if anything, do these customers have in common? In contrast to the quantitative process of ranking customers by sales and profitability, the best-customer profile is a qualitative tool. Over time, you will be able to define several classes of best customers. That in turn will help determine the sorts of things you need to know about anyone you do business with. Figure 3.1 shows the profile form Capitol Concierge uses.

In cyberspace the term *customer profiling* has a negative connotation because it usually means compiling data without the knowledge or explicit consent of the customer. In the context of customer chemistry, however, customer profiling is a systematic way of documenting customer interests, preferences, future needs, and buying cycles that absolutely depends on the customer's participation.

If your customer base consists of hundreds or thousands of individuals—or if your time and resources are limited—start small. Start with your top-ten customers. But start today. Take advantage of every avenue for contact. With the ideal best-customer profile in mind, your employees should be learning more about individual customers to see if they might fit the best-customer classification. The ultimate goal is to develop a full profile of each customer. Over time, you can also create profiles of promising prospects.

Developing customer profiles is important for a few reasons. You can sit down with staff and say, "This is the information we're going to capture and why." That naturally leads to a discussion of "How are we going to capture it? How are we going to start talking to these customers?" And there are so many ways. The goal is to make every interaction a learning interaction. Even in casual conversation you're trying to pick up a new piece of information to add to the profile and "leaven" the relationship.

The activities that go into creating customer profiles are not carried out in a vacuum. Rather the process should be part of the natural customer-feedback loop. It's all part of the effort to improve products and services. Not coincidentally, the process of learning about individual customers goes hand in hand with rewarding those same customers. For example, frequent-buyer clubs and VIP programs recognize top clients, who in turn volunteer more information about themselves.

Figure 3.1 Capitol Concierge Client Profile

1. Contact Information

Client Name: _____   Title: _____

Company: _____   Business Type: _____

Work Address: _____   Suite #: _____

City: _____   State: _____   Zip Code: _____

Phone # (w): _____/_____   Phone # (h): _____/_____

Fax #: _____/_____   E-Mail Address: _____

2. Personal Service Information

Account #: _____   Client Birthday (mo/date): _____/_____

Single/Married: _____   Spouse's Name: _____

Age Range: _____   Commuting Method: _____

Type: D S T R   How does client contact you: ___ phone   ___ fax

                                                     ___ at desk   ___ e-mail

Children:	Name	Age	Birthday (mo/date)
	_____	_____	_____/_____
	_____	_____	_____/_____
	_____	_____	_____/_____
	_____	_____	_____/_____

Conversational Interests:

3. Concierge Service Information

Entertainment Preferences: Sports, Concerts, Theater
Client has expressed interest in or has purchased event tickets for the following:

Sports	**Concert Preferences**	**Theater Preferences**
___ Baseball	___ Rock/Pop	___ Drama
___ Basketball	___ Jazz	___ Musicals
___ Football	___ Symphony	___ Dance
___ Golf Tournaments	___ Country and Western	___ Opera
___ Tennis	___ R&B	___ Comedy
___ Hockey	___ Alternative	___ Alternative
___ Soccer		
___ Ice Skating		
___ Other: _____		

Favorite team:	Favorite entertainer:	Favorite show:
_____	_____	_____

Client purchases tickets for   ___ him/herself   ___ clients

                                ___ premium tickets   ___ face value only

Recreation/Hobby Interests:

___ Water Sports   ___ Boating
___ Winter Sports   ___ Horseback Riding
___ Hiking   ___ Fishing
___ Biking   ___ Other: _____

Favorite leisure activity: _____

Washington Area Interests:

___ Nightclubs   ___ Museums   ___ Tours/Festivals   ___ B&B

Other: _____

Restaurants:

Favorite Restaurants: Favorite Cuisine Type:

_____   _____

_____   _____

Your Client's Favorite:

Type of Book: _____   Type of Movie: _____
Flower: _____   Candy: _____
Magazine: _____   Fragrance: _____

Gift Services (Client gift interests):   *Gourmet Gift Giving:*

___ Flowers/Plants/Balloons   ___ Coffee
___ Cigars   ___ Cakes/Cookies
___ Books   ___ Food/Fruit Baskets
___ Sports Items   ___ Chocolates
___ Novelty/Electronics   ___ Wine/Liquor
___ Gift Baskets   ___ Gourmet Meat/Seafood
___ Children's Items   ___ Snack Items (Popcorn Tins)
___ Other: _____

Gift certificates to favorite store: _____

Client's favorite gift(s) to give: _____

Client gives gifts to: ___ family   ___ friends   ___ clients

Personal Services:

Dry cleaning/laundry: shirt starch preference: _____   frequency: _____

Auto inspection date: _____   Auto type: _____

Parks where: _____

Detail schedule: ___ weekly   ___ monthly   ___ quarterly

Travel:

Client travels primarily for: ___ business   ___ leisure

Travel frequency for business: ___ 1 or more times per week   ___ monthly

                        Other: _____

Travel destination/trip interests are:

___ Cruises   ___ Tropical Resorts   ___ Family Vacations   ___ Spa/Sports

___ Weekend Getaways/B&Bs   ___ Tours Foreign: _____

U.S. Region: _____   Other: _____

Recent trips taken: _____

Limo/sedan service: ___ special occasions   ___ airport transfers

Teach Employees to Be Detectives

Retail environments present their own special challenge—the challenge of getting to know a sea of seemingly anonymous customers. But in any company in any industry, there is always more to learn. The effort to bring the right products and services to the right customers often involves detective work.

What should you be trying to learn about your customers? Some companies ask customers dozens if not hundred of questions in surveys throughout the year. To get started you only need a few. Focus on a couple of qualifying questions that you and your staff can use daily in phone conversations, e-mail exchanges, special events, and face-to-face meetings. The questions should be so natural that they don't sound rehearsed. Employees will become more relaxed in their conversations with customers as they get more practice.

What are the best ways to give them more practice? Seek out as many ways as possible to include employees in customer conversations. Make sure every employee gets a chance to be part of customer focus groups, writing thank-you notes, traveling to client sites, and carrying out customer surveys. Talking to customers may come easy enough to you; many employees, however, benefit from having a script to start with, from participating in role-playing sessions, and especially from one-to-one mentoring by the company owner or a manager.

There are really two sides to the role of detective (and some companies liken it to playing investigative reporter): *deciphering the needs of current customers* and *sleuthing out your best sales prospects*. For some companies, those two tasks are one and the same, but for other companies they are quite different. Some companies assign junior level staffers to sales-lead screening while others assign one very senior person. Likewise, learning more about current customers may be everyone's job or it may be the exclusive responsibility of one or two people in the company.

When you ask employees to be detectives *on behalf of valued customers*, they may need to research, say, a customer's corporate culture and industry. Your staff must also know how to make important links among your customers and your product lines. For example, customer service reps at ScriptSave are trained to recognize which customers might be good candidates for special prescription offers or for additional services related to health and wellness.

At Capitol Concierge, if an individual is making dinner reservations, it may well be appropriate to suggest an order of roses waiting at the table. On the other hand, not all links are immediately obvious. For example, someone using the company for catering could turn out to be a perfect candidate for airport pickup. As a business owner or manager, you know the logical links in your service line. Over time you can begin to calculate what all these links are worth for each customer.

To help employees uncover hidden opportunities, you must provide them with the right management tools such as reports that provide the specifics of your relationship history with each customer. The employees need to know the key indicators for each customer, including number of transactions during the year, average transaction value, last purchase date, age of customer, active status, and number of referrals. Such measures can and should be incorporated into a *customer activity report*.

In addition, you'll want to develop a *share of customer report*, as shown in Figure 3.2. When you go *deep* within a smaller group of best customers instead of going *wide* with many customers, it is crucial to know just what share of a given customer's business you're getting. With the help of your staff, identify all *potential* customer purchases across your product and service lines. Many companies obsess about market share when they should focus on customer share. Make sure your employees know the difference between the two.

In the quest to sleuth out the best sales prospects, the role of the employee-detective is to sniff out sales leads that are a good match with the profile of your best customer. In this regard, it is absolutely vital to communicate to staff what that best customer looks like. Never forget that while you're trying to sell more to your existing customer base, you don't stop customer acquisition efforts; they're just a lot more focused and targeted because everyone understands what to look for in potential "partners."

Customer chemistry is not just what happens when you make a sale but what transpires before, during, and after the sale. Thus employees

Figure 3.2 Share of Customer Report

Identify current customer purchases across your different product and service lines.

Customer Name	Product 1	Annual Value Product 1	Product 2	Annual Value Product 2	Product 3	Actual Potential	Customer Rank
		$		$		$	
		$		$		$	
		$		$		$	
		$		$		$	
		$		$		$	
		$		$		$	
		$		$		$	
		$		$		$	
		$		$		$	
		$		$		$	
		$		$		$	

are trying to fill in the opportunity gaps at every stage. At the early stages of a relationship, Custom Research Inc., for instance, focuses some of its customer detective work on finding out why would-be customers are not fully satisfied with their current vendor relationships. Once they are customers, CRI takes the time to do extensive interviews detailing how the new clients prefer to work—research that uncovers numerous opportunities for quickly growing the budding relationship.

Chemistry is fluid, and so too customer chemistry changes states, from fluid to solid and back again, and sometimes evaporates into thin air. A top-tier client today may not be tomorrow. Priorities change. A customer may go away for no fault of yours—mergers and acquisitions (M&A), of course, have pared down the customer list of many a company. But when there is true customer chemistry, you won't be left in the dark about a pending M&A that affects your business. Companies can merge or go bankrupt, but the people at those companies—the ones you've worked hard to forge lasting relationships with—live on and move on. Customer chemistry then is not tied to a company. It is carried from company to company by the people who know you and trust what your company can do.

Perhaps nowhere is that more evident than in the fast-changing world of employee staffing. It's an industry in which loyalty (on the part of clients and talent) can be short-lived and promises can be broken. For companies competing in this arena, the list of top customers can change completely in a year, a month, a week, or even in a matter of hours.

For example, at Connect: The Knowledge Network, a twenty-person technical staffing firm in Littleton, Colorado, there is a daily reprioritization of tier-one customers, says co-owner Kelly Gilmore. She and her partner, Maureen Clarry, constantly confer with their four sales reps about who can be considered a top customer or prospect and why. The two cofounders have even developed an opportunity scoring mechanism based on about a dozen factors. Sales reps are asked to consider how quickly a customer plans to hire in addition to the size and rough profitability of the sale, for instance. But it's not just the size of the opportunity that matters. What counts even more, as far as Gilmore and Clarry are concerned, is how the customer relates to Connect. Will there be a direct relationship with the actual managers doing the hiring (a necessary ingredient to having a real relationship)? Or will Connect face a layer of human resources bureaucracy? If so, that makes it almost impossible to have a relationship with the actual client.

Connect's top customer list is constantly in flux, but Clarry and Gilmore have found some constancy. It lies in their relationship with a core group of individuals that has grown steadily over the years. These are the people who have tipped them off to mergers (and other bad news) ahead of time. They are also the ones who don't forget Connect when they leave one company and join another. They stay in touch and work with Connect over and over again (some for ten years now). Gilmore and Clarry track these relationships very closely. They even have a special designation for these individuals in their database—they call them alumni. To let these people know just how special they are, they even hold alumni events. Once forged, these relationships are never forgotten.

Help Employees Stay Focused

Remember, hours spent on going-nowhere, unprofitable customers take away from the time you have for good customers. Yet your resolve to take only the right customers will repeatedly be put to the test—perhaps each day. Resisting the easy sale isn't easy. Some companies keep their salespeople focused on the right customers purely by altering their commission schemes (paying a higher rate for repeat sales or new sales as circumstances dictate). One successful entrepreneur taught her salespeople to view customers through the "lens" of the contract; signed contracts that matched the company's ideal terms paid out the highest commission rate. But rarely does compensation alone do the trick. Employees need help and encouragement to stay on the straight and narrow.

At advertising agency Fallon McElligott, employees get a daily reminder of what's important. The first thing employees see when they power up their PCs in the morning is the company's mission statement: "To be the premier creative agency in the world producing extraordinarily effective work for a short list of blue chip clients." The mission is further bolstered by Fallon McElligott's seven core values. One is "the necessity of having fun." It's a whole lot easier to have fun in business when you are working with customers you admire and who admire you.

Many companies get distracted by spending too much time on every lead that comes in the door or over the transom. Consider creating a screening process for qualifying cold leads by composing a series of interview questions. Here are some you might want to consider asking would-be customers:

- *How'd you hear about us?* A bad answer: "I found you in the Yellow Pages." If someone was just flipping through the phone book, there's no compelling reason why they should use you over anyone else. You're a commodity as far as that caller is concerned. A good answer: "A colleague of mine recommended you."
- *What kind of work is it?* You know you can't be all things to all people. Asking this question will quickly let you know if the work is outside your scope or right up your alley. The answer may also reveal if the caller is trying to price a quick, one-time project.
- *What's your budget for the project?* Admittedly this is an uncomfortable question to ask, but you can ease the discomfort by bouncing off a ballpark figure—and gauging the response.
- *What's your decision criteria?* Many companies don't fare as well in blind bidding or in drawn out, committee-style decisions. Avoid anything that smells like a bidding war. You won't find any customer chemistry in such lowball tactics.
- *Who else do you work with—who's our competition?* If you don't hear the names you consider to be your competitors, it could be the caller isn't buying what you're selling. Be sure you're in good company. You can also gauge the caller's budget for the project by the number of competing companies it uses. Too many suppliers can be a sign of constant churning.
- *Is there something wrong with your current supplier?* Another tricky question, so listen carefully. You want a customer who doesn't switch suppliers easily, yet you also need a way to break in.

At companies where such questions are routinely used to screen callers, it may be that only a handful of callers each month answer enough questions right to warrant more attention. Regardless, train employees to be courteous to every person who calls regardless of their status as a sales prospect. There is an art to saying no, and employees need to practice how they will gently refer would-be customers to the competition. You may even want to assign one point person to act as your "referral desk." Indeed, when you handle the rejection process respectfully by providing contact information for a competitor, your company wins points for being helpful.

The Customer-Chemistry Team

The whole point of involving employees is that getting closer to customers should be a team effort. Making contact with customers is too big and too important a role to be left to one part of the company, whether that's upper management, marketing, or the sales department. Rockford Construction, for example, does not even have a sales force. Yet the company has grown more than 800 percent since 1994. How is that kind of growth possible without dedicated salespeople? Rockford's charismatic CEO, John Wheeler, is no slouch when it comes to making sales, but he attributes much of the company's success to the repeat business generated by a half dozen company teams devoted to tracking the needs of individual clients.

In fact, one whole team is dedicated entirely to Rockford's largest retail client. Another team is devoted to Rockford's health care industry customers. Yet another takes care of video store clients. Wheeler created the teams about six years ago instead of hiring commissioned salespeople. He's never regretted that decision. "We groomed the team to the customer and asked the customer for feedback," he explains. They had one request: "Just take care of me." One of his largest customers even asked if it could "borrow" a Rockford team member for two months of the year. Wheeler said yes. You can imagine the elevated level of goodwill and dialogue that resulted from sharing an employee. Sales rose to $125 million in 2000, up from $12 million in 1994, the year Wheeler adopted the team concept for catering to customers.

In truth, the job of learning about customers and their needs is too impor-
tant to be left exclusively to a company's owners. Customer chemistry tran-

scends corporate titles and departments. It happens person to person and builds one employee at a time.

Capitol Concierge Best Practices

- *Proactively pursue employees who excel at customer service.* With the ideal employee profile in mind, Capitol's managers began seeking out exemplary retail workers in malls, handing out business cards listing four reasons they should work for Capitol Concierge.
- *A week-long training program for new hires.* All new hires undergo five days of training on subjects such as suggestion marketing. The company devotes one day to teaching product, for example, and two full days to teaching new concierges how to identify customers, build rapport, and develop customer profiles. There are also specific pointers on how to be a detective. There's homework, a test at the end, and a graduation party. Figure 3.3 shows Capitol's training schedule.
- *Rehearsing conversation starters.* Concierges are trained to ask simple questions: "Tell me about the company you work for." "What is your role within the organization?" "Which concierge services would be most valuable to you?" From there, the questions are more specific: "Tell me about the special events you are planning within the next quarter." "What are the special occasions you want to be reminded of?" "What do your clients like to do when they're in town?"
- *The customer scrapbook.* Some of Capitol's best-performing concierges kept scrapbooks filled with photos of their clients and prospects taken during company events. The scrapbooks became great training tools for the other concierges.
- *Assigning managers to top accounts.* Capitol Concierge's most seasoned managers are assigned to its most profitable accounts. Each manager covers a certain group of buildings and becomes familiar with the various corporate accounts within each of the buildings. Working with the concierges, managers identify the most profitable and active accounts and focus their efforts on growing those accounts. The managers conduct office manager luncheons and special one-on-one presentations with select corporate accounts that are either best customers or show the most potential for growth.

Figure 3.3 Capitol Concierge Orientation and Training

Monday

10:00 A.M.–1:00 P.M.	Introduction to Capitol Concierge and Our Service Standards
	History of Capitol Concierge
	Who are our customers?
	The role of the Concierge Club
	Capitol Concierge's five service standards
	Capitol Concierge S.T.A.R. program
	Capitol Concierge dress code
	Orientation and policy handbook
1:00 P.M.–2:00 P.M.	Lunch at Service Partners
2:00 P.M.–5:00 P.M.	Desk Observation (team leaders)
Homework Assignment	Read service menu, procedure manual, and One-to-One article

Tuesday

10:00 A.M.–1:00 P.M.	Concierge as Service Consultant: Product Knowledge
	Client-product-matching exercises
	Role-playing
	Suggestive marketing
	Developing your product portfolio
1:00 P.M.–2:00 P.M.	Lunch
2:00 P.M.–5:00 P.M.	Order Placement and Financial Procedures
	Computer system demo; how to maximize potential
Homework Assignment	Study marketing manual and marketing articles

Wednesday

10:00 A.M.–1:00 P.M.	The Fundamentals of Relationship Marketing
	What is relationship marketing?
	How to identify and target clients
	How to calculate share of customer
	Developing client profiles—the Concierge as detective
	Study client service plan and activities notebook
1:00 P.M.–2:00 P.M.	Lunch
2:00 P.M.–5:00 P.M.	Concierge Desk Observations
Homework Assignment	Study marketing manual and marketing articles

Thursday

10:00 A.M.–1:00 P.M.	Relationship Marketing Part II
	The art of pacing: personality profiling and rapport building
	Using the client service plan
1:00 P.M.–2:00 P.M.	Lunch
2:00 P.M.–5:00 P.M.	Concierge Awareness Tools, Effective Follow-Up, Activities Planning
Homework Assignment	Study marketing manual and marketing articles

Friday

10:00 A.M.–1:00 P.M.	Capitol Concierge Opportunities
	Ongoing training
	Recognition programs/Bonus Bucks/S.T.A.R. program
	Tracking your success
	Team participation
	Effective incident resolution
1:00 P.M.–2:00 P.M.	Lunch
2:00 P.M.–5:00 P.M.	Concierge Test and Graduation!

• *Forms for helping employees gather information.* "Executive Focus" is a two-page form for gathering information about individual customers. Concierges adopted the Client Profile form (Figure 3.1) and used it to collect information on key executive clients. The management team decided to focus on executives in the office buildings for two reasons: executives had the most disposable income and they influence corporate purchasing decisions. The first time Capitol tried this, each concierge was assigned to complete five Executive Focus forms on existing customers each month. The company helped the concierges choose the five. In fact, they had weekly conversations about it. (Who is someone you think fits our best-customer profile? Is it a partner in a law firm who passes your desk every day and doesn't know what we do?) The objective was to use strategic and proactive questions to obtain key personal preferences, including favorite gifts to give, favorite restaurants, top travel destinations, preferred method of being contacted, and special occasions for which they wanted reminders.

In turn, the information was used by the concierges to provide their busy executives with targeted information on services and events as well as reminders and specials personalized for each individual. A version of the Executive Focus form is maintained online in the form of a website-based "Personal Preference Profile" (see Figure 3.4). The company asks executive clients to fill this out themselves, but concierges are still happy to do this for them.

• *Forms for staying ahead of the curve.* Every company that sells to corporations has received a frantic phone call from a client asking for numbers for the new budget. Every summer, as property managers rushed to meet their budget deadlines, Capitol's office was flooded with calls requesting projections for the next year's concierge expenditures. The Capitol team would have to respond overnight with some sort of estimate on the percentage increase. The company broke the cycle by using the client's budget-planning season as an opportunity to learn about needs for the coming year. The result was a new form called the "Property Management Budget Planner" (shown in Figure 3.5 on page 68). The form is exactly what it sounds like—a spreadsheet with the months of the year and a list of services Capitol provides, from desk flowers to office tenant gifts and lobby events. The budget planner is sent, along with a small gift (a prod-

Figure 3.4 Personal Preferences Profile

ASK THE CONCIERGE **Go**

VIPdesk
Helping busy people get things done.

CHANGE CITY Chicago **Go**

| Home | Shopping | Household | Sports & Recreation | Dining | Entertainment | Travel | Tourist & City |

You are here: Home > Member Services   Member Services | Feedback | Customer Service

Personal Preferences

Tell us more about yourself by completing or updating your Personal Preferences Profile. The more we know about your gift and lifestyle preferences, the better we can be of service.

My Lifestyle Interests
(Check from one or more of the following)

☐ Food/Wine   ☐ Health/Fitness   ☐ Theatre/Music
☐ Art/Culture   ☐ Business/Finance   ☐ Toys/Games
☐ Home/Garden   ☐ Sports/Recreation   ☐ Travel/Leisure
☐ Fashion/Beauty   ☐ Electronics/Technology

My Gift Preferences
(Check from one or more of the following)

Favorite gifts to give:
☐ Flowers   ☐ Chocolate/Gourmet food   ☐ Gift baskets
☐ Gift certificates   ☐ Toys and games   ☐ Children
☐ Bar, wine and cigars ☐ Home and garden   ☐ Bath and body
☐ Fragrances   ☐ Electronics   ☐ Jewelry
☐ Books/Magazines/Music ☐ Pet gifts   ☐ Features of the day
☐ Luxury gifts

Favorite gifts to receive:
☐ Flowers   ☐ Chocolate/Gourmet food   ☐ Gift baskets
☐ Gift certificates   ☐ Toys and games   ☐ Children
☐ Bar, wine and cigars ☐ Home and garden   ☐ Bath and body
☐ Fragrances   ☐ Electronics   ☐ Jewelry
☐ Books/Magazines/Music ☐ Pet gifts   ☐ Features of the day
☐ Luxury gifts

Ticket Preferences
(Check from one or more of the following)

Sports:
☐ Basketball   ☐ Football   ☐ Baseball
☐ Soccer   ☐ Hockey   ☐ Golf
☐ Tennis   ☐ Auto Racing   ☐ Ice Skating

Theatre/Performing Arts:
☐ Drama   ☐ Musicals   ☐ Opera
☐ Comedy

uct sample) to all property managers. The return on this simple form has been easy to measure: smiles all around and a response rate as high as 97 percent.

A similar four-page form called "Corporate Concierge Service Planner" (shown in Figure 3.6 on page 70) was created for collecting crucial data on the buying cycles of office managers. Capitol Concierge puts on luncheons during which office managers are asked to complete the corporate planner—for instance, checking off events such as anniversaries, Secretaries Day, recruitment fairs, holiday parties, conferences where they could use Capitol's services. This strategy has enabled Capitol to stay ahead of buying cycles, increase the

---

Concerts:

☐ Alternative	☐ Blues	☐ Children's Music
☐ Classical Music	☐ Country	☐ Folk
☐ Hip-Hop	☐ International	☐ Jazz
☐ New Age Music	☐ Opera & Vocal	☐ Pop/Top 40
☐ Rock	☐ Rhythm & Blues	☐ Soundtracks

Favorite Group: [   ]

Dining Preferences
(Check from one or more of the following)

Cuisine Type:

☐ American	☐ Belgian	☐ French
☐ Health Food	☐ International	☐ Italian
☐ Japanese	☐ Mexican	☐ Seafood
☐ All Cuisines		

Travel Preferences
(Check from one or more of the following)

Travel for:

☐ Business	☐ Leisure

Travel Frequency:

◔ 1 or More Times Per Week	◔ 1 or More Times Per Month	◔ 1 or More Times Per Year

Destination/Trip Interests:

☐ Cruises	☐ Tropical Resorts	☐ Family Vacations
☐ Spa	☐ Adventure/Sports	☐ Weekend Getaways
☐ Tours	☐ International	☐ US
☐ Airline Packages	☐ Hotels	

My Home
(Check from one or more of the following)

I am interested in:

☐ Auto Care	☐ Grocery	☐ Pharmacy
☐ Home Furnishings	☐ Cleaning	☐ Appliances
☐ Home Improvements/Repair		

< Save >

probability of closing a sale, and, most important, impress clients with proactive service.

- *Employee bonus plan.* Capitol created an incentive program called the "$1,000 Club," the goal of which is for each concierge to reach a baseline of at least $1,000 in gross service revenue per month. This program was designed to jump-start new concierges eager to ramp up quickly and leverage the historical knowledge of their buildings. Membership in the $1,000 Club has grown from fourteen to forty concierges.

- *When good employees leave.* The company conducts an exit interview to review the employee's success in building customer relationships, obstacles encountered, customer likes and dislikes, as well as their suggestions for improving client relations. This ensures a smooth knowledge transfer for the new employee and prompts new reasons to contact customers.

Figure 3.5 Property Management Budget Planner

In an effort to provide a higher level of service, we have developed this Property Management Budget Planner. Our goal is to achieve the following objectives with this time-saving tool:

- Proactively create an annual calendar "at a glance"
- Create a unique series of tenant retention activities
- Ensure adequate advance planning
- Address tenant interests and needs

Property Manager: _____

Building Address: _____

Concierge: _____

Date Completed: _____

Building No.: _____

CAPITOL CONCIERGE, INC.
1400 Eye Street NW, Suite 750, Washington, DC 20005
Phone: 202/223-4765 • Fax: 202/833-2287
www.capitolconcierge.com

Figure 3.5 Property Management Budget Planner (continued)

Simply place a check mark (✓) in the month

	Jan	Feb	Mar	Apr
Lobby Events—				
CC, Inc. will submit proposal	☐	☐	☐	☐
_____	☐	☐	☐	☐
_____	☐	☐	☐	☐
_____	☐	☐	☐	☐
_____	☐	☐	☐	☐
_____	☐	☐	☐	☐
_____	☐	☐	☐	☐
_____	☐	☐	☐	☐
_____	☐	☐	☐	☐
Office Managers' Luncheon	☐	☐	☐	☐
Community Involvement Events	☐	☐	☐	☐
Art Show—high school and senior citizens	☐	☐	☐	☐
Book Fair	☐	☐	☐	☐
Vacation Fair	☐	☐	☐	☐
Sports Fair	☐	☐	☐	☐
Cyber Fair	☐	☐	☐	☐
Local Musicians—during lunch hours	☐	☐	☐	☐
Health—wellness fair	☐	☐	☐	☐
Charity Events	☐	☐	☐	☐
American Cancer Society	☐	☐	☐	☐
Blood Drive	☐	☐	☐	☐
School Supply Drive	☐	☐	☐	☐
Can-U-Care Drive	☐	☐	☐	☐
Clothing Drive	☐	☐	☐	☐
Angel Tree Program	☐	☐	☐	☐
Thanksgiving Family Meal	☐	☐	☐	☐
AIDs Walk	☐	☐	☐	☐
Grandma's House	☐	☐	☐	☐
Tenant Gifts	☐	☐	☐	☐
Holiday	☐	☐	☐	☐
Lease Signers	☐	☐	☐	☐
Tenant Orientation/Roundtables	☐	☐	☐	☐
New Tenant Move-Ins	☐	☐	☐	☐
Renovations	☐	☐	☐	☐
Lobby Decorations (December)	☐	☐	☐	☐

Building Population: _____   Number of Tenants: _____

Annual Tenant Retention Budget: $ _____   Tenant Anniversary List: _____

Figure 3.6 Corporate Concierge Service Planner

Corporate Concierge Service Planner
(completion time: only 10 minutes)

ABOUT CAPITOL CONCIERGE:

Capitol Concierge has 9 years of experience in assisting over 5000 companies like yours with a variety of time-saving services. Working behind the scenes with your concierge, is a dedicated management team of corporate service managers and an extensive network of service partner vendors. *Our primary goal is to save you and your organization time and money* by delivering quality services and a wealth of information through one-single source — Capitol Concierge. Let us help you and *Consider It Done!*

What We Can Do for You and Your Company:

- ▶ Save you time, effort and money
- ▶ One-stop service ordering and order tracking service
- ▶ Conduct research and secure proposals for corporate services
- ▶ Provide a corporate occasion reminder service: remind you of key dates and assist with service planning
- ▶ Participate in new employee orientation; the concierge is a human resources benefit
- ▶ Suggest marketing ideas to assist you in growing your business and keeping your clients happy
- ▶ Assist you with employee recognition and retention programs
- ▶ Provide you and your clients with Washington Area entertainment and attraction information
- ▶ Conduct complimentary workshops and seminars
- ▶ Provide content for your in-house company newsletter

Let Us Assist You:

In order for us to provide you with proactive service, we ask that you complete the following Corporate Service Planner information. Capitol Concierge will enter this information into a computerized Corporate Service Planner which will enable us to provide you with reminders of key dates, special service offers, and to present service information/proposals for your unique needs.

ABOUT YOUR COMPANY:

Name of Company: _____

Company's main line of business (i.e. legal, financial, association, technology, etc.): _____

Number of staff members: Management:_____   Support staff:_____   Total number on staff:_____

Key Staff Members:

President _____

President's Assistant _____

Office Manager _____

Human Resources Mgr. _____

Marketing Manager_____

Receptionist_____

Other: _____

Office Status:

- ❑ Only location in entire organization
- ❑ Headquarters of multi-location organization
- ❑ Branch/division of multi-location organization
- ❑ Other:_____

How do you want to receive info on services (circle one):

fax	e-mail	interoffice mail
receptionist	mail	telephone
other_____		

CORPORATE SERVICE PLANNER:

We can assist you with planning, research, *offers* and reminders of the following:

Corporate Gifts: Staff

Do you give gifts to staff on any of the following occasions?

| | What we do now: | | Gift Preference | | | | | | | If you don't give gifts now for this occasion, would you like more information? |
	Monthly	Weekly	cake	basket	flower	desk access	gift certificate	engraved item	other	
a. Birthdays	❑	❑								❑
b. New employee welcome	❑	❑								❑
c. Promotion	❑	❑								❑
d. Awards/recognition	❑	❑								❑
e. Employee anniversaries	❑	❑								❑
f. Holidays	❑	❑								❑
g. Retirement	❑	❑								❑
h. Get well; new baby	❑	❑								❑
i. Other:_____	❑	❑								❑

Corporate Gifts:Clients/Customers

Do you give gifts to clients on the following occasions?

Gift Preference

	What we do now:		cake	basket	flower	desk access	gift certificate	engraved item	other	If you don't give gifts now for this occasion, would you like more information?
	Monthly	Weekly								
a. Birthdays	❑	❑								❑
b. New account	❑	❑								❑
c. Anniversary	❑	❑								❑
d. Logo imprinted items	❑	❑								❑
e. Holidays	❑	❑								❑
f. Marketing promotions	❑	❑								❑
g. Renewals	❑	❑								❑
h. Other:_____	❑	❑								❑

What is your most important consideration in your corporate gift giving: ❑ quality   ❑ creativity   ❑ price   ❑ other:_____

EVENTS PLANNING:

Which events do you have on your corporate calendar: (check the month in which the event *is* planned)

	Jan	Feb	Mar	Apr	May	June	July	Aug	Sept	Oct	Nov	Dec
Company Anniversary	❑	❑	❑	❑	❑	❑	❑	❑	❑	❑	❑	❑
Staff holiday parties	❑	❑	❑	❑	❑	❑	❑	❑	❑	❑	❑	❑
Corp./Staff retreats	❑	❑	❑	❑	❑	❑	❑	❑	❑	❑	❑	❑
Annual/Board meeting	❑	❑	❑	❑	❑	❑	❑	❑	❑	❑	❑	❑
Open House	❑	❑	❑	❑	❑	❑	❑	❑	❑	❑	❑	❑
Summer associates	❑	❑	❑	❑	❑	❑	❑	❑	❑	❑	❑	❑
Retirement events	❑	❑	❑	❑	❑	❑	❑	❑	❑	❑	❑	❑
Client parties/events	❑	❑	❑	❑	❑	❑	❑	❑	❑	❑	❑	❑
Secretary's Week	❑	❑	❑	❑	❑	❑	❑	❑	❑	❑	❑	❑
Partners' meeting	❑	❑	❑	❑	❑	❑	❑	❑	❑	❑	❑	❑
Staff meetings	❑	❑	❑	❑	❑	❑	❑	❑	❑	❑	❑	❑
Sales meetings	❑	❑	❑	❑	❑	❑	❑	❑	❑	❑	❑	❑
Other:_____	❑	❑	❑	❑	❑	❑	❑	❑	❑	❑	❑	❑

Please provide us with the following event information/resources/ideas/pricing for:

❑ catering   ❑ flower arrangement   ❑ weekly drop off breakfast/lunch
❑ decorations   ❑ entertainment   ❑ off-site locations
❑ invitations   ❑ event staffing   ❑ equipment rental
❑ transportation   ❑ logo gift items

CLIENT/CUSTOMER ENTERTAINMENT:

	Do now	Would like info		Do now	Would like info
Event tickets					
concerts	❑	❑	Transportation	❑	❑
sports	❑	❑	Hotels/exec. retreats	❑	❑
theater	❑	❑	Travel	❑	❑
Sedan/Limo Service	❑	❑	Restaurant Dining	❑	❑
Tours	❑	❑			

FINALLY, ABOUT YOU...

YES, I want to receive announcements of special offers, discounts and services.

Your name: _____
Your title: _____
Organization: _____
Address: _____ Suite: _____
City: _____ State: _____ Zip: _____
Phone: _____ Fax: _____
E-Mail: _____

❑ I completed the Service Research survey on the back page and I want to be entered into the prize drawing.

THANK YOU for your time and interests.
Simply forward this information to Capitol
Concierge and *Consider It Done!*:
1. Fax to 202/833-2287
2. Give to your concierge
3. Mail to: Capitol Concierge
   1400 Eye St., NW #750
   Washington, DC 20005

Chemistry Checklist

1. *Remember that customer chemistry begins with the first person you hire.* Invest time in finding employees your customers will love; provide ample training on the specific, quirky, and unique needs of individual customers. Make a conscious and ongoing effort to match the right employees to the right customers. The ability to make good matches will rely on your understanding of employees' skills, experience, personality types, and working styles. Find out how customers like to work and create a document that can be used to train employees.

2. *Incorporate your best-customer profile(s) into all employee training.* Employees can't target best customers unless they know what your company is looking for. Provide team members with tricks to help them seek out best customers. Examples include customer job titles, industry types, and purchasing frequency.

3. *Make the transition from market research to customer profiling.* Once you prepare a list of best-customer attributes, create a list of all key pieces of information that you would like to know about your customers. Think about buying cycles, product and service lines, customers' contact methods, likes and dislikes, and basic demographic information.

4. *Take your market research from the feedback of specific customers.* Instead of relying on surveys from random strangers in the market, limit your survey and customer feedback efforts to your customers and prospects that meet your best-customer profile.

5. *Teach employees to be detectives on behalf of customers.* Armed with your best-customer profile and list of key pieces of information you need to capture, develop a list of methods your employees can use to collect data. These include learning questions related to your products and services (i.e., what corporate events is the customer planning in the next quarter? What's his or her favorite restaurant or vacation spot?), minisurveys, prize drawings tied to data capture, review of past purchases, and visual clues (i.e., publications a customer reads, communication preferences, etc).

6. *Train workers to recognize the related products and services top customers will value.* As employees begin to know your customers, you need

to train them to link customers' preferences and interests to related products and services you offer. If a customer, say, places numerous catering orders, there is a good chance he or she will be interested in flowers, rental equipment, audiovisuals, and entertainment services.

7. *Recognize employees' efforts to go above and beyond the call of duty for customers.* Be creative! Establish regular times and occasions to reward serving the customers. Hold monthly award meetings; write up customer service case studies and put them on your intranet and bulletin boards and in your company newsletter. Always post customer testimonials and thank-you notes in prominent places around the office.

8. *Engage your employees in conversations with customers in as many ways as you can.* There are countless ways to start learning dialogues, from simple follow-up telephone calls and thank-you notes to best-customer focus groups and VIP events that employees can plan.

9. *Develop a customer chemistry team.* Dedicate groups of employees to the needs and satisfaction of particular customer groups. If possible, assign some employees to individual clients as needed. Create specific objectives and methods to measure outcomes—such as retention rate and share of customer's business.

ENGAGING CUSTOMERS IN A CONTINUAL CONVERSATION
RULE 4: NEVER STOP LEARNING ABOUT YOUR CUSTOMERS

In the early years of Capitol Concierge each of us had our own way of learning about customers and taking note of what we found. Some concierges kept a marketing notebook, others maintained handwritten calendars noting customers' birthdays and anniversaries. And at least one concierge compiled a scrapbook filled with customer photos and information. Many concierges kept Client Service Cards (see Figure 4.1) that tracked birthdays, anniversaries, and who was interested in which services. The card system was crude, but it was at least some record when concierges left us. We had paper forms for everything you can imagine. Cards for prize drawings asked customers to tell us a few details, like their travel and recreation preferences. The information gathered was powerful and the concierges who leveraged that information were heroes.

So that's how our customer data collection process started: on paper. The paper trail, however, proved to be unwieldy to manage after a while. The management team could not easily get at information from the field. And a new concierge was left to make sense of her predecessor's client records. Any attempt at consistency was more than a challenge. Oh, we had a customer database, but it was pretty crude. Part of the problem was that managing technology was not one of my strengths—or so I felt at the time. It seemed like all the entrepreneurs I knew were light years ahead of me.

Figure 4.1 Client Service Card

The company has come a very long way since its first stabs at automation. We can now collect information about customers as things are happening and we can respond in real time. Our customer database isn't crude any more. It's Web-enabled and quite sophisticated.

However, even after having sunk quite a few dollars in information technology (I/T) at my company, I want to stress that technology is no panacea. A database, no matter how slick, can't tell you how to think about customers. There's no substitute for the actual physical process of learning about customers one by one and face-to-face. First things first: get all of your employees on the same page before you take any technology leaps. A company's customer database may prove to be its most important asset, but when all is said and done, a customer database is only as good as the customer relationships it is built upon. Don't bite off more tech bytes than you can chew. Think about how you're going to use the customer information before you automate. But above all, never stop learning about customers.

The underpinning of all of Capitol Concierge's customer contacts was to create an ongoing customer dialogue that enabled the concierges and the management team to learn about customers' preferences. The personal and corporate profiles we maintain of our customers are the keys to our relationship-building efforts. Only by consistently creating opportunities to learn about our customers' needs, likes, and dislikes— and maintaining that information in a centralized profile—can we proactively anticipate customers' needs. It is exactly this anticipating that builds customers for life. Once we know a customer's preferences and deliver "wow" service, it requires too much time and effort on the customers' part to go and re-create that learning relationship with other service providers. We have found that to be true time and again.

Yet in my company's early years, my employees sometimes hesitated to ask customers to answer even a simple survey. They were scared not only of being rejected but also of seeming intrusive. The concierges were definitely anxious when I first introduced the executive focus program to them. I discovered that some of them were afraid to ask questions. They were afraid they would come across like uncouth salespeople. The turning point was when Capitol Concierge held its first-ever executive roundtable. It was very liberating for concierges to meet face-to-face with executives and hear them talk. It was the encouragement they needed to call a football fan about Redskins tickets or to remind some-one of a car-inspection date—and take care of it. "That's not selling," I always told the concierges. "That's proactive service." They started to believe me after that first focus group.

We've always found clients willing to fill out surveys—even lengthy ones—if we make it worth their while. We also make it fun. There's so many ways to be creative. We've done ice-cream socials, catered lunches, wine tasting, and even pumpkin-carving contests. These events have been a great way to bring together customers with similar professional interests. Of course they've also been great ways for us to get to know people in a more relaxed setting.

Make Every Customer Contact Count

There are a million opportunities to learn about customers. Many opportunities occur naturally in the course of a business day. You can create other opportunities. Really, every interaction with a customer is an opportunity to capture new data to grow the relationship. But obviously, there's some serendipity at play. A customer phoning to complain is an unforeseen chance to resolve a problem and learn something new. Structure plays a role too; some companies make a point of surveying all their customers once a year.

However, customer complaints and annual surveys are like two extremes on the customer-education spectrum. It's not enough to tabulate the results of one huge survey and gather up the unsolicited feedback from disgruntled customers. In between the two extremes are many other potential contact points. The reality is every customer contact counts whether planned or not. (How you respond is what one CEO called "moments of truth" in his bestselling business book of the same name.)

Many contact points occur in the normal course of a business day. When there's a problem or an opportunity (and some CEOs see every problem as an opportunity), how do you respond to your customers? Whether it's by phone, in person, via electronic chat, or through e-mail, each choice says something about you in a particular instant with a particular customer. And of course, there are rules for each medium. For example, customers who correspond with you via e-mail expect to get a reply by e-mail within twenty-four hours; two hours is considered cutting edge. While e-mail is not as formal as a business letter, it is more formal than online chat. Conversations via chat take on a different tone than other electronic media. Chat seems to bring out people's playful side, like passing a note about homework, complete with emoticons (little faces, etc., created with keyboard characters to convey emotions). With online chat, speed is most important.

RULE 4: NEVER STOP LEARNING ABOUT YOUR CUSTOMERS

The customer-chemistry-building process employs methods to continually understand and stay on top of your customers' needs and expectations. By applying what you learn from the methods, you will always be one step ahead of your customers. The result: long-lasting customer relationships.

Some businesspeople like the term *touch points*. Think of touch points as all the ways a customer comes into contact with your company. Consider everything from how you answer the phone to the design of your fax cover sheets, reception room, and even the information included with your e-mail signature. Are you sending a friendly message? Do you make it easy for customers to get in touch at each touch point? You lose points when you don't list a website address on your fax sheet or an 800 number on your package—or when you neglect to list a phone number at all at your website. A toll-free phone number is the norm in many industries. Some predict it won't be long before the younger generation expects every company to offer e-mail and online chat. And it will probably happen much faster than the decade-long rise of 800 numbers. Brainstorm with your team to create new ways to leverage each customer touch point.

Regardless of *how* you interface with clients, *what* you learn is the most important aspect of fostering customer chemistry. You need a strategy for how customer information is going to be gathered and used throughout the company. Employees should not only be comfortable with the prospect of speaking directly to customers (which gets back to training), they should be ready to seize the moment.

Such a philosophy starts at the top. Take, for example, Stew Leonard Jr., the CEO of Stew Leonard's, the Connecticut grocery store chain famous for its customer service standards. Leonard personally replies to signed notes left in the store suggestion box. He does so to set an example for his employees but also to remind himself of his personal accountability to customers. Leonard says you need to ask yourself, "Do you as a company owner have that contact with customers?" He makes a point of weaving customers into his conversations with employees. In the store locations where Stew Leonard Jr. is not personally present, a variety of managers and staffers respond to suggestion box comments.

Jeff Parker, CEO of Corporate Communications Broadcast Network (CCBN) in Boston, is worlds away from a gourmet grocery store, but he's also a staunch believer that nothing happens without the right attitude in the corner office. "The whole concept of the customer and how you feel about the customer has to pervade an organization, has to be part of the fabric and philosophy, and it has to come from upper management. If the CEO says the client is why you have a job, the client is important, and the CEO likes interacting with clients, then that will trickle down to employees and you'll have a better base for good customer care." To make his point, positive comments by customers are logged, tracked, and published internally in CCBN's Monday morning report. "Two pages of our fifteen-page Monday morning report contain quotes that have come in from customers relating to service," says Parker. "What's important: the folks who are not quoted are motivated to be on the next list. That's a positive feedback mechanism to get other people to know service is an important aspect of the job."

At USAA, a highly respected insurance agency that serves the military community, there's a favorite customer service slogan. It goes like this: every contact has opportunity—ECHO for short. It's a neat acronym because it conjures up an image of the customer's voice echoing throughout the organization. Which is of course exactly what you want to have happen whether your organization is one employee or one thousand.

Let's take the ECHO idea a step further. Every contact has opportunity *for building customer chemistry*. Of course, the cornerstone of customer chemistry is communication. Without constant communication you have no relationship. To truly realize the potential of customer chemistry, you can't depend on a one-time sampling of customer sentiment. You need a proactive plan for customer dialogue: a *customer chemistry communication plan*.

That's the approach Wade Harris has taken at Phase II, a chain of personal-training facilities in Raleigh, North Carolina. Proactive contact begins the minute a first-time customer steps through the door. CEO Wade Harris likes to ask two questions of newcomers. How did you hear about us? And have you done personal training? "If they've worked out with a trainer somewhere else, we want to know why they left the last place. That tells us how we can meet their expectations." To make new customers feel comfortable about offering feedback, the CEO sends a personal letter saying, "Please call me, the president of the company, if you ever are dissatisfied with the service you receive, and give me a chance to correct that."

A true learning relationship is like time-motion photography; it develops in stages over time. A customer chemistry communication plan attempts to capture the relationship as it unfurls. You can start very simply. One CEO wanted, for starters, to rise above the poor reputation of his industry—tuxedo rentals. The poor man was haunted by the image of a TV advertisement. "There used to be an Alka-Seltzer commercial with a heavyset father. He was the father of the bride, and his tuxedo didn't fit and he was so upset, he was taking two Alka-Seltzers." It was a sad commentary on the industry.

To raise the company's profile, the tuxedo shop started attaching quality assurance cards onto every order so customers could rate stores, service, and other elements. Many customers took the time to fill out the cards and return them.

A customer chemistry communication plan might begin with the goal of improving customer satisfaction. The sincere desire to measure customer service can in turn lead to more far-reaching conversations with customers and impressive results.

At Grand Circle, the travel company that serves the senior market, customers have reached the point that they are less like customers and more like consultants to the company. Upon their return home they receive a detailed questionnaire about every aspect of their recent trip. The one-hundred-question survey is customized for each trip with names of hotels stayed at, restaurants visited, the name of the group's guide, and more. Travelers are asked about the quality of the airline, hotel, food, pacing of the trip (too fast, too slow), the discovery element of each trip, and value of the trip (was it a good buy for the dollar), and so on. Amazingly, 70 percent of customers complete the survey. The company received back some one hundred five thousand surveys in the year 2000. According to the company, this information is invaluable in helping it refine its travel products, uncover any problems with a particular trip, and learn what parts of the trip were especially interesting to travelers. For example, people loved an in-home meal with a local family, but they weren't crazy about spending the night with a local family, so Grand Circle changed the itinerary. In 2000, 69 percent rated their trips "excellent," up from 64 percent in 1999. The goal is 75 percent by 2005.

Opportunities for Customer Contact

Customer contact opportunities are everywhere. We've compiled a listing of twenty-four, but our list is hardly exhaustive. Use the examples to jump-start your own communication plan. A few qualifiers are in order. The suggestions in this chapter don't rely on using outside consultants, but that said, there are times when you will want or need to hire professionals to get more objective customer feedback. By the same token, technology can enhance almost any contact opportunity, but the process of learning about customers does not depend on technology.

1. *Conduct short surveys on the phone.* This can be done with both customers calling in and by dedicating yourself and your employees to calling so many customers per month. The key is to keep these surveys respectfully brief. The phone is also great for following up on a written survey. For instance, the St. Paul Saints, a minor league baseball team that has won kudos for its customer service, conducted a satisfaction survey of fifteen hundred fans two years ago. Though the team hit a home-run response rate—fourteen hundred returned the survey—the front office called back a number of fans. (More than a few people willingly supplied their names and phone numbers.) The Saints front office staff interviewed any identified fan who scored the team a 3 or lower (on a scale of 1 to 5) on any service attribute.

2. *Assemble a customer advisory board.* A handful of customers can't speak for all your clients, but these boards are a great way to get the kind of direct, honest, and complete feedback you might not get anywhere else. The meetings can be as formal or informal as you and your customers want, but to get the board started, send out official invitations.

3. *Organize client focus groups.* You might convene focus groups as often or more often than your advisory board. Rather than outsourcing the whole event, you can and should conduct the groups yourself. It's not scientific results you're after but meaningful conversation about upcoming products, customer service issues, past problems,

etc. That said, it can help to have or hire an experienced moderator, particularly when you're conducting a large focus group with customers who might also be competitors (such as a manufacturer that invites a roomful of competing store owners to review upcoming products). Breaking a large group into smaller ones can also help keep the meeting cordial and productive. Definitely use the opportunity to get written as well as oral feedback. It's also worthwhile to bring several employees for every one customer you invite. (A sample customer-invitation letter and focus-group agenda are shown in Figures 4.2 and 4.3.)

4. *Hit the road.* This is another way to conduct informal focus groups with key customers that gets you out of your comfort zone and into

Figure 4.2 Sample Customer-Invitation Letter

Mr. Bob Jones
ABC Corporation
123 Main Street
Denver, CO 02134

Dear Mr. Jones:

Our goal is to be the best provider of consulting services in the Denver market. Your comments and suggestions are vital to assist us in achieving this goal. We are inviting valued clients from varied industries to participate in a series of focus groups over the next year. The focus groups will engage in small informal discussions to obtain your opinions on our service.

_____ would like to invite you to participate in the first of our Client Focus Group series on Thursday, February 17 at 12:00 P.M. at the Omni Hotel. The Omni is located at 125 Spruce Street, Denver, Colorado. Complimentary lunch and beverages will be served. The topic of our discussion will be a review of the current service offerings of _____ . Additionally, we hope to glean advice on continuously increasing our level of service. Please respond to _____ by February 14. We look forward to seeing you on February 17.

Sincerely,

Kelly Gilmore

Figure 4.3 Sample Focus-Group Agenda

   I. Welcome and Introduction of Attendees

   II. Purpose of Meeting
     [Introduce new product or service and assess customer needs]

   III. Overview

   IV. Potential Questions:
     How well do we deliver on what we promise?
     What are the three changes that would make it easier for you to do business with us?
     Are you personally involved in making decisions about loyalty programs?
     What other departments are involved in making those decisions?
     What kinds of loyalty programs do you presently have in place?
     What drove your decision to use this service?
     How valuable overall would you say this service is for you to achieve your goals (somewhat, fairly, very, extremely)?

The focus groups can be done very cost effectively with a breakfast or luncheon, or done after work with hors d'oeuvres.

theirs. Some CEOs believe so strongly in the value of road trips that they schedule one or two each year. Some companies stage mini–trade shows on wheels. Skyline Displays, a maker of trade show booths, stages free or inexpensive workshops on topics related to trade shows in cities around the country.

5. *Form a frequent-buyer club.* Examples abound—both good and bad—but the clubs' popularity shows no signs of waning. Just make sure your club is distinct and rewarding. When they are well thought out, frequent-buyer clubs are a great way to create a community and learn more about when and why customers buy. The best frequency/loyalty programs offer both hard and soft benefits. The more tangible benefits include merchandise, travel, or services; the soft benefits might encompass special discounts, advance notices of sales, and other courtesies.

6. *Create a VIP program.* This could be instead of or in addition to a frequent-buyer club. At any rate, it's your chance to reward specific customers for specific actions (such as making referrals) while learning more about their personal likes and dislikes. Plus, everyone likes to win a prize. Preferred-customer plans serve the same purpose.

7. *Birthday clubs and anniversary circles are another way to get customers' attention.* Send a special offer on special days. If it's appropriate, you might use such occasions to bring together groups of customers.

8. *Write a thank-you note within forty-eight hours of a new purchase, contract signing, reorder, or referral.* It's easy to customize a standard thank-you letter on the computer, but handwritten notes still score major points with many buyers. Thank-you notes might seem like one-way communication, but they can also be the start of something more. A thank-you note can also be accompanied by a book or magazine article of interest to the client—anything to spark the next conversation or e-mail exchange.

9. *Follow up after a sale with a phone call thirty days later.* What better excuse to pick up the phone and take a quick read of customer satisfaction. Planner books—online or on paper—make this task a cinch.

10. *Schedule checkup visits.* Offer to return to the customer site at regular intervals for routine maintenance. It's an opportunity to fix any lingering problems the customer might be hesitant to raise. Such repair work might also lead to new work.

11. *Write an annual service plan* for every new contract. Update the plan throughout the year by checking in with the client.

12. *Create a budget planner* that anticipates a customer's purchases and tallies the costs involved. Naturally the process involves sitting down with the client at least once and probably several times throughout the year.

13. *Postcard surveys* can be tucked into purchases and thank-you notes. They can also be mailed out to mark a special occasion—such as

the anniversary of a purchase or contract signing—but you don't have to wait that long to make use of the short-form survey. Postcard surveys can also accompany raffles at special events.

14. *Get the maximum value from client reviews.* Whether you hold them monthly, quarterly, or annually, these are built-in opportunities for detailed dialogue. Some companies also use these events to conduct their own industry research.

15. *Make monthly touch base calls to customers.* Divide up the call list among your key executives. Since customers are often assigned to midlevel account managers, it's critical for senior staff to keep their hands in the customer relationship as well. A simple "How are we doing?" call can reap huge rewards and uncover potential pitfalls in the relationship.

16. *Do "Lunch and Launch" events.* Invite key customers to preview new products and services. Solicit feedback that can assist your team in improving the product. Learn which features bring the greatest value to your customers and emphasize those in targeted, individualized marketing pieces.

17. *Actively solicit customers to serve as references.* You'll get immediate and invaluable feedback. If the customer isn't willing to be a reference, you'll know why. Those who agree to send you business will help further cement your relationship. Rockford Construction, a $100-million-plus builder in Belmont, Michigan, never misses a chance to get a new reference. In fact, on the last day of a job the company immediately sends an account executive to the construction site to get a letter of recommendation. Rockford's customer-account teams are rewarded for each letter collected.

18. *Enclose a short questionnaire with each invoice.* It saves stamps, but more important, when a client pays the bill, it's the ultimate evaluation. If there are any unresolved issues with the customers, better to hear about them quickly than after your invoice has sat on somebody's desk for ninety days.

19. *Take them out to the ballpark.* One creative company invited key clients to a baseball game and made a product presentation in the stands before the first batter was up. Then everyone sat back and

enjoyed the game. The company not only had a chance to get to know its clients as individuals, but the clients got to talk to each other. And they had fun.

20. *Take the customer-suggestion box seriously.* Whether the comments come by phone, fax, letter, or e-mail, they should be acknowledged with a phone call or at least a short thank-you note and perhaps a follow-up question.

21. *Don't underestimate the value of asking a first-time customer for help.* You may find to your surprise that people are flattered to help—especially if you make customers feel like they have a stake in putting your company on the map. For example, Next Monet, which sells original art through a catalog and on the Web, sent one hundred surveys to its first group of customers in 1999. The accompanying survey letter was worded as an appeal "to help Next Monet." Customers complied; the response rate to the twelve-question survey was 100 percent. "We found out we had a tremendously loyal following," says Next Monet cofounder Myrna Nickelsen. "They wanted us to succeed." Though it's rare to see customers wax poetic in a written survey, Nickelsen says customers wrote long paragraphs about the service they had received and even named their favorite customer service reps.

22. *Vet purchases at the point of sale.* At Sunny Fresh Foods, a supplier of egg-based food products to hotels and restaurants, customer service reps pore over orders that come in electronically, looking for potential omissions. "If the order doesn't look right, we call," says Mike Luker, CEO of the Monticello, Minnesota–based company, which won the Baldridge Award for Quality in 1999. "We might say, 'You buy this every week, but you didn't this week. Is this a problem?'" The CEO views customer service as a crucial communications opportunity. In fact, the service reps "touch" the company's two thousand regular customers more frequently than the sales reps do, Luker adds.

23. *When you lose a sale,* put your pride aside, and you may just save a customer. It takes guts to ask customers what they *don't* like about you, but you'll learn so much more. At the same time you've got a

second chance to establish a stronger bond with customers who care enough to tell you the unvarnished truth. Take the time to create a "Lost Job Survey."

24. *Create a reminder service for customers* based on past or future purchases. Talk to customers about what they bought this time last year or last month. To prompt a reminder, use both historical orders and "proactive dates," secured by asking clients about special events.

The Role of Technology

Once upon a time entrepreneurs knew everything there was to know about their customers because they weren't just customers; they were neighbors and friends. What possible need did the corner barber have for a PalmPilot or a contact-management program? He carried what counted in his head, or in the collective memory of his small shop. Wireless communication? Well, how about shouting down the street?

Of course, those days passed many eons ago. In the new millennium it's clear that nearly everything about the way we relate to and communicate with customers has changed. How we come into contact with customers has been forever altered by one technical innovation after another. Today no one can imagine life without electronic mail. A popular book on business manners now devotes a chapter to e-mail etiquette. Contact-management programs are affordable to all, which means keeping a customer database is easier than ever.

Meanwhile, clever direct mail solicitation letters are typeset in script fonts that look convincingly like someone bothered to pen a personal message. The mass personalization of the direct mail pitch letter is a fitting symbol for the true promise of technology: that we can have it both ways; we can be personal in our interactions with customers even as we connect with dozens or thousands of them at the same time.

Where will all the technology lead? How far should a company travel on the technology curve to attract and retain the best customers? For every I/T investment there's a cost-benefit calculation a company must do as well as an internal audit. You have to ask yourself first and fore-most how paramount is it to forge individual relationships? With how many of your customers? For example, a company that sells mainly through distributors may or may not have a compelling reason to get in touch with the actual end users or consumers of the product. Per-haps distributor feedback is enough to give the company the inside scoop on how customers are thinking and feeling, but such an assump-tion can also be very dangerous. There is a real tradeoff to outsourc-ing any aspect of customer contact. Another example: *call centers* can be a great way for a small company to train more "ears" on the customer. But call centers can also present a barrier between you and your clients. On the one hand, call centers let you make sales twenty-four hours and gather new insights on customers you might never have gotten other-wise. On the other hand, no call center will ever know your product or service the way you do.

You should view technology as a means to carrying out your cus-tomer chemistry communication plan—but not the only means. At its best, technology makes the promise of a continuous learning relation-ship with customers a reality. That doesn't mean, however, that you must become a 24/7 operation. Consider some of the opportunities for making contact brought by technology, from the simple to the more complex. Based on information gathered from customer service gurus, other company owners, and on our own customer service research, here's our tally of the best ways to use technology to enhance customer retention.

- *Automate the customer reminder service.* This can take the form of a fax or e-mail message.
- *Customize your response to customer comments.* With the ease of cut-and-paste and the speed of e-mail there's no reason any company should send the same response to every customer who takes the time to write, call, or send e-mail. Stew Leonard Jr., the grocer, person-ally answers about ten e-mail messages from customers each day.
- *Respond to orders by e-mail.* Fulton Street.com, a seller of seafood products online, routinely sends a customized thank-you note after each order is received. Repeat customers are acknowledged as such.

CEO Stratis Morfogen explains: "We started by doing five orders a week, addressing each customer by name. 'Thank you, Mrs. Jones, for your recent order; my name is Joe, and I will be your personal customer service rep.' My goal was to break down the computer barrier and make the online experience as simple as a handshake."

- *Send your postcard customer surveys by e-mail.* It's faster.
- *Solicit opinions via an e-mail newsletter.* Electronic mail is a great publishing medium for a variety of reasons. An e-mail newsletter is immediate and cheap to produce. You can ask a weekly or monthly question to solicit opinions on pressing business issues of the day or to solicit product feedback. The newsletter can also be positioned as a perk for joining an online fan club or frequent-buyer club. As a prospecting tool, e-mail newsletters allow you to politely ask would-be subscribers to identify themselves and answer a few pertinent questions. The answers give you at least a starting point for comparing the new prospect's profile to that of your ideal client.
- *Allow customers to register their personal preferences* on a secure area of your website. (Refer to Figure 3.4 for a sample form.)
- *Put the frequent-buyer club online.* Let customers check their status as often as they want.
- *Post interesting spot polls at your website.* Lids, a specialty retailer of baseball hats, has done a great job interacting with its teen and pre-teen audience at its website, lids.com. A poll last December consisted of two words: "Holiday Shopping?" Respondents were asked where they were buying gifts—online, in stores, in catalogs, or a combination. While such topical questions don't yield specific product feedback, there's still great value in asking them. Lids's holiday shopping poll, for example, revealed that teenagers are not the mall rats many think they are.
- *Design your website for customer feedback.* Encouraging public discussion is one way to do this. Of course, with discussion groups you lose some measure of control; angry customers may also pop up online, but that's not a good enough reason to dismiss a potentially very powerful tool. A more private alternative is to set up an extranet for certain customers who'd benefit from posting messages to each other and to you.

- *Get customer feedback in real time.* If you're selling to a big enough base of consumers, you can get customer feedback at the point of sale by signing up with a third-party rating service online (such as Bizrate.com). Or you can do a version of what Bizrate does yourself. For example, you can send a short survey by e-mail immediately following a key event. Many off-the-shelf contact-management programs let you automate the process of sending out surveys on a timed basis.
- *Talk to customers all day long for free.* E-chat programs are easy to install and most are free or very cheap. AOL's Instant Messenger (AIM), Microsoft's MSN Messenger, and ICQ ("I seek you") from Mirabilis—to name three programs—are all free and independent of your choice of Internet provider. AIM is used by sixty-four million chatters internationally, according to AOL. Some companies, like Granny's Goodies, are offering live chat from nine to five—a good option for any company with a limited number of employees who can answer chat while also manning the phones. Chat sessions can also be used to convene virtual focus groups. You won't capture the body language, but you will get pages of verbatim responses from your assembled group of preselected customers while saving a ton on travel and hotel bills.

Of course, it's easy to get carried away with the latest technical twists. All those bells and whistles can be like a siren song drawing you in and taking you under. Consider a potential technology investment from the viewpoint of both your employees and your customers. Online chat, for instance, is a subject that polarizes many people. They seem to either love it or hate it; some find it one of the most useful tools on their computers, others regard chat as nothing more than a distraction.

"In my experience, the advantages of using chat are numerous," says Maggie Etheridge, cofounder of IRIS, a $4-million developer of residential real estate software in Anaheim Hills, California. For eight years Etheridge directed the company's customer support department. During that time she found that chat "erases former imaginary obstacles to communication. It suggests preferred status. And it has advantages over both the telephone and e-mail."

USING "CHAT" TO MAKE CONTACT:
IRIS, ANAHEIM HILLS, CALIFORNIA

Problem: How to make proactive contact with customers on a limited budget.

Overview: IRIS is a fast-growing developer of software for residential real estate agents. A few years ago Maggie Etheridge, IRIS cofounder and then head of customer support, was looking for an informal, inexpensive way to keep in touch with customers. The approach had to be convenient for all concerned and cheaper than giving out her mobile phone number to everyone.

Solution: Online chat immediately appealed to Etheridge, but putting a chat function at the IRIS website would not have been feasible for the $4-million company. So she did the next best thing: she installed three popular, free chat programs that she and others on the IRIS help desk could use. With their customer's permission to chat, Etheridge and her staff began initiating conversations. Before suggesting chat as a means to correspond, Etheridge went through a "delicate process" of feeling out an important customer. She observed clients for signs of their propensity for trying out creative technologies and the degree to which casualness was encouraged at the client's company.

Results: Chat proved invaluable for helping clients who have only one phone line and need instruction while online. Etheridge and her staff were able to help several customers at once by participating in multiple chat sessions. Another measure of success is the fact that Etheridge's name made its way onto the "buddy list" of numerous clients. "There was a closeness implied right away," she says. "My customers felt I was allowing them into my preferred circle, that they were elite insiders." When a customer's name showed up on her buddy list, Etheridge says, it was like bumping into a friend at the grocery store, but not being obligated to stop and talk. She considered her workload and what she knew of the customer's situation, and then made a decision. Many times she decided to say hello and ask how things are going with the software. "Chatting with customers reminded me they were out there, and they seemed to feel grateful that someone cares enough to ask from time to time."

Chat serves another role in communication—it reduces people to their "written personality," and showcases eloquence, intelligence, and wit—often expressed through emoticons—sideways faces made of text characters. (See Figure 4.4.)

The Mechanics of Customer Contact

While all contact with customers is invaluable, the techniques for going about it are numerous. You must determine how much you can spend and how to get the most bang for the buck. Here are some of the most important factors to consider: cost, how to use customer satisfaction surveys, whether to hire professional help for surveys, and determining the best mix of survey methods for your situation. Finally, you need to organize the data in some kind of customer database.

Cost

What does it actually cost to talk to customers on a regular basis? Of course, the cost will vary widely depending on the methods you use and whether you tap your own staff or outside consultants. Consider the cost of carrying out customer satisfaction surveys. E-mail is now the least expensive method, followed by mail, telephone, and face-to-face.

The telephone may not be the cheapest way to conduct a survey, but it's hard to beat for convenience. Simple phone surveys continue to be popular with all size companies but especially smaller ones. Roger Nunley, managing director of the Customer Care Institute in Atlanta, estimates that a five-question telephone survey will run about $7 per call if you do it in-house.

Figure 4.4 The Many Faces of Chat

Etheridge: hi! how's it going?	**Proactive**
ClientFriend: Just fine, are you in CA now	
Etheridge: yes	
ClientFriend: Did you hear from [office] about getting the file to work for them? I have been out of the office and have not contacted them	
Etheridge: I sent it but I haven't heard back.	
ClientFriend: I will call them tomorrow and check. We have tickets to the Cubs game tomorrow pm. It will be fun as the weather is gonna be 80	**Personal**
Etheridge: oh wow. how cool.	
ClientFriend: No, how hot. We are not used to this nice weather this early.	
Etheridge: thank you global warming. hahah	**Humorous**
ClientFriend: You got that right	
ClientFriend: [Your rep] is coming out next week, I have to call him tomorrow and get the agenda straight	
Etheridge: does he need anything special? everything basically going smoothly?	
ClientFriend: I guess he is going to do [presentation]. Does he bring the projector and a laptop or use the office pc's	
Etheridge: My guess would be projector.	**Casual, human**
ClientFriend: Well I will call him and make sure. The offices are very delighted to have him come out again. By the way, I have tried [certain function of program] but no dice. What could be the problem?	**Telling**
Etheridge: i [do that] fine, so must be something up with your setup. are you using [specific settings]?	
ClientFriend: Thanks I will try it but later as I have only one lonely little old-fashioned phone line. My area is not connected for cable access yet or dsl. The sticks, that's where I live. ha ha	**More humor**
Etheridge: you can use this exact connection we are talking on, so you don't need to hang up to try it.	**Multitasking**
ClientFriend: Oh, that is right, it is going through the internet not the modem. I am still thinking of dialing. oops, don't tell anyone that, they will fire me. ha ha	
Etheridge: no way—you're pure gold.	
ClientFriend: Excellent. It worked great. I must have to put [those settings] at work. I will be a hero at work tomorrow. In my own mind at least	
Etheridge: cool!	
ClientFriend: LOL	**"Laugh out loud"**
ClientFriend: bye	

The Role of Customer Satisfaction Surveys

Satisfaction surveys are effective in a number of ways, to gauge the success of a particular customer transaction, for example, or to take the pulse of the relationship with the customer as a whole. The customer satisfaction survey is a must-have item in any customer chemistry communication plan. Luckily the survey can be carried out in a number of ways.

Do It Yourself or Hire Professionals?

When objectivity is crucial, it pays to seek out survey experts. Customers may be willing to reveal more to a third party about certain issues—particularly a bad experience. Wade Harris, the owner of the personal-training facilities, checks in with people who have missed workouts on a consistent basis. He uses an outside agency to make the phone calls so clients can be assured that their comments are anonymous "and they don't have to feel bad about hurting their trainers' feelings," he says. "As business owners, we have to accept criticism of our business. If we use it the right way, it can become positive." For every new site he opens, Harris says it's the "first twenty to thirty clients who come in" who make or break the business.

While there are times when you will need or want to hire experts, there is still a lot you can do on your own. Myrna Nickelsen, the entrepreneur who scored a 100 percent response on her first survey, says her survey wasn't strictly scientific. She admits she broke "a lot of the rules" when it came to designing her first customer satisfaction survey for Next Monet. "I was after something completely different." She was interested, for instance, in the free-form responses to suggestions for how the new company could improve. She was also interested in seemingly minor questions that revealed a lot about her customers, such as whether they acted alone in making their art selection or sought the advice of another. She used the survey responses to help motivate her customer service staff, many of whom received glowing reviews from the customers surveyed. Qualitative feedback—while not to be confused with results that are statistically significant—has a value all its own.

Survey Methods

In 1997 Advanced Micro Devices, a $2-billion global supplier of integrated circuits, conducted one of the first annual, worldwide customer satisfaction surveys on the Internet. It was a huge success: more than two hundred of AMD's largest customers responded. Most of the invitations were sent out by e-mail; customers had the option of responding by Web, e-mail, fax, or postal mail. A whopping 93 percent chose the Web.

The Internet is clearly catching on as a way to quickly dispatch customer satisfaction surveys. But not every company will enjoy the level of success experienced by AMD. Plus, there's a fair amount of preparation that goes into doing your first Web-based survey. Nor is the Web or e-mail the right choice for every occasion. Depending on your customer base, sometimes good old snail mail is best. The fax hasn't disappeared as was once predicted, and there's nothing like a phone conversation to encourage customers to go beyond simple yes/no responses. And yet the Web and e-mail share some distinct advantages: cheap and lightning fast. Surveys can be sent out, returned, and tabulated—sometimes without human intervention—before a mail survey reaches its destination. Some experts predict that an e-mail survey with Web link is the direction all surveying is headed. Answers can be downloaded right into survey software, which has been coming down in price.

Online surveys can make a lot of sense, but those who conduct surveys for a living say the best surveys use a combination of methods. A short telephone interview can direct customers to a lengthier survey on the Web. When the results of a Web or e-mail survey come in, the telephone can be used to follow up on selected questions. Mail surveys balance out phone surveys.

Before you mix and match, it's worth it to compare the relative pros and cons of each survey method. Each method is considered here for its usefulness in carrying out customer satisfaction surveys.

SURVEY METHODS: PROS AND CONS

Face-to-Face
➤ Best for small number of clients
➤ Ideal for also gathering one-to-one market research
➤ Good excuse to go to client's office
➤ Most expensive
➤ Some questions hard to ask in person

Telephone
➤ Good for ongoing minisurveys or for a limited client base
➤ A "live" connection
➤ Can get higher response than mail
➤ Can tape verbatim responses (with customer permission)
➤ Can probe for more complete answers to open-ended questions
➤ Relatively expensive (about $7 per call)
➤ Subject to interviewer bias

Mail
➤ Relatively inexpensive
➤ Ideal for large sample size
➤ Can include a catchy marketing piece and/or incentive item
➤ No interviewer bias
➤ Not ideal for open-ended questions
➤ Extra work—written responses to be scanned or typed into computer
➤ Some level of inaccuracy—some questions may be misunderstood or two answers chosen
➤ Could be mistaken for junk mail

Fax
➤ Most of the same advantages and disadvantages as mail
➤ Can be automatically sent out by computer
➤ Some responses may be unreadable
➤ Hand tabulation required

continued on next page

E-Mail

➤ Fast and easy to deploy

➤ Cost almost $0

➤ Easier for customers to answer questions than with written surveys; respondents simply edit the original message and send back

➤ Can ask more questions and more fill-in-the-blank ones

➤ Can get up-to-the-minute responses

➤ Low-cost software available to instantly tabulate results and capture verbatim responses

➤ Risk of looking impersonal

➤ Incorrect or incomplete list of e-mail addresses slows the process

➤ Not practical yet for surveying large number of households

➤ Risk of being mistaken for spam (junk e-mail)

➤ Can't probe customer for additional detail

Web

➤ Same pros and cons as e-mail

➤ Uses hypertext markup language (HTML)

➤ Can improve accuracy—use of check boxes can limit respondents to one choice per question

➤ Can spice up the survey by incorporating graphics, sound, animation, and links to other Web pages

➤ Self-contained questions—data-entry fields box in open-ended questions

➤ More efficient and personalized—can design to recognize customer by name, pre-answer some questions, and automatically skip past those that don't apply

➤ Requires an e-mail invitation containing the Web link

➤ Have to take special precautions if "ballot stuffing" is an issue; may need to provide unique Web address and password for each customer

➤ Not everyone has access to Web

➤ Lower response rate than e-mail although the gap may be closing

➤ Potential confidentiality issues with transmitting data over the Internet

How to Conduct a Telephone Survey

The Customer Care Institute (at www.customercare.com) has some pointers. First of all, keep it short on the phone. If you want to survey a lot of customers, follow the 5/5 rule—ask five questions and finish up in five minutes. Keep the questions basic: Were you satisfied with the service? Would you recommend us to others? The questions should be easy to answer with a yes/no response or on a scale of 1 to 5. Make sure you're measuring what's important to the customer satisfaction of *your clients*. Some things aren't as important as you might think—so ask, don't assume. Measuring what's truly important to your customers will help you focus your time and resources.

If you have the time (or fewer customers), the ideal is to leave a few minutes for one or two open-ended questions. The open-ended questions can reveal which customers are only satisfied (and why) and which customers are truly loyal (and why). Of course the more probing questions will keep you on the phone longer and drive up the cost of the call, but taking a few extra minutes could pay off big. As a general rule, keep phone surveys to ten minutes tops and no more than ten questions, Nunley says. But there are exceptions to the rule. "I've seen fifty-minute phone surveys with a pretty high response rate," he says.

The Customer Database

Once you begin to deploy your customer contact strategies, you may soon have more data than you bargained for. It may go without saying, but you need some way to organize all that precious information—there are plenty of cases of entrepreneurs who continue to maintain manila files filled with handwritten notes long past the company's start-up stage. There's no arguing that in order to effectively manage and use the information, every company needs a systematic way to store, sort, and retrieve the information. A solid database solution is invaluable for making sense of your learning and for reaching your ultimate goal of developing unique service and marketing plans for your best customers.

The bottom line: no company should be without a customer database, no matter how elementary. If you don't have an automated solution, you're at a competitive disadvantage because any company can afford a contact manager these days. Even the corner florist has one. "We see lots of small companies taking advantage of contact-management software for automating customer surveys and personalizing e-mails" that go out at regular intervals, says Nunley of the Customer Care Institute.

If you are absolutely allergic to technology of any sort, you can outsource the work: have a direct mail service bureau or similar outfit store and maintain the database for you. Janene Centurione, the owner of two Great Harvest Bread stores and a self-described techno "boob," opted to have an outside firm maintain her database of customers belonging to her Bread Zealot club. It costs just pennies to add a new name to the database.

Patti Glick, a business soloist, likes to keeps things simple and portable. Glick is a registered nurse who six years ago went into business as the Foot Nurse. She serves a professional clientele of Silicon Valley companies that hire her to conduct foot safety training and wellness seminars for their employees. From her home office in Cupertino, California, Glick takes meticulous notes on the computer of all things related to her customers. She uses a scheduling program called Anytime Deluxe, which she can also download to her PalmPilot, to enter details on speaking engagements and client information.

Even a simple database can pay off big. Certainly there's nothing fancy about the system in place at Connect: The Knowledge Network, an I/T staffing firm in Littleton, Colorado. Co-owners Kelly Gilmore and Maureen Clarry use a Lotus Notes database they've souped up a bit over the years. Five years ago the company (which is located in a vacated convent complete with a day care center) was just seven people; today there are twenty and everyone depends on the customer database daily. "We can really look at our database all sorts of way. Every contact is logged," says Gilmore.

The database includes detailed information on the people and companies who make up Connect's two customer bases—I/T consultants and the companies that hire I/T consultants. Current customers as well as prospects are all in the same system. The database has become a hot property. "When we're approached by potential buyers," says Clarry, "the database is what people are most interested in." The database became all the more valuable as demand for I/T talent began to slow with the economy in 2001. "We haven't had to cold call until now—so the database is really crucial now," says Clarry. "We're able to open warm doors instead of cold ones."

The Connect partners admit, however, that the database is only as good as the data is accurate. The number of tier-one clients can change weekly. The skills and needs of the I/T consultants seem to change just as rapidly. To keep up with the swirl of new information coming in, the company hired someone just to keep the consultants' information current. Several dedicated account reps are responsible for updating the status of their corporate accounts. Says Gilmore: "It's all of our jobs to keep data in the database current."

In many ways database records are like the ultimate barometer of customer relationships. All the hard work of differentiating customers comes to bear in a good database; you can see at a glance just how things stand between you and a customer or prospect. While some companies maintain one database for customers and another for prospects, others integrate all leads into one marketing database. That makes sense since most companies are simultaneously marketing to current as well as would-be customers.

The more complete your database, the greater a business asset it becomes. At Green Hills Farms, a grocery store in Syracuse, New York, the customer database is used to track about 90 percent of the transactions in the store and to capture invaluable information on the shopping habits of different classes of customers—from the extremely loyal to the occasional shopper. The database has become a secret weapon for quietly rewarding Green Hills's best customers and fixing problems as fast as they arise. The database—or rather what's in the database— is the key reason Green Hills has been able to hold its own against six larger grocery stores in the area.

How do you know when it's time to build a more sophisticated customer database? The answer depends in part on how important cutting-edge service is to your business. It is everything to LexJet, a fast-growing Sarasota, Florida, provider of high-end inkjet printing products. LexJet cofounders Art Lambert and Ron Simpkins started with one goal: that every employee should be able to help any customer who calls with any matter, whether it's a technical question or a billing issue. No more passing the buck or the phone.

The solution, they decided, was to develop a "one-touch" system for maintaining customer relationships. What that means: with one touch at the computer, you can call up everything on a customer. Every form of communication is integrated into one system. Invoice records, shipping details, and technical issues are all together. No more passing the phone or searching for files.

That kind of functionality sounds expensive. LexJet could have spent millions on the ultimate one-touch system. Instead, the company got what it needed by linking popular off-the-shelf programs like ACT and Quicken and adding a browser-based interface. Putting the pieces together wasn't cheap—LexJet has invested more than $100,000 on outside programmers. But the more expensive alternative was to buy the parts from various vendors of customer relationship management (CRM) software. Simpkins says the new system is working: any of LexJet's twenty or so employees can now comfortably handle customer calls.

Everyone would like to have employees as well informed about customers as the workers at LexJet, but when it comes to technology, you've got to walk before you can run. One of the first big questions you will confront is whether you can make do with an off-the-shelf database solution or whether you really need to start from scratch.

Before You Invest in a Customer Database, Ask Yourself These Questions

- *What do you want to know?* Map out the information you want to capture about customers and prospects. Consider what you are trying to accomplish with your database. Your goal should be to "own" your customers' preferences and capitalize on them. That's your starting point in all this. A word to the wise: nail down all the pieces manually before you introduce technology.

- *What do you already know?* Where does customer information currently reside? In various contact managers? In your accounting system? In the heads of your sales reps?
- *Profit from the experience of others.* It can't be stressed enough: visit other companies. Organized field trips are worth every moment. Find out how other companies use their customer database. You'll get a firsthand take on what you really need and what you can live without.
- *If you build it, you will pay more.* Much more. So if you can find a database off the shelf that meets 90 percent of your needs, buy it because technology changes too fast. If you have an existing database, determine whether it can be improved with new off-the-shelf tools or whether you should start over. By all means, look at the store shelf first. Established and reliable database platforms such as Oracle and others can be customized.
- *Understand the hardware requirements.* The hardware costs add up too. Be sure to project future uses and development, always the hardest part of planning.
- *Consider total costs.* If you go the custom route, take what you think it's going to cost and double it. Take the staff you think it's going to need and double that. And don't forget the cost of ongoing maintenance. (For Capitol Concierge, upgrades to its customer database turned out to be a huge expense.)
- *Hire a dedicated technology specialist.* Don't make the mistake of trying to manage the whole project yourself. Sometimes it's worth it to spend $50,000 on an outside consultant. Trying to do it all with a small staff can be a very costly mistake.
- *Take your time rolling out the new database.* Roll out small, five or ten people at a time. Run two systems concurrently. If you can't afford to hire a consultant, dedicate someone on staff to the transition for about six months.

Developing your own customer database has certain advantages and costs. Be sure to vet any outside consultants carefully. Your request for proposal (RFP) should be well thought out and probe all the potential areas for conflict. Some general questions to ask vendors: How many software developers do you have? Have you received funding and how much? Which of your customers have implemented your solutions? Will your database, operating system, and servers be compatible with ours? Can we license the software at a later date?

The Web Difference

At one end of the tech spectrum, you have an inexpensive contact-management program you can pick up at any office supply store and learn in a half hour. At the other extreme is the Web-enabled customer database you cannot buy at any store. A Web-enabled customer database is exactly that—anything you do on the web automatically downloads or is integrated into the database. Here are a few arguments for a Web-enabled customer database:

1. *It's vastly more efficient:* no more typing in faxes or orders from the Web. Surveys, orders, and e-mail generated on the Web are all neatly collected and sent on their electronic way.
2. *You can expand your product offerings in near–real time.* When orders are electronically transmitted, the hassles of making product changes disappear.
3. *Information is at your fingertips* or within a few mouse clicks. Remote employees can easily be given access to log in to the customer database from home or on the road. You can also design things so customers can access their own records via the Web.

But a Web-enabled database doesn't come cheap. So how badly do you need it?

Clearly, there are many compelling technologies out there, all promising to improve your customer relationships. (CRM solutions are now a multibillion-dollar market.) In a growing company, it's not easy to decide how the precious few I/T dollars should be spent. One bad investment can sink a small business. Yet the right technology can elevate customer chemistry to new heights.

"We're trying to foster a long-term forever kind of client," says Gary Artis, explaining why his company has invested heavily in a company-wide CRM system aimed at automating every conversation and transaction with customers. "We're 90 percent there," says the CEO of Artis & Associates, a business consulting company in Charlotte, North Carolina. Such an aggressive investment is admittedly rare among smaller companies. Artis recorded sales of $3.6 million in 2000, however the CEO has done his math. He values the average customer at $100,000 over a three-year life cycle. Some clients have stayed with Artis since its start twelve years ago.

Put any investment in customer database technology into perspective—the customer's perspective. How many times have you found a cool new tech tool with great power and value, only to find that in the real world of running a small company, the cool new tool is impractical? There are so many logistical issues to contend with when you're growing. When it comes to implementing new technology, no company is able to move as quickly as the owner would like. But consider how one technology change could impact your employees. You always have to ask yourself, "How much can a small company absorb, roll out, and evaluate?" Don't lose sight of the ultimate goal: to continue learning about customers so you can respond to their needs in the best way possible. In that light every contact is truly an opportunity for building customer chemistry. Each new piece of information gleaned is another brick in the foundation. If you can capture the "chemistry" in your customer database, you will build a very valuable asset indeed. Consider the database your customer chemistry scorecard.

Chemistry Checklist

1. *List your opportunities to make customer contact, considering all customer touch points.* Starting points include at point of sale, incoming calls, reception area, website, fax, voice mail messages, signs, company events, e-mail, and face-to-face presentations.
2. *Develop a customer-chemistry communication plan.* After you have made your touch point list, get together with your team and list five ways that you can use each touch point to gather customer information. Example: Include a survey in outbound e-mails or provide an option on your voice mail system to leave comments for customer service.

3. *List the critical, initial pieces of customer data you want to track—also known as data capture components.* Start with the basics such as contact information and how the customer prefers to be contacted. Note types of purchases, frequency of contact, and service preferences. Companies selling to other companies want to track industry type, size of company, and titles.

4. *Determine what information is already captured today and how.* Review all existing customer records. Is your data in one centralized location or is it gathered from a variety of sources? Prepare a list of all data items your company currently collects.

5. *If you are not capturing much data today, make a list of ways you plan to gather information* (i.e., surveys, Web profiles, sweepstakes, etc.). Identify five easy starting points for collection. What types of gathering techniques would your customers respond to? Select the methods that are easy for your staff to administer and manage. Make sure that your plan is relevant to your customers.

6. *Develop a wish list of your data capture system features and functionality.* Now that you have a list of the type of data you want to collect, start to prepare an outline of software requirements. Think through the order and flow of data fields. Consider the types of reports and outputs you need from your system to effectively use in the field to grow relationships.

7. *Check out off-the-shelf solutions first.* Start with your industry association to get recommendations for software solutions developed for your industry. Talk with other company owners and managers to secure their recommendations.

8. *Solicit proposals from various providers.* Prepare an RFP that details your objectives, business rules, required functions, optional features, and elements for pricing.

9. *Prepare total software system budget checklist.* The software is just the beginning. Be sure to include consultant fees for integration, staff training, future upgrades, and the hardware required to support your solution.

CHAPTER 5

HOW TO REACH YOUR BEST CUSTOMERS
RULE 5: CREATE TOP-OF-MIND MARKETING CAMPAIGNS

In Capitol Concierge's first four years in business, my staff and I attempted our own version of mass marketing. We plastered office buildings with fliers announcing discount offers. $5 off flowers! Shirts dry-cleaned for 99 cents!

What we discovered following a series of customer surveys was (1) very few people in a building were familiar with the services the concierge offered, and (2) our special offers were attracting one-time price shoppers.

When we started to actually talk to customers and potential customers, it was the same kind of thing. Many were familiar with only one of the many services we offered, or none at all. Here we were putting all this money into this mass attack of flyers and information. What was worse, our marketing expenses consistently exceeded our budget.

As we focused on our best customers and prospects, a funny thing happened. Our marketing campaigns became more low key, more grass roots. It was like turning the volume down several notches. If we wanted to be taken seriously, we had to lower our collective voice and reach customers in a more direct and personal way. A special presentation for a small group of office managers goes over much better than any amount of mass advertising. Some have been fancier, catered lunches where we also invite our suppliers to talk about what they do. These presentations are particularly effective when office-manager clients are getting ready to plan some event. We've come to learn what those events are, and we try to help customers prepare for them in advance.

As discussed in Chapter 3, to assist clients in planning important events, my staff and I developed a budget planner that we customize for different groups of customers. We pass out this planning guide to clients at the beginning of their budget season. Let me tell you, there's no better way to get around the old "it's not in the budget" objection than this. The budget planner makes us look professional and prepared. It's a chance to educate customers about all our services, and my staff gets more time to write up proposals and source products for a specific client. Some of our best property management clients used to call us at the last minute looking for numbers they could plug into their new budgets. Using tools like the budget planner, we've eliminated a lot of those frantic calls. We always review the budget planner in face-to-face meetings and then schedule phone calls thirty to sixty days prior to an event listed on the budget planner. The return on this simple form has been easy to measure: smiles all around and a response rate as high as 97 percent.

In short, when customers go to make a purchase we want them to instantly think of Capitol. I call this approach *top-of-mind marketing*. The goal is to be part of the customer's buying process. I want my customers to think of the concierge as a goodwill expert who can select the best suppliers for whatever occasion. If you don't stay top of mind, there's always the danger the customer has met someone else. By simply reminding a client about an upcoming sales staff meeting or other event, we have an advantage over our competitors who don't take the time to learn or remember such details.

Striving to be top of mind with customers really does pay off. I'll never forget one occasion involving one of our top clients. Capitol provided concierges for this particular property management firm in all of its buildings but one. Truly one of our best customers, this firm appreciated great service and even paid its bills early. However, one of our key competitors provided the concierge service in this one building. That was like a thorn in our side, and there was almost nothing we wouldn't do to get 100 percent of this client's business. Over a five-year period my staff continued to pursue this last building; we contacted the client on a regular basis, being careful, however, not to make a pest of ourselves. Without seeming too cocky we tried to act as if getting the building was inevitable. We sent over one of our budget planners for this building, and we offered additional services such as complimentary floral arrangements for the lobby desk, additional events for the tenants, and a customized newsletter. The continued communication effort paid off. One day we were given the opportunity to provide a temporary concierge in the building. That was just the in we needed. After years of trying, our proactive service finally won Capitol the account.

Top-of-Mind Marketing Is a Mind-Set

The customer chemistry approach to marketing is different. Perhaps the best way to sum up the difference is to say what this approach is not: it's not mass marketing and it's not the traditional rationing of marketing dollars. It is simply a shift away from marketing as traditionally taught in business school and practiced by many large corporations. Where TV commercials and other mass marketing often seem like a series of impersonal and random hits, the customer-chemistry approach to marketing is personal, customized, and timely.

RULE 5: CREATE TOP-OF-MIND MARKETING CAMPAIGNS

Learn to map your customers' buying cycles and timetables. Deploy a communication plan that plants reminders with your customers just in time and capture every potential selling opportunity.

We call it top-of-mind marketing because the phrase neatly sums up the objective: to keep your company front and center in the customer's mind.

Remember the old saw about catching a husband? It goes like this: "The best way to a man's heart is through his stomach." We beg to differ. The best way to your customer's heart is through his mind—which is, after all, where the chemistry begins. Remember that falling in love is actually a very heady event; it's a *chemical* reaction in the brain's wiring. Top-of-mind marketers understand this and look for ways to continually make that mental connection with customers. And they do it without spending big bucks on slick advertising.

Chapter 4 presented advice on how to proactively communicate with customers as a way to stay in touch and continue to learn more about all customers but especially your best ones. Top-of-mind marketing revolves around the customer chemistry communications plan and builds on it using a variety of media.

Top-of-Mind Marketing Is Personal

Brian Farley, owner and president of Pride Mortgage Co. in Provincetown, Massachusetts, is a firm believer in top-of-mind marketing. As he puts it, "I'm always looking for ways to buy brain cells." In fact it's almost impossible to forget about Farley once you've completed the process of getting a home loan through him. For example, Farley's photo appears in the ads he takes out in small local newspapers that reach the gay and lesbian communities from which Pride draws many of its customers. He sponsors events important to the gay community. Once a year he throws a huge party at his Cape Cod home inviting all his customers; in 2000 more than one hundred attended.

In the last year Farley found yet another way to keep customers thinking of him; he sends them a magazine subscription that's memorable because the magazine includes a little message from him on the cover. After closing on a loan, the customer automatically gets a subscription to *Traditional Home* magazine courtesy of Farley, whose photo and short message appear in one corner of the cover of the bimonthly magazine. Every other month hundreds of home owners open their mail boxes to find Farley's smiling face looking up at them. The cost: $12 per subscription, a price Farley considers dirt cheap considering that customer referrals generate nearly 85 percent of his revenues.

Farley explains his philosophy toward marketing this way: "There's separation anxiety when the deal is done. We have to find a way to stay in front of people. It's the lender-for-life theory. We want them to call us for anything finance or real estate related. I'm very gratified by the number of people who call me and say 'Brian, I think it's time to refinance, what do you think?'"

As for results, Farley personally writes more loans than just about anyone in the country, making the list of the top two hundred mortgage originators since 1998. In 2001 he was on track to broker more than $60 million in loans. He also oversees a growing company with nineteen employees and $2 million in revenues. Pride Mortgage has succeeded in staying top of mind with customers without resorting to aggressive telemarketing or shelling out the big bucks to advertise in major newspapers. Rather, customer chemistry is kindled through personal interactions and smaller but more intimate advertising campaigns.

Farley is not the only one who's figured out how to stand out in the marketing jungle. Some catalogers are also starting to place special messages on the mailing label. Road Runner Sports, for instance, also includes special greetings when it mails out catalogs. The message might be "Happy Birthday" or "Your ASICS shoes on page 82" or "Eric, you're a VIP and its's time to celebrate YOU!" Although the technology for inserting such custom greetings is about two years old, it's still not commonly used. For repeat mailers it's one way to rise above the crowd.

Top-of-Mind Marketing Is Timely

Traditional mass marketing relies on building *brand awareness* through expensive mediums: TV and radio ads, print placements, and large direct-mail campaigns. Ultimately, the mass marketer hopes a certain (usually small) percentage of the population will respond to the message. Top-of-mind marketers create brand awareness in a very different way: by communicating on a small scale at well-planned intervals.

As in many pivotal points in life's relationships, the old adage "timing is everything" applies to building customer chemistry. If you've identified key customer touch points (see Chapters 3 and 4), then you can also identify when key customer data capture opportunities will occur. As much as possible, you want to time your communications to key events in the customers' life cycles.

Companies that are in tune to their customers' buying cycles make a point of touching customers just prior to the time key purchase decisions are made. One classic case: Day-Timers Inc. makes sure customers never run out of pages for their Day-Timer planners. For instance, advance notice arrives via fax with a message that typically reads "Renew now—get a reward!"

Don't assume you know when customers will be ready to make a purchase or request a service. Your estimate could be off by a lot. Capitol Concierge surveyed office managers and found out that buying decisions for Secretary's Day gifts were made in February. Previously, Capitol had sent out Secretary's Day offerings in mid-March. By taking the extra step of asking when buying decisions were made, Capitol was able to send out relevant information when the customer would act on it—resulting in 50 percent more orders.

Likewise, you can boost your response from potential customers simply by making sure your message reaches them when they are thinking of hiring someone in your industry. Even before you've established a relationship with a prospect, you want your message to arrive *just in time*.

For instance, Cavanaugh, a $12-million promotional products company in Pittsburgh, studies what current customers are ordering at different times of the year to help time mailings to potential new clients. What customers have ordered in the past helps determine in part which prospects the company will send an introduction letter (and small promotional item) and when. "Having a customer database that can generate reports about what kinds of products certain kinds of businesses ordered in the past and when during the year they placed the order is very, very helpful," says business development manager Kimball Smith. He spends time correlating customers' Standard Industry Codes to their purchases to be sure he's reaching hot new prospects at just the right time in the planning cycle. He knows, for example, engineering firms tend to order promotional products for spring trade shows—"so right after January 1 is when you want to contact them," he says.

Top-of-mind marketing programs evolve as you get to know your customers better. The important shift in thinking here is that you are timing your marketing to meet their schedules, their deadlines, and their budget cycles rather than your own need to make a certain level of sales by the end of the quarter. Think of yourself as the customer's personal planning assistant. And as with technology, walk before you run. Try out your marketing ideas on one or two customers at a time.

It's not just knowing when to place the phone call but how to get customers' attention when they are preparing for a busy time of year. For example, Joshua Frey, cofounder of Granny's Goodies in Washington, D.C., targets two very specific gift buyers with promotions geared to their very different needs. He sends "Move In Survival Kits" to his property manager clients during the summer, the busiest time of the year for this group. College recruiters are also good customers for Frey; they typically have gift and giveaway needs during the second, third, and fourth quarters, with peak demand for gift items in spring and fall when the recruiters stage career fairs and need giveaways like pens and stress reliever "toys."

Conventional advertising depends on repetition to be successful, and so does top-of-mind marketing. The difference here is that you aren't blasting your marketing to everyone but quietly broadcasting it to the customers who need or want your message most. Today that goal can be accomplished through a combination of face-to-face meetings, postcards, phone calls, and, increasingly, e-mail.

Frey enjoys sending electronic mail because it lets him reveal a little bit of his personality to his customers. "E-mail has been very helpful as we are able to send our proposals with funny little messages to brighten the recipient's day as opposed to leaving long-winded voice mail messages."

Capitol Concierge Best Practices: The Top-of-Mind Marketing Campaign

The bulk of Capitol Concierge's marketing dollars and concierge time goes to staying top of mind with great frequency with its best customers. Here's the schedule of what Capitol does for its tier-one corporate clients on a regular basis:

Weekly
- Phone call to touch base
- Review customer anniversary and birthday list and send any appropriate cards
- Update customers' personal profiles

Monthly
- Visit from a Capitol Concierge manager
- Monthly service activity report to highlight key achievements of concierges and service activity for their specific buildings

Quarterly
- *Breakfast or lunch with a key contact.* The management and concierge teams regularly schedule informal outings to review service, to program progress, and to provide another opportunity for learning conversations with best customers.

Semiannually
- *Written survey.* In June and December of each year, ask clients to complete a two-page survey to assess several key areas of our service performance; follow-up with a telephone call or meeting to specifically review each comment and map out plans to improve service elements that received less than excellent ratings.
- *Complimentary training.* Provide customer service workshops for customers' frontline staffs (the building engineers and porters) led by an experienced Capitol Concierge trainer.

Annually
- *Budget planners.* In June of each year, distribute budget planners listing all services.
- *Seasonal gift.* Capitol Concierge chose to forgo the conventional approach and sent out our client gifts in June to accompany our budget planners. (Summer is also when Capitol celebrates

anniversaries, and sometimes top clients are invited to these events as well.)

- *Event or outing.* Typically, a holiday preview event in which the concierges showcase holiday catering menus, gifts, and floral arrangements. This exclusive event allows the staff to interact with best customers in more of a social setting while still creating awareness and sales opportunities for the company's different services.

- *Planning meeting.* Each member of the Capitol Concierge management team is assigned a group of our key client contacts to meet with once a year for an annual planning session. We bring a plan outlining proposed activities for each month of the year. The manager also secures feedback from each client and makes specific additions or changes to the plan based on that particular client's unique needs.

Top-of-Mind Marketing Online

If you're a customer of Mark Zimmerman, who owns a Great Harvest Bread franchise in Chapel Hill, North Carolina, you won't miss out on getting your "Honey Bear" whole-wheat dinner rolls in time for Thanksgiving. That's because he sends out an animated e-mail message two weeks before Turkey Day reminding all customers who've opted in for e-mail that their last day to place an order is fast arriving. The message lays out the store's mouth-watering menu of breads, cookies, and pies. Some of the holidays reflect the store's unique personality. For example, August 5th is Greatful Bread Day in honor of Jerry Garcia's birthday. Zimmerman's just-in-time e-mail message promises a free loaf of bread to all who wear a tie-dyed T-shirt to the bakery for the occasion. For Zimmerman the e-mail missives have been an inexpensive way to stay in touch with customers who've clearly expressed an interest in learning more.

Janine Giorgenti presents another striking example of how far you can effectively incorporate e-mail into your top-of-mind marketing plan. She's the owner of an eponymous firm in Melville, New York, that does image consulting and produces its own line of clothing for professional men and women. Giorgenti makes the most of the tickler feature in her sales force automation program, SalesLogix. The company uses dozens of automated marketing processes to send out customized letters at regular intervals to thirty thousand prospects. Trade show prospects receive e-mail follow-up the day of the show.

Online the perspective is a little different because so many companies are still in customer acquisition mode. It seems that anyone who opts in to an e-mail list is a hot prospect. Or anyone who's willing to identify himself or herself online. Sometimes that thinking makes sense. For example, British Airways ran a raffle-type promotion on its website that asked contest entrants to fill out a survey. The customer information was so important to the airline that it was willing to give away a round-trip ticket. And for good reason: travelers willing to fill out a survey on the Web are the very same travelers likely to book their travel online in the future—exactly what British Airways wants to have happen. It's a good bet the airline is following up with a targeted pitch to everyone who entered the contest.

Event-Based E-Mail

Furthermore, some of the event-based e-mail marketing out there is quite good. For example, anyone who signs up for the e-mail newsletter at babycenter.com does so by filling out a short form that includes your child's birth date. When the monthly e-mail arrives from Baby-Center, there's no missing it in your e-mail queue. It's timed to your baby's age to the day, with a recurring subject line each month: "My Baby This Month—Your 16-Month-Old." What mother (or father) could resist learning whether the baby is right on course developmentally or lagging behind? You can also link up to other parents with a child the same age as yours. There is something for everyone to click on in this fast-paced newsletter that is designed naturally to get you to the website—where there's all matter of baby products for sale as well as pages and pages of expert advice. And reportedly many of the approximately seven hundred thousand BabyCenter subscribers do click through to the website. How many actually buy something once they're there? BabyCenter's not talking. Or not yet.

It remains to be seen whether this particular information-heavy business model will succeed. It did not succeed in the case of garden.com, which offered newsletters, a community of fellow gardeners, and lots of expert help for developing that green thumb but, alas, came up short on actual online sales. However, BabyCenter stands a better chance of surviving the dot-com downturn since it's been acquired by Johnson & Johnson, which obviously values the direct pipeline to parents that BabyCenter has created via its e-mail newsletter.

You can't lose when you create e-mail campaigns for what you know to be your best customers and prospects. Animated e-mail greeting cards can be sent anytime but seem especially effective after making contact with an important customer or prospect. In addition, e-mail clubs can be used to qualify a buyer's interests and potential buying power and to provide a way to track actual sales.

Boston-based music retailer Newbury Comics, for instance, rewards customers who join its e-mail club with discounts and advance notice of new recordings, concerts, and other events. (The chain got its name because it was founded by two MIT roommates, Mike Dreese and John Brusger, with $2,000 and a comic book collection; their store quickly became the region's leading specialist in alternative music and now consists of twenty-three locations throughout New England.) E-mail club members receive 5 percent discounts on CDs and DVDs and other perks in exchange for letting the chain track their purchases. Eventually that information will be used in future targeted marketing promotions. For now, subscribers receive information on as many as twenty artists they've chosen, as well as unadvertised specials. There's one line on the sign-up form that's especially telling. Newbury Comics asks, "Where else do you buy music?" There is a box to check that says "NOWHERE ELSE." If the chain is as smart as it appears to be, those customers should be in for some extreme VIP treatment. As for covering the costs of the program, Newbury Comics charges club members $5 a year, although in the first year of the program the chain wisely charged just $2 for a trial membership. Both membership fees and discounts are subject to change each year. The chain does not sell customer information.

BIRTH OF AN E-MAIL CLUB

We asked Trish Kane, the director of Newbury Comics Interactive who heads up the store's innovative e-mail club, to fill us in on the challenges and results of reaching out to customers online. She responded by e-mail.

Q: How many customers are now in the club?
A: The trial program that we had launched previously expired on March 1, 2001. At that time it had more than sixteen thousand members. We relaunched the program and now have approximately twelve thousand members. Most of the active customers who were in the trial program joined the new program.

Q: Does the $5 fee cover your expenses?
A: No, and it is not intended to do so. We have a staff of four people working solely on this program. The approximately $60,000 we've collected wouldn't begin to cover the labor and materials costs. The fee is in place so as to give the card a sense of value. We've found that with a fee in place we get customers who are interested in the program and find it worthy. When the card was free we had a large percentage of club members who only used the card once or oddly enough never at all. Since there wasn't a value attached to it, customers viewed it as a discount card and would join and then discard the card after that one-time shopping discount was received. We also had a high percentage of phony/bad addresses and "lost" memberships resulting in customers joining multiple times, which in turn resulted in more work for our staff and burn through of materials. Now, more than 80 percent of club members have used their card more than once.

Q: Have you taken the club to the next level?
A: We are currently undergoing segmentation analysis to drill down into the purchasing data so we can come to better conclusions about what our customers are interested in. We currently make very simple conclusions such as "Since you've purchased CDs by Radiohead, we thought you would be

interested to know that there is a new Radiohead CD coming out tomorrow." With the segmentation analysis we hope we can make conclusions about people who would be interested in receiving that e-mail but have never actually purchased that particular artist. We have done special things for customers who are very profitable. We have offered the most profitable customers the best offer/discount and then staggered it down the line to the least profitable, who don't receive the discount at all.

Customer Preferences for E-Mail or Snail Mail

While Capitol Concierge has found e-mail reminders to be a time-saver when it comes to helping customers with their routine and regularly timed purchases such as a catered corporate lunch, it's important to note that Capitol always asks clients how they would prefer to be contacted. Like it or not, snail mail is still what many people depend on. Gary Hawkins, the CEO at Green Hills Farms in Syracuse, says the majority of his customers—including a large elderly population—prefer to get their promotional specials through the mail. Fewer than 10 percent have requested information by e-mail. Regardless of the medium used, Hawkins's marketing pitches are truly top of mind and just in time for the next shopping trip since every promotion is tailored to the person's past buying as well as his or her status in the company's four-tier loyalty program.

Still, in many industries e-mail has become a vitally important way to communicate with customers. Steve Leveen, the president of Levenger, a direct marketer of upscale reading and writing products, reports that electronic mail now represents 30 percent of his customer communications. E-mail is certainly not going away. According to the Electronic Messaging Association, we sent more than 5.5 trillion e-mail messages in 1999. Electronic mail makes top-of-mind marketing even more timely. Yet as e-mail communicators, many companies are flunking. Among the mistakes: taking too long to respond, being too long-winded, giving incomplete answers, and being too informal or too forward.

Many people could benefit from a short course in e-mail etiquette, a phrase that seems like a new-age oxymoron since so many e-mail messages come uninvited. Yet even when our customers opt in, it's worth establishing guidelines for e-mail correspondence.

- *Don't send e-mail to a customer or sales prospect unannounced.* By now everyone's heard of *permission marketing*. Basically, consumers grant companies permission to send them e-mail pitches in exchange for some sort of reward. But permission marketing means something entirely different when you're selling to other businesses. You can never be too careful, says Marguerite Sallee, chairman of Bright Horizons Family Solutions and the founder of Frontline Group, a corporate training company she started in Nashville two years ago. She is particularly cautious about approaching corporate executives online. She always gets permission to send e-mail, she says, usually through an executive's assistant—increasing the odds that the message will be read. Good manners have paid off for the Southern-bred Sallee. In Frontline's first year alone she brought in more than $5 million in sales.
- *What could be construed as rude in the real world might be savvy in cyberspace.* In their book *The Etiquette Advantage in Business: Personal Skills for Professional Success*, Peggy Post and Peter Post write: "The business etiquette of electronic communication is still being developed, and what passes for manners in this brave new world of electronics often reflects the enthusiasm of the media's youthful masters." That enthusiasm can spread to your customers. At least it did for Timbuk2, a San Francisco manufacturer of messenger bags. One customer openly praised the company for its unconventional writing style. The customer commented by e-mail:

  "As a copywriter for an ad agency here in Seattle, I appreciate the tone of your corporate communications. You project a consistent attitude and style befitting to your products and customers. I also appreciate the 'risks' you take in the copy on your website, few companies have the balls to write edgy stuff like that."
- *Bend the rules to fit the situation.* Pat Cavanaugh, the CEO of the aforementioned promotional products company, is not shy about writing a personal e-mail message to someone he really wants to reach. While

watching a basketball game one night, he was inspired to fire off an e-mail message to a VIP sales prospect. It was midnight. Needless to say he didn't get permission to send the message. But at 1 A.M., the prospect e-mailed back and even included a personal note: "You didn't miss much of a game . . ." Cavanaugh won a sales meeting—and the chance to bid on a big piece of business—all because someone "liked the fact that I was working my ass off," he says. His just-in-time marketing paid off: the client extended a deadline for selecting a vendor because of Cavanaugh's dogged persistence. A few months later, the Cavanaugh company won the account. In this case breaking the rules of e-mail etiquette paid off, but don't try this one at home unless you have a very good feel for the person you're trying to reach.

As much as e-mail helps automate the whole process of keeping your name in front of customers and prospects, it's just one way of getting out the message. It's no substitute for the kinds of careful thinking that you must put into any marketing you put out there—but especially the marketing messages that you place in front of your most-valued clients. Top-of-mind marketing should be as thoughtful as it is timely and personal.

Top-of-Mind Marketing Is Value Added

It's also important to create ways to stay top-of-mind that don't always result in direct sales, but that instead deliver value-added services to your best customers. Consider, for example, offering free educational workshops on some topic of interest to your customers. Other value-added strategies include free service evaluations. The best way to gain insights into the types of programs that your customers will perceive as high value are to ask them directly what areas within their own businesses they find challenging or frustrating or for which they cannot identify a service provider to assist them. You want to be the resource they turn to again and again, even if it means finding a supplier you don't currently work with.

Little Nell Hotel in Aspen, Colorado, reaches out to customers in the crucial weeks before they're scheduled to arrive. The hotel's concierges call some ninety-two guests to go over and arrange the little details like dinner reservations, concert schedules, and activities best suited for children. The concierges fax menus, trail maps, and theater lineups. Who's going to forget a hotel that goes that far to help you? The hotel considers it one of the most welcoming gestures it can do. It's a way to personalize the stay of VIP guests. The effort has clearly paid off—customers often comment on the concierge phone calls. What's more, a full 70 percent of customers are returning guests of the eleven-year-old hotel. You can imagine the kind of chemistry the hotel must have with those repeat customers.

Figure 5.1 provides a quick summary of the differences in the traditional and top-of-mind methods of communicating with customers.

Figure 5.1 Marketing Models

Out with the Old . . .

Under the old mass-marketing model—based on selling a single product to as many customers as possible—communications can be best described as:

One-way
Loud (TV, radio)
No memory of the customer
Encourage one-time purchases
Junk mail
Spam
Anonymous ("To: Current Resident")

. . . And in with the New

Under the new relationship-marketing models—that rely on building customer chemistry and share of customer—communications can be best described as:

Two-way dialogue
Discreet
Customer-database driven
Encourage repeat purchases and customer referrals
Customized and handwritten letters
Individualized e-mail
Personal (never "To: Current Resident")

The Top-of-Mind Marketing Budget

At most companies the majority of the marketing budget is usually earmarked for customer acquisition. Many businesses not only pour lots of money into securing new customers, but direct their internal resources and sales incentives to that goal as well. The price is paid to capture customers but not to keep them.

One big advantage to knowing your customers well is you can strategically plan your chemistry-creation efforts. By planning to be proactive, you can devote more time and money to your best prospects without increasing your overall marketing budget one dollar. Chances are you'll have to reallocate your marketing budget to accomplish the goals of top-of-mind marketing.

As shown in Figure 5.2, here's how you should think about divvying up the pie. Basically, a company has three target markets at all times.

1. *The universe:* every customer in your market. Allocate 10 percent of the company's budget and time to this customer group.
2. *Prospects:* potential customers that fit your best-customer profile. Allocate 30 percent of the company's budget and resources to this population.
3. *Current customers:* the smallest group of the three, yet the one that offers the greatest potential for profitability and long-term

Figure 5.2 The Marketing Budget

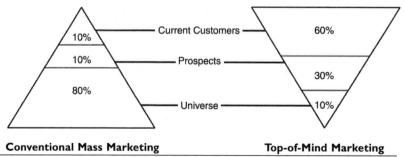

10%	Current Customers	60%
10%	Prospects	30%
80%	Universe	10%
Conventional Mass Marketing		**Top-of-Mind Marketing**

relationships. Allocate 60 percent of your budget and efforts to this invaluable group.

While it's crucial to allocate dollars, to really maximize a tiered approach to building customer chemistry, you need to develop different marketing plans for different customers and touch points for each tier following the same 10/30/60 allocation of time and materials. The top-of-mind marketing plan revolves around touch points for each customer level. The key is to design and deliver relevant information to different customer groups at different times and at different points of contact. Just as you want to stay in your customers' mind as much as possible, you also want customers to know they are top of mind for you as well.

Chemistry Checklist

1. *Create a marketing budget using the 10/30/60 formula.* Slice the pie differently this year when planning your budget, giving the biggest piece to your existing customers. Meet with your team to create and price a list of marketing events, mailers, surveys, and other communication tools that will grow your current customers. Because you already have an existing relationship with these customers, the return on your money will be far greater than the dollars used to chase new customers.

2. *Consider what you can do for specific tiers of customers, and assign specific employees to oversee the plans for each tier.* Start by breaking your customer base into no more than three tiers. Make a list of all of the possible activities and touch-point plans. Drawing from this master list, allocate the different activities to the different customer groups. Remember to place emphasis on your best customers.

3. *Create customized marketing plans for as many individual customers as possible within each tier.* The key to creating chemistry is to deliver personalized and relevant messages to each individual. Take small steps by selecting specific clients within each tier and create unique promotions for each based on profile information collected.

4. *Map your customers' buying cycles and other key events.* Using a tool such as the budget planner, determine the frequency for specific product and service purchases. Plan your just-in-time communications to touch the customer four to eight weeks prior to the event. Map out other important dates in the customer's buying cycle and how you plan to keep in touch at each juncture.

5. *Create staff guidelines for marketing communications.* Be particularly clear about the tone you want to set in e-mail messages, and be sure it's consistent with the overall image you want to present to customers.

CHAPTER 6

HOW TO ENHANCE THE CHEMISTRY

RULE 6: TREAT YOUR BEST CUSTOMERS LIKE YOUR BEST EMPLOYEES—RECOGNIZE AND REWARD THEM

Best customers, like star employees, need to be recognized on a consistent basis. All too often the customers who keep our businesses thriving do not receive the appreciation they deserve. A friend of mine once gave me a popular book on dating called *Are You the One for Me?* As I was reading it, I couldn't help thinking about business. In the pages of a self-help book I could see parallels to how we get to know our customers. The parallels are not only amusing but also highly instructive. You know, at the start of a personal relationship, we're wined and dined. That first six months or a year it's all very magical and happy. But in truly successful marriages over time, there's a conscious awareness of the need to continually show appreciation and to communicate. There are just amazing parallels in the business world. I always say we pay the price to capture a customer but not to keep the customer.

During the go-go start-up years at Capitol Concierge, the need to ramp up revenues took precedence over everything else. We were in a race with a new competitor to land new building accounts for the concierge service. For many entrepreneurs and salespeople, the thrill

of closing a sale is exhilarating. And so it was for us. While our existing clients were receiving super service from their on-site concierge,
they were not getting the attention they needed from me and my management team. We were a very small team and it was all we could do
to keep our heads above water. Then one day during a networking
event I was attending for property managers, a valued client commented that she had not heard from me in a long time. This client
had several new buildings to send our way but was concerned these
buildings would not get the attention needed. This encounter was a
wake-up call for me, reminding me how important current clients are
to fueling growth.

Such experiences, as well as the results of our study of current clients'
contribution to revenue and profit, led us to develop the tools, communication activities, and support mechanisms that we use to ensure
the majority of our time and resources are allocated to those who matter most—our current customers. I show customers they count by
devoting more staff time to them, but there are many little ways to show
we care as well. Just as our concierges used the client profile form to
track the birthdays and unique interests of their individual customers,
the management team also started to collect the same type of information from our property management clients. We've learned that our
clients' hobbies and interests are wide ranging, from duck hunting and
golf to fine wines and gardening.

The extra effort to send an interest-related gift versus a "one size fits
all" raises the customer-chemistry bar. John W. was a golf enthusiast
and we sent him a golf-theme clock, for example, on the anniversary of
our contract. CeCe B., an existing client, was always sending us referrals for new buildings. To express our appreciation, we sent her a beautiful bouquet because she loves getting flowers. Simple gestures related
to what you have learned about your customers have a powerful chemistry-building effect. You demonstrate that you value the relationship,
you are paying attention to personal details, and you remain top of mind
with your very best customers. In addition, we are always looking at our
product and service line to develop extra touches. The frontline team
is by far the best source for creative ideas.

Customers Need Recognition

Why don't companies take the time to do something special for customers after the wine-and-roses stage? It's simple: they don't know how to quantify the payoff of such ongoing efforts. However, if you've taken the time to identify your best customers, you do have a way of measuring your return on investment. Share of customer is a powerful measuring tool in addition to repeat business, order frequency, and sales per customer.

Your ability to effectively reward customers stems naturally from the process of (1) identifying tiers of customers and degrees of loyalty; (2) training employees to truly listen to customers; and (3) developing a top-of-mind marketing plan that stresses one-to-one communications. Customer recognition, then, is the culmination of all your efforts to get closer to your most valuable customers. It's the final step in building customer chemistry.

How many ways can you say "I love you"? Customer rewards come in a variety of forms. First and foremost, don't forget to simply say thank you after each and every sale. In between sales there are numerous ways to let customers know you're thinking of them and are thankful for the referrals they send your way.

RULE 6: TREAT YOUR CUSTOMERS LIKE YOUR BEST EMPLOYEES— RECOGNIZE AND REWARD THEM

Everyone likes to be appreciated. No one deserves recognition more than the customers that fuel your growth. Relevant rewards that demonstrate your knowledge of your customers will result in unsurpassed levels of loyalty.

Customer loyalty programs are another popular way to give something back to customers. While you can't buy loyalty—and shouldn't waste your time trying to—you can reward it when you see it. After all, why should price shoppers get all the prizes? Be sure you're not inadvertently rewarding customers who only buy from you when you're offering a discount.

What's more, a customer loyalty program can include extra services or perks as well as frequent-buyer discounts. Since no two customers are exactly the same, cutting-edge loyalty programs strive to customize the rewards. If you can somehow personalize your own customer recognition program, you'll no doubt be ahead of the competition. In many cases creating personal perks is a matter of responding to customers' personal preferences.

Of course, gifts, notes, discounts, and other extras cannot in and of themselves build strong, lifelong customer relationships. However, once you have sown the seeds for a relationship, customer recognition is kind of like Miracle-Gro; it helps the relationship bloom a whole lot faster.

Finally, reward customers for choosing you by devoting yourself to continuous improvement. Consider upgrading your computer system, for example, or enhancing customer service so you can better handle special requests and fast turnaround times. Feedback from your best customers will help you prioritize your ongoing efforts to run a better operation. When you make customers part of your quality control team, you are recognizing their value to your company.

Simple Ways to Recognize Customers and Show Appreciation

- *"Saw this and thought of you" cards.* Print a supply of cards with this message and attach to a newspaper or magazine article related to a customer's interests. Mail or personally deliver the information. This technique keeps your employees looking out for customers' best interests and gets you in front of customers in a nonsales manner.
- *Referral thank-you gift.* Every time you receive a referral send a bouquet of flowers or other noticeable but simple gift.
- *Recognize positive feedback.* Whenever your company receives a letter from a client commending an employee's performance, always contact the customer immediately and thank him or her for taking the time to send a positive word. Typically, most companies drop every-

thing to respond to negative feedback. Remember that customers complain more than they praise. When a customer takes the time to extend kind words, it is imperative to respond and share the feedback with your entire staff.

- *Special-occasion reminders.* By tracking key dates for customers, you can send special-occasion reminder postcards. You may also be able to make purchase recommendations related to the event.
- *Personalized gifts.* Noting customer birthdays and sending gifts tailored to their interests and hobbies helps you deliver the personal touch. Every contact provides an opportunity to discover preferences.
- *Special-offer certificates* that are personalized based on the client's interests or purchase history.
- *Customer testimonial features.* Feature customers in your newsletter often.
- *Customer hotlines.* Provide best customers with special telephone numbers and access channels for after business hours. Nothing is more frustrating to a customer than not being able to get assistance after hours when something important is at stake.
- *Reward a significant order.* At some companies any purchase more than a certain amount automatically triggers a gift with the order. Unexpected freebies are appreciated all the more.
- *Handwritten thank-you notes.* Hands down the most powerful recognition tool in this age of the electronic pen. Write the notes as orders are fulfilled.

Customer Loyalty Programs

A good loyalty program serves several purposes at once: it educates customers about your product even as it pays them back for their patronage; it rewards customers just as they are rewarding you with the kind of repeat business that often equates to higher margins; and the best loyalty programs let customers be part of a special, self-selecting community.

- At Road Runner Sports, a popular source of running shoes based in San Diego, members of the company's Run America Club pay an annual membership fee of $20. In return, they qualify for a 5 percent discount, free shipping, and a free magazine. By joining the club, customers are indicating to Road Runner that they intend to make repeat purchases (or they wouldn't pay to join). Road Runner basically breaks even on the membership fees but more important gets an instant list of best customers that benefits its store and catalog operations. The list changes from year to year but more than a few customers have stayed in the club since its start. They're very avid buyers and the company goes all out to make them feel special.

- At Green Hills Farms in Syracuse best customers self-select by spending $100 or more per week; when that's sustained over twelve weeks, they get special treatment in the way of unadvertised discounts, 5-percent-off coupons, and holiday gifts such as a free turkey and Douglas fir tree. One year Green Hills threw a semiformal holiday party for its top two hundred customers (and their spouses) based on spending levels. About two hundred people attended the after-hours soiree and were treated to a huge buffet spread.

- In the world of minor league baseball, the St. Paul Saints of St. Paul, Minnesota, rewards its most loyal fans—the two thousand or so season ticket holders—with team merchandise, special events that let fans mingle with the team, and an occasional newsletter known as "The Gospel."

- Fanatical baseball fans are not so different from the bread zealots who spread the good word for Janene Centurione, the owner of two Great Harvest Bread bakeries in Michigan. She amply and regularly rewards the loyal customers who belong to her "bread zealot" club. Between the two stores, there are about fourteen thousand customers in the club, and they tell hundreds of their friends about Great Harvest. She mails a newsletter with recipes and coupons to everyone on the list three times a year. Once a quarter she also gives "lavish and loving goodies," as she calls them, to the most frequent patrons of the bakeries—those who buy bread about once a week—or forty to sixty loaves a year—as well as other goods at the bakery. She has given posters of prairie scenes done by a well-known regional artist. There are free loaves of bread in the summer. One Christmas the customers received a one-of-a-kind "floatie" pen featuring a small loaf of bread sliding into a hungry man's mouth. She spends so much more on top customers because they are spending so much more with her. Each year the top 20 percent of customers spend about $450 each—that's nearly twenty times that of the bottom 20 percent. Centurione likes to keep customers guessing about her next surprise. "No one knows what's coming next," she says.

HOW TO MAKE EVERY CUSTOMER A BEST CUSTOMER: GREEN HILLS FARMS STORE, SYRACUSE, NEW YORK

Problem: How to reward loyal customers—including those who can't afford to spend as much, such as senior citizens on a fixed income

Overview: One time-honored way to reward your best customers is to identify the proverbial 20 percent of customers who generate 80 percent of your sales and lavish them with attention and rewards. But Green Hills Farms's CEO Gary Hawkins decided to do things a little different. He wants every customer of the grocery store to have a shot at making it to the top rung. So he doesn't focus on deciles or quartiles per se, as many retailers do. His system is based on how much each customer actually spends in hard dollars, designing his storewide promotions and individual discounts accordingly.

Solution: In Green Hills's loyalty program there are four levels of customers, named for gemstones: Diamond at the top, followed by Ruby, Pearl, and Opal. Moving up to the next level is not only possible but encouraged through one promotion after another. Or rather, the next level is attainable if you, as a consumer, do the majority of your grocery shopping at Green Hills. On the other hand, if you're a habitual price shopper, jumping from one store to the next, you won't reap many rewards from shopping at Green Hills.

The store makes the bargain explicit: the more you shop with us, the more we'll reward you. The loyalty program and promotions are explained in the store and at its inviting, clear website, greenhills.com. How about senior citizens on a limited budget? They are not forgotten. Green Hills's most popular promotion, the Great Gobbler Giveaway (see Figure 6.1), is based on dollars spent for ten weeks leading up to Thanksgiving. The first level of rewards is attainable by most anyone; all you have to do is spend $30 a week (senior citizens) or $50 a week (families) to win. Even the top award is something many families can reach.

Results: The store used to sell turkeys below cost to anyone who walked in the store around Thanksgiving. Not any more. Both sales and gross margins have gone up since the Great Gobbler Giveaway began eight years ago. Almost everyone who shops at the store participates in the loyalty program on some level, providing the store with invaluable information on what customers buy and when. "My gut belief was that all this customer data should be a gold mine," says Hawkins. And it has been. Green Hills has turned to its best customers time and again to help the store successfully survive the expansion of much larger competitors.

Figure 6.1 Examples of Customer Loyalty Rewards

Green Hills Farm's Great Gobbler Giveaway
Spend $300 and get a free turkey breast
Spend $500 and get a free turkey
Spend $750 and get a free turkey and wreath
Spend $1,000 and get a free turkey, wreath, and tree

Frequent-buyer clubs are all the rage in stores and airlines, and now various prizes and rewards are all the rage in cyberspace. But are loyalty programs or frequent-buyer clubs appropriate for everyone? There are legal considerations, such as the issues addressed in this loyalty program caution.

> *Caution. If you are rewarding some customers and not others with special price discounts, you must check with a lawyer to be sure you are not inadvertently engaging in illegal price discrimination. There are federal laws that protect certain industries from predatory pricing practices.*

Can they work in a service firm? Yes. After all, even when your customer is a corporation, you are still dealing with individual buyers. They are real people, not corporate cogs, and they yearn to be recognized like anyone else. Of course, there is an art to corporate gift giving. You've got to be careful lest your reward be perceived as a kickback or your point system as degrading.

Designing a Loyalty Program for Service Firms

Dan Miller, founder and CEO of a recruiting service based in New England, wanted to recognize and reward clients for actively referring their colleagues to his company. He awarded clients—mainly human resources directors—anywhere from 100 to 500 points for six different beneficial actions. Agreeing to appear in a company testimonial ad was worth 100 points, for example. Moreover, each customer referral that netted actual business in thirty days was worth 500 points. Miller first surveyed some of his clients to arrive at appropriate rewards, and then he designed three levels. At the first level, or 500 points, the winner could choose between a $150 gift certificate to one of three top-rated restaurants in Boston or a $150 gift certificate to Macy's. The grand prize, for earning 1,500 points, was two nights stay at a top hotel and dinner or an $850 Macy's certificate. The program details were sent via e-mail. Miller included an important caveat: "If you choose not to receive an award . . . we will donate a comparable amount to the charity of your choice." It was a point system with principles. After a year about 120 of 180 clients were earning points. Suddenly Miller had information that had been nearly impossible to collect before. All he asked them to do was report back on their success with his recruiting service. Customers were glad to do it.

For a recent variation on the same theme, consider the approach of RightNow Technologies. The start-up software company in Bozeman, Montana, wasted no time creating what it calls "The Inner Circle." Customers who sign up immediately receive a "Montana gift basket." The benefits, spelled out at www.rightnow.com, include training discounts, quarterly gifts, and media exposure in return for serving as a reference for the company or entering into a comarketing arrangement.

At Custom Research Inc. in Minneapolis, there is no official customer loyalty program, but the most valuable customers are clearly treated differently: top clients, called partners, are on a track of their own with separate marketing initiatives and rewards for continued patronage. CRI makes a continuous attempt to discover what extra services and perks it can give these customers without the customer even asking. CRI devotes managers to figuring out the bigger things clients need that they might not have clearly verbalized. Managers sift through project notes, interview customers, and sit in on account-team meetings. For each of about forty clients, CRI creates what it calls a Surprise and Delight plan. The plan is reviewed and amended every quarter. Account teams prepare the plan, with other managers often weighing in. At year end all Surprise and Delight plans undergo a major revision after CRI's review of all its key clients.

What if you have dozens of highly valuable clients and a very small staff? What then? How can you possibly recognize and reward all your VIP customers? Andrea Keating, who employs a staff of just eight at Crews Control, describes her method of giving thanks: "We run client A/P reports on a quarterly basis to track our top clients' billings. Out of the top forty we will pick a rotating ten or so that become our 'Clients of the Quarter.' We will then send them something special based on the client. We've sent everything from a "breakfast on us" spread from a local bagel place to gift certificates to take them all to lunch to a big goodie basket that they can munch on in the office, along with a note thanking them for helping us have a great quarter." Incidentally, she reports that "clients who are acknowledged as being part of our success and sent something special increase their bookings the next quarter an average of 25 percent." Give and you shall receive. Yes, it's a good maxim in business and life.

Operational Rewards

How can key areas of your company better serve your VIP customers? Conduct a quality audit from *their* perspective. Take stock of your company's strengths in various areas and consider how you might infuse an element of customer recognition. What additional efficiencies could you be delivering to your top clients? For instance, does it make sense to "lend" any of your employees to a client? Consider these four functional areas ripe for customer recognition and rewards—order and fulfillment, sales and marketing, public relations, and customer service.

Order and Fulfillment

Simply making it easier for clients to do business with you makes a strong statement. For example, Road Runner Sports makes it almost impossible for customers to run out of their favorite model shoes. The company's "discontinued shoe notification service" gives customers plenty of advance notice that their favorite shoe is being phased out and monthly updates on remaining inventory should a runner want to stock up. This is both a valuable extra service and top-of-mind marketing rolled into one.

To make it easier for consumers to reorder its beauty supplies, a retailer called Blue Mercury, in Washington, D.C., decided to sell online and mail out a limited number of catalogs to repeat customers. The idea was to make it easier for those who lived outside of the Washington area to get what they wanted without having to order blindly.

Sales and Marketing

Equip your salespeople with the knowledge and power to cut special deals for special clients (within your guidelines, of course). If your product or service can be tailored for a VIP prospect or current customer, it's so much more powerful when the salesperson can illustrate that on the spot using a laptop computer.

Public Relations

Whenever you're tooting your own horn, look for ways to get the word out about your customers as well. Presenting customer case studies at your website is a great way to do this—assuming the client doesn't mind the exposure.

Another way to get PR for both of you: hold a creative contest for customers and publicize the winners. Mail Boxes Etc. sponsors an annual contest for small-business owners (its best customers) with the winner appearing in a commercial during the Super Bowl. Granted, few companies can afford to give a customer that kind of recognition, but it's possible to get local or national press with a far cheaper promotion. An organizational consulting firm once held a contest for the messiest desk and the prize was a free desktop "makeover."

If you are strong on community events, invite some of your clients to get involved as well, or volunteer to join them in one of their special projects. Volunteering together can forge deep bonds between your employees and theirs. Such efforts obviously take more time and planning than actual money. By all means include your employees in the discussion. Community-building events can attract the local media with good write-ups for you and your clients.

Customer Service

Providing superior customer service may be the ultimate way to show your customer appreciation. How can you bring your service to the next level? A phone number to reach you after hours, an intranet for best customers, dedicated customer service agents . . . the list goes on. Here you are limited only by your staff and technology budget, and research has shown that even small companies are spending plenty on devices like cell phones and pagers to stay in touch with customers. If we haven't quite reached the level of twenty-four-hour service for all, top customers certainly deserve it.

Levenger, an upscale catalog of all things related to reading and writing, decided several years ago to create its own twenty-four-hour contact center that ties together phone calls, e-mail inquiries, and Internet orders. Now Levenger's discriminating customers can get real help (not just place an order) when it comes to picking the right fountain pen or reading light no matter what the hour. Many orders are placed at lunchtime or between 4 and 5 P.M., but the catalog company is extremely busy until 2 A.M. throughout the year, according to Wanda Cieri, Levenger's customer service director.

At Phase II facilities, personal trainers will go the extra step of booking your medical appointments for you. Phase II maintains an unusually long list of referrals for everything from neurosurgeons to masseuses. Phase II owner Wade Harris says offering a higher level of customer service is crucial because he believes his biggest competition is not the other health clubs or other trainers. "Our biggest competition," he says, "is the very best service that our customers have ever received anywhere."

It's that fanatical diligence to the details of a customer's experience that sets great companies apart, according to professor Leonard Berry, an author of books on customer service and marketing professor at Texas A&M. He says that meeting customer expectations is not enough. "You have to find a way to exceed them at least some of the time."

Capitol Concierge Best Practices: Saying Thanks

Over the years, Capitol Concierge has developed many simple and cost-effective ways to reward its best customers. Here are a few:

- *Themed visits.* The Capitol team has been known to dress up in costume (snowman, Easter Bunny) and deliver gift baskets to best customers' offices. Not only do customers appreciate the effort but everyone in the customer's office gets a kick out of the visit too.
- *Complimentary magazines. Concierge Recommends* quarterly guide is distributed free to customers. The magazine includes lots of content that is not about specific products. Capitol Concierge also includes a

feedback form in each issue to generate new ideas directly from customers.

- *Extra touches.* When making a dinner reservation, concierges arrange for a complimentary dessert or beverage for best customers.
- *Fifteen minutes of fame.* Best customers are featured in "service post-cards." The company takes a photo, prints a postcard with the customer's picture and quote about Capitol, and distributes the postcards throughout the buildings.
- *Preferred client cards.* Capitol provides best customers with access to special dining discounts cards. In one case one of Capitol's vendors developed the card. It's a win-win. The vendor increases distribution while Capitol provides a unique perk to clients.
- *Prize drawings.* All of Capitol's concierges have held prize drawings for customers. Each concierge collected business cards of customers and awarded customers complimentary gifts and services from our product lines.
- *Piggyback offers.* For frequent customers the company created a series of "piggyback" fliers. The piggybacks are small certificates with special discounts and offers that the concierges send in a note card or attached to an order like dry cleaning. Delivering a product whether it is an event ticket or deli platter always provides a chance to give more information to customers.
- *TGIF candy.* Every Friday each concierge places a bowl of candy at his or her desk in the building lobby. Customers help themselves and often stop to chat.
- *Special events.* Customers are asked to accompany Capitol Concierge staff to events such as theater previews, restaurant openings, and luncheons. Spending time with customers outside of the normal work environment opens up communication channels in a more relaxed fashion. Special events are a valuable opportunity to create a learning dialogue and in the process increase customer chemistry.
- *Seasonal bonuses.* Almost every year concierges do complimentary gift wrapping and package delivery during the month of December for best customers.
- *Just because.* The best gift comes for no particular reason but to say thank you. Capitol Concierge keeps a variety of logo-imprinted items

in stock to send to customers. As in personal relationships, nothing is appreciated more than recognition that is not tied to any occasion. The surprise and delight element of a "just because" reward is what makes it memorable.

Doing Something Special— Customer Events and More

Clearly, some customers warrant going well beyond the usual forms of rewards and recognition. Successful companies versed in the art of customer chemistry continually dream up new ways of doing something extra special.

Lisa Buksbaum, owner of Boxtree Communications in New York City, is a big believer in throwing special events her clients won't soon forget. "Think of creative ways to say thank you that have a strategic tie-in with the project, are clever, and reinforce the uniqueness of your relationship," she advises.

She has found that most people love to go to "exciting venues or have experiences they normally would not have the opportunity to have," she says. For example, for many years she's invited Boxtree clients to join her at the Cannes Film Festival "Best Advertising from Around the World" at New York's Lincoln Center. Sounds like a pricey affair, but it's not, she says. And there's a direct tie-in to Boxtree's business as a marketing-communications firm. To save money and make the event more personal, Buksbaum holds a dinner party at her office prior to the gala. The office dinner is an intimate opportunity to have clients mix with each other and with Boxtree staff. Then everyone heads over to the Lincoln Center for the screening. Buksbaum pays just $20 a ticket for the screening instead of the $150 for the gala dinner and screening. Yet her clients still get the glamour and excitement of Lincoln Center. To mark the special night, she sends a framed photo of clients and the Boxtree team enclosed with a note to keep Boxtree top of mind in their offices long after the event is over.

She's also organized many events for her clients' clients. For an investment-firm client, she arranged a product-launch party at the

Guggenheim Museum that included a private viewing of a popular exhibit. The event attracted the kind of high-net-worth individuals the investment firm wanted but didn't cost an outrageous sum. By joining the museum as a corporate patron, the investment firm was able to get seventy-five spots for dinner and the tour for just $75 a person. Buksbaum says she's always on the lookout for cleverly staged events that can be pulled off on a budget. For her own clients, she also puts on creativity workshops. "The residual value is they start thinking more expansively." Plus, newer clients get to meet older clients who "adore" Boxtree, she says.

There are lots of ways to do events that bring your employees and clients closer together. For instance, Springfield Remanufacturing Corp. (SRC), a company recognized for its innovative open-book management, brings some of its dealers to Missouri for SRC's annual fishing tournament—only dealers who make the sales goal are invited. Many have been coming for years.

FMS, the software developer, throws a kickoff party when a project is completed and it's time to celebrate the success—the best time to get to know customers better and say thank you. On a similar note, Joshua Frey of Granny's Goodies says informal settings like dinner after a trade show are the best times to dream up client gifts that are personal. "We ask lots of questions to get a better understanding of what our client's needs are, as well as what the specific gift buyer's interests are on a personal level. A recent example: one of my customers has a dog that required surgery. She was very concerned about getting the appropriate medical opinions, and we were able to put her in touch—through our network—with a very knowledgeable and respected vet who was able to advise her and help her out."

A more extreme example of customer bonding comes from Smed, the office furniture supplier in Calgary. When the company flies VIP clients to Smed's facility in the Canadian Rockies, it also flies in the client's sales rep. There's a lot of bonding that goes on during company tours, dinners, and special events at night, including Smed's version of a pajama party. Customers leave feeling very pampered and say so in the Smed guestbook, providing powerful testimonials to the next group of visiting customers. Not an inexpensive way to say thank you, but then again, Smed's furniture is a major investment for its clients. The prize should fit the circumstances.

After winning a local business award, Kelly Gilmore and Maureen Clarry wanted to savor the good news with the folks that helped them land the award: their employees and clients. So Gilmore and Clarry, co-owners of Connect, The Knowledge Network, a twenty-person I/T staffing firm in Littleton, Colorado, staged a fancy "client appreciation" dinner. The invite list included sixty-five people the partners considered tier-one clients. About fifteen clients and their spouses attended. All clients received bottles of wine imprinted with the Connect logo and a special message.

In addition, every year Connect throws a memorable event for its top independent consultants (whom the company also considers customers). Connect's western-theme "Casino Night" features real blackjack tables, craps, roulette, and door prizes such as a vacation getaway. About forty-five consultants came to the last Casino Night.

Custom Perks and Services

Roth Staffing, a fast-growing temporary staffing firm, took another path to reward its biggest customers. Roth created special on-site partnerships with top clients that vastly improve those clients' ability to staff up quickly. If such a customer offers one of Roth's temps full-time work, Roth usually doesn't charge a referral fee. Roth effectively extends the reach of its customers' human resources departments. Roth Staffing's CEO Ben Roth believes, "If you figure out how to enhance the satisfaction of the customer more consistently than anyone else, you are going to win."

Kepler's bookstore scores points with its Menlo Park, California, patrons by keeping less popular inventory in stock at the request of individual customers, such as locals who are hosting a party for an author or other special event. (Stanford University is three blocks away.) "It is very expensive for bookstores to stock customer requests—expensive to order and risky to have less popular books in stock," explains owner Clark Kepler. In general, chain bookstores won't do it. Kepler's advertises the service in their catalog. Coincidentally, Kepler's is the lone independent bookstore competing with a slew of chain bookstores in the Menlo Park area. While their independent counterparts have gone under, Kepler's has managed to stay vibrant because of the attentive customer service and its position as the bookseller that also loves books.

Jeff Parker of Corporate Communications Broadcast Network believes the ultimate perk may be giving customers greater autonomy. "We provide customers the ability to control products themselves without having to always go through us. For example, they can publish news directly to streetevents.com [a CCBN service], and they can make changes to the website. We've enabled the customer to have some control over the end product."

Individual Recognition

Consumers and corporate clients alike want recognition as individuals, not just as customers. Green Hills, the grocery store, once used its customer database to generate a list of best customers by store department (deli, bakery, etc.). A direct mail piece went out that included a letter thanking area residents for being best customers and a gift certificate to be redeemed at the store. Each gift tied back to the customer's favorite department. When the customer arrived to receive the gift at the service desk, the department manager was paged so he or she could actually meet the customer and deliver the gift.

Lisa Buksbaum of Boxtree Communications does something many wouldn't think to: she lavishes recognition and rewards on her client's administrative staff, the people who often toil away in obscurity. She has found that the secretaries and marketing assistants who work for her clients are often crucial to helping Boxtree do a good job. As such, they win their share of Boxtree Brilliance awards that go to individuals who help Boxtree by making a new-client introduction, helping to champion a project, or simply doing their job well. Buksbaum says many of her clients are happy to hang their Boxtree Brilliance certificates in their offices. The framed gift is not only a memorable memento, but a wonderful way to keep the customer chemistry flame burning bright.

But how far should you go? CEOs have different philosophies about where to draw the line on gifting. Use common sense. Andrea Keating recognizes her clients' personal milestones only when it seems natural to do so. "If one of our regular clients is getting married or has a baby, we send a personal gift from all of us," she says. The gift becomes an extension of daily interactions. "We're talking to many of them daily throughout the wedding planning or pregnancy—probably more than they are talking to their family or friends —so we want to send them something personal to help celebrate the event. We also send a sympathy card or flowers if there is a death in the immediate family." And sometimes Crews Control succeeds in recognizing two influential people at once. "We had one big client where our two key contacts had birthdays the same week so we threw them a surprise birthday party. Their secretary recommended a local bakery that we had deliver a cake and balloons to their weekly staff meeting. It was a huge surprise and a big hit. We don't do this for all clients but only for the ones where it is a natural, genuine gesture." Keating stresses that the gifts are presented by the Crews Control employee who is the client's main contact. "It's not a company gesture or marketing opportunity."

Chemistry Checklist

1. *Offer customers extra perks.* Make a list of your current products and services. Schedule a brainstorming session with your team to create a menu of extras related to each product or service. Then select one value-adding item for each product to deliver at the time of purchase.
2. *Make it easy for employees to thank customers.* Provide all staff with logo-imprinted thank-you notes. Encourage employees to write a personal note following a purchase. The goal for each of Capitol's concierges is to write a minimum of five notes per week. Track the responses from happy customers.
3. *Create a system to track new business referrals from existing customers.* Designate at least one team member to acknowledge the referrals by sending the customer a note and/or gift. This should be done within one week of receiving the referral.
4. *Test various ways of showing appreciation.* Start with three tips from our list that are most relevant to your business and easiest to do.

After you try one method, measure progress by tracking, for example, customer feedback, increased sales, and number of referrals at the conclusion of ninety days. Make adjustments to improve results or test other ideas.

5. *Strive to be relevant.* Don't send generic gifts—no matter how nice!—as a token of gratitude. Be sure that any appreciation actions are related to either your company's primary product or service (e.g., customer newsletters, publications, special events) or are relevant to your customers' interests. A golf gift sent to a nongolfer will not create goodwill. Remember to listen and learn your customers' favorite pastimes and preferences. The ideal gift is one that ties in somehow to the work you've done or an experience you've shared with a client—such as attending a nonprofit event together.

6. *Develop a customer loyalty program.* Many of the tips in this chapter can be integrated into a comprehensive loyalty program. The best place to start is to review your customer-chemistry communications plan and look for natural occasions to express appreciation. Be sure to include your best customers in the creation of your loyalty program. Ask them via surveys or in person, what types of perks they would like to experience. There is no stronger chemistry builder than giving the customer what he or she wants.

7. *Tailor individual rewards to individual clients.* When your customer loyalty plan kicks into high gear, it's possible to give every customer a different combination of rewards.

8. *Ratchet up your customer service.* If you can't afford to offer a higher level of service for all your customers, consider what more you can do for your very best. Some top clients may even be willing to pay more for the additional service.

CHAPTER 7

WHEN THE RELATIONSHIP DOESN'T WORK
RULE 7: SAY GOOD-BYE TO BAD CUSTOMERS AND DYSFUNCTIONAL RELATIONSHIPS

I have had to say good-bye to a few clients and consider myself lucky that it was only a few. No matter how many times you experience it, letting go of a customer relationship that no longer works has to be one of the greatest challenges a business owner faces. First of all, it's not as if you wake up one morning and a bell goes off. Like marriages that tumble, business relationships rarely go downhill overnight. But there comes a time when there's no denying it: the chemistry with a particular customer has faded. There are lots of reasons why this happens. A change in company mission, a change in price, shifts in the industry, technology demands, or new service requirements. It's particularly painful, of course, to lose your first customer after years of growing together. Customers for life? It's still the ideal we all shoot for, but in business as in life, few relationships last forever.

As I've discovered, relationships rarely fall apart over one event. There are warning signs along the way that something is changing. It's up to us as business owners to pay attention to the signs and form an intelligent response. At Capitol Concierge, we have stressed the importance of maintaining a learning dialogue in order to grow our best customers. This dialogue also serves the purpose of monitoring the health of customer relationships and allowing us to candidly work through difficult situations with valued customers.

Capitol Concierge had one particular property management client we had worked with for years. When the client merged with another company it was forced to reduce its concierge budget. After countless attempts to make the numbers work, we simply could not reach a point that would give the client the price they needed and allow us to continue to provide the same level of service. Ultimately, we had to resign from a highly valued account. We finally met face-to-face with the client and reviewed our reasons for ending the relationship. It was important for us to be able to substantiate our reasons. We did this by preparing a spreadsheet that demonstrated the financial impact of reducing the concierge budget and our inability to be able to deliver service profitably. The next step in ending a relationship is to offer to provide assistance with a transition. In this case we worked with the client as they moved to adopting an in-house guard service.

At the other extreme I've had the experience of being the jilted customer. One day the call center we used told us good-bye. Capitol Concierge had worked with this call center to provide after-hours service and to process our customer orders. We were one of this company's first clients. As a result, they offered us very competitive pricing. They continued to be very flexible, and worked with us on various pricing schedules. There came a point in time, however, when we were not a good profitable fit for them, and after three years of handling our business this call center advised us it was shifting its business model to focus on larger clients. Essentially, they changed their best-customer profile. They broke the news to us by saying, "We're happy to keep you here but now you're going to pay more." It was smart on their part. It was a pretty good relationship while it lasted, and I would highly recommend this call center. It's just that we'd reached the point where we weren't a good customer fit for them and they weren't good for all of our needs. The customer chemistry died when our needs no longer matched up. It was as straightforward as that. The company gave us ample notice and assisted us in transitioning to a new call center. I learned a lot from that experience about the right way to say good-bye.

Today, I try to sit down with my finance manager a few times a year to do what I call a *scope-of-work overlay* on all my accounts. The customer who sets off alarms is the one that requests an excessive amount of meetings and requires more and more from my management team without a corresponding increase in sales. When the overrun costs start climbing, you have to question whether it's an issue of managing customer expectations. Raising prices is a simple way to say good-bye. The customer will either pay up or leave. There are also things you can do to avoid getting to the point of firing a customer. For example, we became more strategic about our sales prospecting by using our best-customer profile.

My company has also worked hard to accommodate customers that other companies might have turned away. For my company and probably for yours, regularly rejecting customers would be the kiss of death. I found ways to improve my profits that didn't involve raising prices or cutting off a customer. From the beginning my staff has invested a great deal of time cultivating our supplier network so that we're more efficient. Capitol has a manager dedicated to the task of identifying new and innovative vendors. Before you take the big step of formally saying good-bye, be sure there isn't another way to resolve the situation within your company.

More times than not, however, we bend over backward for a poor customer even when it has become clear that the chemistry is gone and there's no getting it back. Have that one last meeting to clear the air. If there isn't a way to make both sides happy, don't hesitate to do what's right for you and your company.

Dealing with Dysfunction

Chemistry is something shared by two. Some customers start out as good companions. There may even be the promise of "love" in the air, but then the relationship changes. The amiable customer becomes boorish over time, or worse, a bully that beats up on your staff.

Consider what happened in the case of FMS Inc., a company accustomed to dealing with very large and very demanding clients. FMS is a developer of software tools for Microsoft Access and Visual Basic. The customer list ranges from Fortune 100 companies to government agencies to international organizations. In one division FMS offers consulting services for clients seeking custom database solutions. FMS CEO Luke Chung describes a difficult situation the consulting division faced: "We had a project that we'd worked on for a couple of years. The client had been very difficult to work with but still was valuable to our company. Finally—after they had most of our staff ready to mutiny over the project—we turned down additional work from them."

RULE 7: SAY GOOD-BYE TO BAD CUSTOMERS AND DYSFUNCTIONAL RELATIONSHIPS

Parting is never easy, but smart companies need to systemically shed customers who are a drain on time, resources, and profits. Plan regular reviews of the quality of your customers and end poor relationships on a positive note. And never burn a bridge. Today's bad customer may be a best customer sometime in the future.

Do *you* have clients that would make your staff consider mutiny? Is it worth it to let a customer relationship deteriorate that far? Sometimes employees know best, so consult them. A client who becomes a dictator doesn't love you; he's abusing you.

Still, it's painful when push comes to shove. Realize that while saying good-bye is very difficult, if the relationship cannot be salvaged to both parties' satisfaction, the long-term drain on financial and human resources will lead to long-term damage to your business and your team.

When you embark on a customer-chemistry program, saying good-bye to an ill-suited customer isn't necessarily the last step. Sometimes it's one of the first things you need to do to get on with the program.

The wake-up moment may come when you complete your best-customer profile and profit analysis of each client. Many companies focus on top-line revenue without paying attention to the profitability of each individual customer. One of the first actions after completing your P&L analysis is to prepare an action plan to change course with challenging customers or if that's not feasible, prepare to say good-bye.

Ultimately, the best strategy is to focus your time, energies, and marketing dollars on reaching your best prospects. If you don't waste your time soliciting the wrong types of business to begin with, you won't often have to say good-bye.

HOW TO SAY GOOD-BYE WITHOUT LOSING YOUR WHOLE BUSINESS: DIAMOND COURIER, PHILADELPHIA

Problem: Can you say good-bye to unprofitable jobs and unprofitable clients without forfeiting the whole farm?

Overview: Claudia Post loved to bring in new business and in three years grew her package delivery service to $3.1 million in sales. Chronic cash-flow crunches, however, made her reevaluate all of Diamond's services. Post hired a consultant to do a profit-center analysis using *activity-based costing,* a process that essentially assigns overhead costs to the various business lines in proportion to their respective use of the company's resources. As a result of the analysis, Post learned that her core bike-messenger service was a huge money loser, but deliveries made by car were turning a nice profit. She agonized for weeks over how to close down the cash-draining bike-messenger service without permanently damaging her reputation.

Solution: She prepared to say good-bye to several of her oldest and biggest volume (but unprofitable) accounts—those that made heavy use of Post's bike messengers. Post and her sales manager drew up a list of clients to visit, and they rehearsed what they'd say in person. Post made the same speech to dozens of big-name clients: "I'm sorry, but after some careful analysis, I'm forced to make a difficult decision—I have to relinquish part of my business with you."

Results: Post basically said good-bye to four of Diamond's top accounts that were unwilling to pay more or switch to delivery by car. However, she kept all the large accounts that used her drivers more than her bikers, and her revenue per job doubled, from an average of $13 to about $28. By being honest and up-ront with her customers, Post believes she gained credibility with them. Today Diamond Courier is more profitable than ever.

Saying good-bye to customers is especially painful when it means also saying good-bye to some employees. When Post made her momentous decision to shut down the bike division, she had to let go of forty couriers, but she knew she couldn't delay the decision because every second she waited was costing her company money. She also needed to free her mind and the remaining staff to focus on the customers that would help rebuild the business.

Circumstances for Saying Good-Bye

When you think about saying no to any kind of business, it's useful to draw some distinctions. Some customers are just all wrong from the first project. (If the honeymoon is hell, you don't need the repeat business.) Saying good-bye is a matter of discipline. It's also an act of faith: you must believe a better customer will come along. Some customers take longer and longer to pay their bills until they don't pay at all. These days, smart companies are not waiting until they get stiffed to say good-bye to customers whose credit-rating reports show a steady slide—after all, you didn't go into business to become a collection agency. But in many ways, "bullies" and "deadbeats" are the *easy* cases. What's harder is when you want to hold on to customers though you know in your heart that they're not a good match for your company product-wise and/or philosophically. Consider these circumstances and how you might resolve each:

Account Is Not Profitable

After you have reviewed the gross sales and profitability of each customer, you may discover accounts that are losing money or are on the borderline. A once-profitable customer is no longer giving you the sales that justify a high level of service and expense. What do you do? These demand special attention for corrective action and provide insight for prevention measures in the future

Possible resolutions: First look at potential internal causes. Are you allocating expenses correctly? Is overhead too high in general? Are there ways to streamline expenses and reallocate resources? Can the marriage be saved? If not, a face-to-face meeting is in order. Document the financial condition of the account. Inform the customer that you value the business and want to continue, but your company is losing money and you are concerned about the long-term viability of the relationship. Ask the customer for ways you might compromise. Could you reduce services offered, increase price, adjust pricing at contract renewal time, share resources to offset expenses?

Change in Customer Strategy and Mission

Sometimes, especially in business-to-business sales and services, a client may shift direction. Your product or service is no longer a top priority. You are not getting the attention and time with the customer required to grow the account over time. In addition, budgets may be cut or reallocated.

Possible resolutions: Be proactive. Prepare alternative plans that align with the customer's new direction and budget. Can you maintain your relationship at a lower price point? Is there a new service that you can add to maintain the relationship? Can you participate in your customer's strategy sessions to contribute ideas and be in the loop? In annual account reviews, always ask clients if any significant changes in their business are planned for the coming year that might impact your relationship.

Requirements Change

Your customer may want to access your product or service through a new channel (e.g., Internet, wireless). Or your client may require you to provide 24/7 service or use one of their technology platforms. The challenge you may face is that you do not have the budget or resources to meet new requirements to maintain the relationship.

Possible resolutions: Meet with the customer to review why they need to make the change and the time frame in which it must occur. Is it possible for you to outsource the new requirement and maintain the relationship? Does your customer have a resource that you can leverage? Is the customer willing to pay you more in order to meet the new requirement?

Key Contact Switch

Your contact within the customer's company is reassigned or leaves. You have spent months or years building a strong relationship. The new contact is not as supportive or interested in your product or service. You are back to square one.

Possible resolutions: Start your chemistry building immediately. Schedule time to review the history of your relationship with your new contact and start the dialogue to understand this person's unique preferences. Then assess whether there's still the potential for customer chemistry. An important reminder that will assist avoiding this situation in the future: always develop multiple contacts within an organization beyond your designated contact. Use some of the strategies outlined in Chapter 6 that will keep your name and product in front of the entire client company.

Unethical Requests

Such requests are usually rare, but do occasionally happen: your customer asks you or your team to do something questionable.

Possible resolutions: Immediately address the issue with the customer and advise them that you are not comfortable complying with their request. Take it up the ladder if required. This may result in the customer saying good-bye to you, but it is better to address these issues head on in order to protect your staff and your company's reputation.

Should you give bad customers a second chance? Yes. Follow resolutions such as the ones suggested in the previous pages and monitor the outcome closely for ninety days. If the new solution does not correct the situation, proceed to the good-bye stage.

THREE UNFORGIVABLE
CUSTOMER-CHEMISTRY SINS

1. Unethical behavior
2. Lack of follow-through
3. Abusive behavior toward employees

Kelly Gilmore and Maureen Clarry, co-owners of I/T staffing firm Connect, have severed ties with a few customers. "We fired customers who really didn't want customer service, they wanted the cheapest price," says Gilmore. They also fired one customer on ethical grounds. "The client didn't respect us," says Clarry, "and went around us to hire one of our consultants behind our back. This was an offense to our ethics." Gilmore and Clarry approached both the client and the consultant to try to resolve the situation, but they were unsuccessful so it was time to say good-bye. The partners stopped calling on the account. They took another important step as well. In their customer database they "red-listed" the people involved so there would be a permanent record of what had happened. "Life's too short and there are too many other places to get work," says Clarry.

Today Connect has more protections in place so that firing a customer should be an exceedingly rare event. "We've got more protection contractually all the way around," says Clarry. "We get expectations out in the open." Connect does something of a Do's and Don'ts orientation for each customer that takes into account how each side likes to work. They pursue customers that are willing to sign up-front agreements aimed at creating partnerships. The agreement lays out some rules for how each side will behave and the consequences if the rules are broken. Salespeople undergo training to teach them how to stand up to customers in a healthy way. After all, says Gilmore, "If you're going to have a relationship, you have to have communication. Client behavior can change. That's why we constantly review our customer tiers."

Companies hesitate to terminate unworkable customer relationships because they get caught up in sales growth. This process is especially hard for salespeople; turning away customers offends every cell in their body. But company owners have to take a more balanced approach. Growth for growth's sake is the ideology of a cancer cell. Problem customers are often a case of diminishing returns: it's taking every last ounce to service this customer, and the math just doesn't add up.

Joe Jensen took a measured approach to dealing with undesirable clients. Jensen is CEO of Teltronix Information Systems in Eagan, Minnesota, which installs cabling and provides network services and support to corporate clients. His solution for dealing with customers "who were just plain difficult to work with" is simple and diplomatic. "Rather than humiliate them, and totally lose the possibility of a reference," he says, "we typically would increase our rates to the PITA (Pain In The Ass) labor rate. Many could not afford it and stopped doing business with us."

Of course, the PITA principle can't be applied across the board. Retailers, for one, can't conveniently charge higher prices to burdensome customers. They can and do, however, control who gets the rewards through their loyalty programs; they also have discretion over who they issue credit to and how much. The way retailers say good-bye to bad customers is to simply not extend the special services, coupons, and other perks that good customers get. Over time, bad customers get the message. The other way consumer businesses indirectly give poor customers the heave-ho is to change the product line or simply get into a different niche with better prospects. Service companies in the B2B world have the option of taking similar steps to indirectly fire poor-performing customers.

The Right Way to Break Up with a Customer

1. *Never burn any bridges.* Take the high road and let them know that you have valued the relationship and hope that you may have the chance to serve them again in the future.
2. *Meet in person,* if possible, to deliver the news. Depending on the circumstances, you might want to send a letter to your lower-tier customers. Occasional customers can be dealt with when and if they call you again.

3. *Be a professional.* Provide ample notice of service termination. Offer referrals to other providers. Provide assistance to ensure a smooth transition. Your efforts will be remembered.

4. *Stay in touch.* Unless this was an abusive client, ask to touch base every quarter. You never know when circumstances will change and the relationship can be renewed. Your former customer may even refer you to a new customer.

The Customer Life Cycle

The loss of any customer can hurt—a lot. It helps to remember there's a cycle to many customer relationships. For example, mergers and acquisitions cause sudden and unforeseen cracks in customer-supplier relationships that once seemed rock solid. While such changes seem earth-shattering at the time, it's not always desirable or profitable to chase a once-loyal customer to the ends of the earth. In fact, it may be time to say good-bye. Every company owner must make that call for himself or herself. Sometimes, with a little investigation, you might learn there were rifts in the relationship long before the merger or acquisition came along. Sometimes the chemistry can be rekindled. Other times you just have to let go of what you can't change. To paraphrase an old prayer, the wisdom is in knowing the difference.

Saying good-bye to any customer is the hardest part of the program, but the most liberating. If you're doing everything else to create customer chemistry, you won't have to say good-bye too often. The experience is less traumatic when you're busy building relationships with your most promising prospects. If you employ the customer-chemistry-building strategies over time, you'll find divorcing a customer to be a rare occurrence indeed.

The relationship process requires constant attention and communication. This is not a short-term idea du jour, but a long-term strategy for operating your business. It needs to be pervasive through your entire culture. You need to invest time in training your team on the principles of customer chemistry and review your communications plan at regular intervals to map your success. If you're actively building a customer-chemistry program, relationship red flags will become apparent before it's too late and allow you time to save relationships.

Again, never burn a bridge. Capitol Concierge had several key contacts move on to new companies. Even though Capitol had terminated the relationship with their previous employers, the company's gracious exit served to maintain positive feelings and resulted in new business when the contacts settled into their new companies.

Chemistry Checklist

1. *Identify your company's potential relationship "red flags."* Create a list of triggers (e.g., reduction in purchase activity, no return calls, late payments) that may signal there is trouble in paradise. Be proactive in approaching customers to see if there are any problems that could be resolved quickly. Train your team to recognize red flags and develop a plan to address each.

2. *Know when to fold.* You have developed your best-customer profile and reviewed customer profitability. Now it's time to deal with customers that don't make the cut. Review your current customers and determine the criteria and factors that may result in terminating the relationship. Once again, by knowing what constitutes good customer chemistry, bad turns and sea changes will not throw you for a loop.

3. *Prepare relationship-recovery resolutions.* If a customer relationship hits the skids, employ one of the resolutions outlined in this chapter. Always strive to work with the customer to secure their feedback and ideas for resolutions versus dictating your terms. Customers will often surprise you with alternative plans that can save the day and create a win-win situation.

4. *Take the high road.* If the relationship cannot be saved, be sure to leave a positive exit impression. Offer to provide referrals and assistance in a transition. Remember to touch base every 90 to 120 days because situations can turn. Most importantly, let them know that you value the relationship and hope to have the opportunity to work together again. Say good-bye to bad accounts but maintain individual relationships.

CHAPTER 8

THE CUSTOMER-CHEMISTRY CHECKUP
RULE 8: TAKE THE PULSE OF YOUR RELATIONSHIPS

The greatest lesson learned by the Capitol team over the past fourteen years is that the customer-chemistry building never ends. Just as our personal relationships require continuous nurturing to thrive, so too do our customer relationships.

Lots of company owners talk about getting to the "next level," but by that they just mean higher sales and economies of scale. Customer chemistry is about more than that. It's a culture and a way of life in a company. It's a daily discipline. Countless times over the course of my entrepreneurial career, I have caught myself being drawn to the lure of new customers. But it only takes me a moment to reflect on the many hard lessons learned over time to catch myself and focus on the path that has always led to the best results—stay close to and nurture your current customers. And the results are real. Capitol Concierge has maintained 85 percent of our best clients for the past fourteen years. The greatest indicator of our commitment to chemistry building is we have fewer clients overall, yet higher-margin business and more buildings from a smaller universe of customers who meet our best-customer profile.

Still, growing current customers requires time and energy—constant time and energy. Top-of-mind marketing, for instance, is designed to be just in time, but maintaining customer chemistry isn't something that you can just plot on a calendar after you've mastered your customers' buying cycles. Customer relationships are fluid. Their needs, requirements, and internal dynamics can change in a heartbeat. A budget is unexpectedly cut, your key internal contact is transferred to another department, or your client has received a new mandate from corporate headquarters. That's why it's so critical to take the pulse of your current customers. What are the vital signs you should be tracking? How can you key into changes that could alter the course of the relationship in the short or long term?

The critical objective of Rule 8 is "don't be surprised by your customers." At Capitol Concierge, we experienced this truth one too many times. One of our client companies was sold and as a result of not being in the loop, we lost a contract we might have salvaged had we known the news sooner. On another occasion a corporate customer was arranging an event with kosher food and assumed we couldn't handle the kosher request. We certainly could have served the customer, but were not "on top of it" at that moment in time.

The most important sign to watch for is what I call the *signal of silence*. It's easy to assume that no news is good news. If the team has not received a complaint and your last interaction with the customer was a positive one, then we think the relationship must be solid. More often than not, silence should be taken as a bright red warning flag. Unhappy customers often keep bad news to themselves and silently change over to your competitor. It is sometimes easier to move on than to take the time to register a complaint. A simple call one of our managers placed to just see how we were performing turned into a two-hour session during which our client laid out several problems he was having with our company. He informed us that had we not called, he was ready to change concierge providers. Several other silent signals we've learned to watch for: a sudden drop in purchasing or overall activity; response rates to promotions that are down significantly; and, perhaps the biggest silent killer of all, unreturned phone calls. All of these critical signs deserve the team's immediate attention.

By staying in contact, the Capitol team has been able to greatly reduce cases of the silent treatment. When there's a problem, we usually know about it sooner rather than later. We use several easy methods to monitor the status of our customers' satisfaction.

- *Touch base calls.* These are as simple as they sound. Each manager is assigned a roster of clients to contact every week. When we spend a few minutes on the phone or even leaving a quick message to "see how we are doing," the customer is more likely to open up and share even the smallest incidents.
- *Issue logs.* Our client managers maintain issue logs that track every item, action, etc., that the client has requested or discussed. It gives our mangers a reason for continuous contact and protects against commitments falling through the cracks.
- *Customer activity form.* One of the items we track is "last contact/activity" with the customer. The team uses this form to proactively gauge if there is any deviation in a customer's pattern of interaction with our company (a purchase, a meeting, or a response to an offer). If too much time has elapsed, we move into action.

Our best long-term clients usually can be counted on to provide glowing reviews of our service. They give us our highest marks on the annual survey, provide powerful testimonials, come to all of our events, and serve as invaluable references. Even with all of this positive feedback, however, we've learned never to be too comfortable or too confident.

At the same time you want to be prepared for the unexpected bonuses that life and customers throw your way. Taking the pulse also means being ready to jump on a new service for a best customer, or perhaps together launching a new product into a new market.

I think about how the relationship with my very first client evolved. The folks at the John Akridge Company took a chance on me and my untested concept more than a decade ago. As we worked together over the years, Akridge moved from client to adviser to partner; the Akridge team has provided us with new ideas and worked with us to change our service offerings over time. Most significantly, CEO John "Chip" Akridge invested in a new venture I launched (with the help of some longtime employees, but more on that in Chapter 9). Like a marriage that has survived the test of time, we've reached a new plateau. The chemistry has climbed to a new level.

At the end of the day, each contact with a customer is a piece of the picture. As you gather more pieces, the picture goes from hazy to clear. The customer is a good match or it isn't. Hopefully, with each piece the picture becomes bigger. For example, if you can develop more than one close relationship within a single client company, you know you're on the right path.

Taking the Pulse in a Changing Economy

Customer chemistry is all about knowing your customers one by one. But will your customers today be the same ones tomorrow? No one's crystal ball is crystal clear. In times of economic ups and downs it becomes especially tricky for company owners and managers to make predictions about their customers' plans. Even CEOs that once depended on some very large clients find that landing the Fortune 500 is no guarantee of their future livelihood. Even the most loyal clients can disappear in an instant following a layoff, a re-organization, or just one bad quarter. Mergers are responsible for customer churn too; everyone has a story about the acquisition that ate the customer.

The customer portfolio changes even for the *Inc* 500, the fastest-growing private companies in America. From year to year you can observe subtle shifts in customer bases. Fortune 1000 businesses invariably provide the primary source of revenue for the *Inc* 500. But in recent years, the percentage depending on the Fortune 1000 for sales has fluctuated from a high of 48 percent in 2000 to just 40 percent in 2001. When the Fortune 1000 goes down, small to midsize businesses take their place in client ranks. No doubt the ratio of large to small clients will continue to change in the years ahead for many B2B companies and not just among the *Inc* 500.

For even the most successful companies, acquiring enough good customers has become a bigger challenge than finding enough good people to hire. Times have changed. Given the new economic reality, the concept of customers for life seems to be, well, dead. Or at least much harder to attain. And yet the cost of acquiring new customers can't be overestimated.

So what's a company to do? Simple: take the pulse of your customers. But what does that mean and how often should you do it?

The Five Ws (Who, What, Where, When, and Why) of Staying in Touch

Taking the pulse means you're in the loop, you know the status, you're up to date with all your current customers. And you also understand Morse code—because the signs customers send can seem like a lot of dots and dashes to the untrained eye. Taking the pulse means monitoring the signals customers send out and proactively finding ways to stay one step ahead. Giving customers what they want before they even know they want it—that's the ideal. Of course, it means being able to digest bad news faster. Remember, it's not always the big corporate events—the merger, layoff, or change in direction—that can cause a customer relationship to end. The little quakes leave powerful aftershocks too. The miscommunication. The little service screwup. The delivery snafu.

Taking the pulse, however, is not just about how to get bad news sooner. It's also about being able to react to positive news. Seizing the day. Making the most of serendipity. Taking the customer pulse makes you better at sales forecasting, communicating the health of the company to employees and shareholders, conducting market research, and creating new products and services.

RULE 8: TAKE THE PULSE OF YOUR RELATIONSHIPS

Your customers' needs are never static. The need to monitor the status of your best-customer relationships is a critical step in maintaining relationships. Employ pulse-taking activities to make sure your customers are happy. If they aren't, you have the insight to change course, make corrections, and keep the chemistry growing.

Still, it's not always easy to take the pulse. Unless you are fortunate enough to be Charles Feghali, the president of Interstate Resources Group, which operates paper mills and box plants. The paper mills have a finite universe of customers. "We know all our customers by name, face, and handshake," says Feghali, "and we know most potential prospect companies." A mill typically has around thirty customers and twenty key sales prospects, he explains.

Everyone should be so lucky. In reality few company builders are, so it pays to be proactive. Clark Kepler gauges the pulse at his bookstore by walking the floor and striking up conversations, and he trains his seventy-five employees to do the same. Every purchase receipt from Kepler's has "We'd Like to Hear from You . . . call Clark Kepler at ###" printed on the bottom. He gets about twenty calls per month from concerned and loyal customers because of this. One customer was distraught by the use of cell phones in the bookstore. Kepler's instituted a no-cell-phone policy.

Company owners agree the best approach is to try several approaches involving a variety of employees. There's a huge ongoing debate about the value of e-mail for staying in touch. While some company leaders believe e-mail is a convenient way to "drop back in" on customers, other chief executives are adamant that e-mail is simply not personal enough. Again, a lot depends on the individual nature of your customer communications.

For now, e-mail is one of those love-hate affairs. Put Andrea Keating, CEO of Crews Control, in the hate column. "We *always* prefer to call our clients," she says. "It's my philosophy that a random e-mail checking-in to see if any business is coming down the pike is almost like a spam. I don't know if it is being sent to just me in an honest effort to touch base or if they are sending it to everyone in their address book. When I receive a phone call to "just say hi, haven't chatted with you in a while" I know that they are specifically interested in me and in my business. I think my clients feel the same way."

Face time may also be overrated. Sure, it's great when you can visit customers in person, but it's not always feasible or even optimal. Keating, who heads a staffing agency that specializes in video crews for corporate clients, has been able to build relationships over the phone, though she concedes, "it takes a little longer than starting out with a face-to-face meeting." Now the company is national and international, so in-person meetings are often just not possible. But she says that's okay. "Because of the nature of our business, we normally talk to a client several times over a two- or three-day period so we can build that relationship very quickly." (She adds that it helps to be naturally cheerful over the phone!)

As for how often to take the pulse, there is some consensus among company builders: for business clients, at least monthly unless you have so many customers that quarterly check-ins are the only way to reach all your current customers. Weekly is even better. Those who sell to large numbers of consumers have to settle for taking a representative sampling of customer sentiments at least once a year. Some pundits predict that online surveying will make it possible to reach out to more consumers more often.

Some companies have their own time clock for when to pick up the phone, which may seem quirky to outsiders but makes perfect sense in their respective industries. For example, C.B.&H. Parts Corp., a $3-million automotive parts and supply store for vehicles and trucks in Wayne, West Virginia, checks in with customers every three thousand miles. By the end of the year they've caught up with all their road-running customers.

Some say it's never too soon to ask customers how they're feeling. That's particularly true for companies competing in industries with a not-so-great reputation. Motoring Services Auto Repair in Richland, Washington, waits just two days after each sale or repair job to make a follow-up phone call to the customer. Brian Johnson says that enables him to get any complaints while they're fresh rather than after they've had time to fester. Johnson uses his own customer satisfaction survey as well as a report card–style questionnaire produced by the AAA. Such diligence gets you noticed. Johnson's company won a state business award from the Small Business Association in 2000. The same year revenues shot up 26 percent to $1.2 million.

What happens when you're not clued in? You can lose customers without a trace. You lose the opportunity to turn one-time customers into something more, maybe even best customers. When you're not in touch with customers' individual needs, you're more vulnerable to price competition.

For company owners pulled in too many directions, the trick is finding a quiet time and space to get back in touch with customers without the pressures of a looming deadline. Sometimes you need a "sea change." Fish Mart in West Haven, Connecticut, chartered a sixty-foot sailboat for a three-hour cruise and invited a few select customers on board to mingle with employees. Talk about getting into the swim with customers!

Here's another way you can cut to the chase: follow the road-tested approaches of CEOs who've been there. We've compiled a guide to the best ways of taking the pulse moment to moment, day by day, and from one season to the next.

Seven Proven Pulse-Taking Methods

Much of how you take the pulse depends on your industry, individual customer relationships, and how long you've been in business, so it's helpful to hear the views of a variety of CEOs at varying size companies and at different stages of growth. We culled our overview from the best practices of more than a dozen growing and award-winning companies. They range from a network services provider to an amusement park. Some of the prescribed methods can work for all companies at any time. A few require a larger staff to pull off effectively, but even soloists and other small businesses can use many of these methods to their advantage.

Method 1: The Critical Question

Who it's good for: All companies

What's involved: Composing a simple key question you or your staff can ask customers in person or on the phone (list of potential questions on page 158)

Company examples: Synergy Networks, Imperial Construction

If you could ask clients one key question, what would it be? Mark Gordon, the CEO of Synergy Networks, was searching for ways to stay current with six of the largest and most profitable customers of his growing, $13-million network services company in Tysons Corner, Virginia. He wanted to do it in a way that wouldn't upset or encroach on his salespeople's relationships with those clients.

Gordon decided he would personally conduct interviews at client sites once a quarter. He briefed all of his salespeople assigned to these most valued customers—MVCs for short—on his plans and asked his reps to set up the appointments, explaining that he wanted to go to the meetings alone.

His favorite way to open up the interview is to ask customers to play entrepreneur for a few minutes. "If you were the owner of my company, what would you change about it?" Gordon says the important thing is he listens and doesn't attempt to do any selling. However, the hour he typically spends with the client provides a great opportunity to spell out his company philosophy of continuous learning and improvement. Laying out his core values helps allay clients' fears that their feedback could be used to reprimand a salesperson, and Gordon gets more honest responses to his questions. "I schedule an hour to talk and some go as long as two hours because some customers become so enthusiastic about telling me what they think." As a way of thanking clients for their time, Gordon surprises them at the end of the interview with a small gift (usually a gift certificate).

After a year of on-site visits he has established relationships with multiple people at six big MVC sites. But some of the face-to-face talks yielded unpleasant surprises. He discovered cracks in some customer relationships that he didn't know existed, and he says meeting in person helped the company save several accounts at risk. "There were a couple of customers on the brink of possibly going away. They probably weren't going to complain. They would have just faded into the sunset," he says. "One client offered a pretty severe critique of some of our business practices and the feedback was valid." Gordon says he learned in that instance that what one customer considers a value-added service may be viewed by another client as a nuisance. He was able to resolve the issue and keep the client.

For many companies the critical question is the one Frank Dominguez, CEO of Imperial Construction Group, Inc. in Elizabeth, New Jersey, puts to his clients. "I ask if they would recommend us or use us again," says Dominguez, whose company provides engineering, management, and "design/build" services. "If they say no, I ask why and fix it." Asking the question has helped Imperial grow 300 percent in the last four years to $97 million.

"JUST ONE QUESTION . . ."

A quick effective way to track your customers' feelings and status is to have one question per month that your entire team asks during the course of customer interaction. Instead of long surveys, develop twelve questions (one for each month) and advise your entire staff of the question and what information you are trying to glean from the customer. Ask the question at the point of sale, post it on your website, send a postcard after a purchase, or make random outbound telephone calls over the course of the month to best customers. Here are some sample questions:

1. What one word best describes our service?
2. If you could add a product or service to our line, what would it be?
3. When and how was your most recent experience with our company?
4. How would you rate our customer service?
5. Are we meeting or exceeding your expectations?
6. How could we exceed your expectations?
7. If you could change one thing about our company, what would it be?
8. If you could improve one thing about our product or service, what would it be?

Method 2: The Customer Advisory Group

Who it's good for: Any company but especially those with lots of corporate clients that don't mind serving as advisers and mentors

What's involved: Setting up a structure that allows customers to rotate on the board and rewards them in some way for their service

Company example: Corporate Communications Broadcast Network (CCBN)

Jeff Parker is CEO of Boston-based CCBN, which enables direct communications between public companies and the investment community over the Internet. CCBN builds, manages, and hosts the investor relations (IR) sections of websites for more than twenty-five hundred public companies, providing in-depth shareholder information through interactive, multimedia solutions. All in all, the company maintains six thousand customer relationships, says Parker, and he can't possibly take the pulse of each one of them each month. That's why he created a Customer Advisory Group a step below his board of directors. The advisory group is so important to the company that members are compensated with CCBN stock options. Parker explained: "It is a small group of interested customers or customer-related people—someone from an IR firm who would refer customers to us—and they meet with us on a quarterly basis to review realistic aspects of new products and give us feedback. We use this board for direction to help us think about what we're doing." Parker must be getting some good advice since the company has grown 100 percent in the last three years, he says.

Method 3: The Online Customer Feedback Group

Who it's good for: Regional or national companies that want to stay in touch with customers spread across the country; an alternative or complement to in-person customer committees, especially if your travel budget is limited; anyone who needs feedback fast.

What's involved: Setting up an online mechanism for polling customers by e-mail; soliciting volunteers from your customer ranks

Company example: Green Mountain Energy

Green Mountain Energy Company, based in Austin, Texas, is a fast-growing residential retailer of energy sources generated from wind, sun, water, geothermal, biomass, and natural gas sources. CEO Dennis Kelly came to Green Mountain Energy having experienced just about every traditional way of gathering customer feedback. He'd racked up more than twenty years of experience in consumer products, including work with Coca-Cola and Procter & Gamble. Now he's trying something new. "We ask for customer volunteers to be an online customer feedback group. It's an opt-in process with a representative sample of customers, and they participate regularly in online surveys. We solicit people from our active customer list." With customers now spanning six states, Green Mountain's opt-in cyber group is an idea whose time has come—at least for those who want to connect with customers in real time.

Consider that Zagat Survey, a leading provider of information on restaurants and lodging, is experimenting with consumer polling online. No mystery why. Zagat Survey was able to complete the entire surveying process for seven midwestern cities—from sending out survey invitations to collecting data—in just a few weeks.

Method 4: Touch Base Calls

Who it's good for: Any company but particularly companies with a small customer base that can afford to spend more time on the phone

What's involved: Establishing a regular routine of calling customers for feedback, not for making sales

Company examples: Sam Whitmore's Media Survey, Fish Mart, ProDriver Leasing Systems

Many first-time entrepreneurs are like Sam Whitmore, the creator of Sam Whitmore's Media Survey in Beverly, Massachusetts. Whitmore, who describes himself as an editor by trade, says he's definitely not a salesperson. In the first year he didn't do much to keep in touch with the customers of his subscription-based website catering to PR and advertising professionals. Around the eleventh month he had to start calling people for subscription renewals. "I felt like a carpetbagger," he says. He had to learn how to view his customers as a source of guidance not as merely a source of capital.

He says that in year two he realized that the business was more than his toy. "This is kind of flowery, but I realized I am the custodian of a service. The first year was all my blueprint and in the second I started to ask customers what they wanted to see on the site."

For one thing, customers asked Sam to send them periodic reminders about the site—often people were so busy they forgot to look at new postings. Sam says he had to get over feeling like a spammer but he now sends weekly updates. He uses the e-mail as a tickler but firmly believes that you have to go to customers bearing gifts. When he makes touch base calls, he's usually prepared to offer some new perk. Premium subscribers get access to teleconferences with industry players, for example, and he often offers standard subscribers access to get them to upgrade or renew. Additionally, Sam generates article ideas by listening to his customers. For example, one woman was interested in learning how to measure the value of PR. Within a week or so there was an article posted compiling data and information. At the end of each article there's a rating system, as shown in Figure 8.1. Sam corresponds with the people who write in with suggestions.

"It's no longer me calling out of the blue to say, 'Hi. Pay me.' I talk with customers either face-to-face, on the phone, or by e-mail at least four or five times a year." He is aware that being a soloist lends him the

Figure 8.1 Real-time rating system

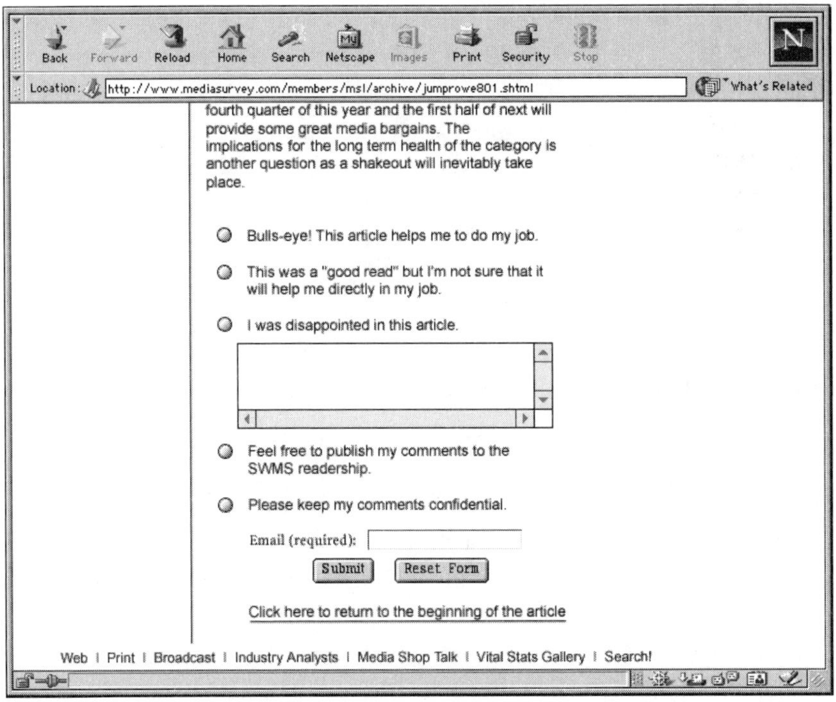

Reprinted by permission of Sam Whitmore's Media Survey.

flexibility to really interact with customers and says that what he does isn't easily "scalable" to a larger company with more clients. "In this world there is a lot of insincere communication. You can call when you know someone won't be there and leave a voice mail. Or e-mail instead of calling at all. It's really effective to conduct a regular dialogue and bring them something they can use."

Laura "Peach" Reid, president and co-owner of the Fish Mart, couldn't live without the phone. The phone is simply a lifeline to her many retail customers. Fish Mart sells fish and related products to some six hundred pet and aquarium stores, nurseries, and public aquariums.

"We're a wholesaler. Our sales staff calls every one of our regular customers on a weekly basis, no matter what," says Reid. "So, there's always that direct contact. Of course, in some ways the call is made to see if we can get an order, and usually we do get orders. But even when we don't, that phone conversation serves as a link that allows us to keep the pulse of our customers. So that clients feel comfortable talking about anything. In addition, we have great retention on our sales staff."

In addition to the regular catch-up calls with about three hundred customers a week, Fish Mart sales reps check in at the half-year mark and full-year mark with all six hundred customers. "At those times, they'll ask about the customer's sales, whether they were up or down, why there may have been a slowdown, what reasons, what they can do," says Reid. "My sales team keeps their eyes open, and observes buying patterns." (A running profile of every company is maintained in Gold Mine, just one of the many sales force automation programs you can buy off the shelf.)

Reid says she also makes a point of singling out best customers, "and I personally make a point during the year to check in with the store owner by phone, or maybe even go out for a golf outing or dinner get-together with that customer." Fish Mart's sales in 2000 were about $5.5 million. In 2001 Reid was named the Small Business Administration Business Owner of the Year for the state of Connecticut.

ProDriver Leasing Systems in Greenfield, Wisconsin, gets both the sales department and the operations department in on the act of making touch base calls. Involving operations people is a wise move because, after all, salespeople can be overly optimistic or hesitant to reveal problems with coveted accounts. ProDriver's approach lends balance. Because the company has grown quickly, there are plenty of people to help make the phone calls. President Christopher Schmus, a 2001 winner of the SBA's Young Entrepreneur award, started his truck driver leasing company in 1996 with a staff of five; in five years the company had 125 employees and revenues of $5 million.

Method 5: Employee Road Trips and Other Special Events

Who it's good for: Companies that spend most of their time conversing with clients on the phone; local companies that can easily stage special events

What's involved: Mapping out the ideal times to visit customers to make the most of face time or creating a memorable event that brings employees and customers together

Company examples: Crews Control, Kepler's

Crews Control is a staffing agency in Silver Spring, Maryland, that specializes in video crews for corporate clients. Those clients span the nation and the globe. Most sales and follow-up are done long distance, by phone, but special visits help bridge the miles. "Our business is a phone business so most of the time we have business relationships with people we have never met face-to-face," says CEO Andrea Keating, who has a staff of eight. "Periodically one of my production managers will go on a client road trip and fly to a city that has a high concentration of their client accounts. They'll spend a few days doing breakfasts, lunches, and dinners . . . meeting with key clients and their staff. Our clients appreciate the special attention of an on-site visit (this is not a sales presentation), and it gives us an opportunity to see their facilities firsthand. On several occasions these visits have not only strengthened our client relationships but also uncovered additional business opportunities."

Like road trips, special events can be a great venue for some concentrated one-on-one time with customers, and they don't have to cost much. Kepler's Books, an independent store among numerous chains in Menlo Park, California, finds that in-store readings are a great customer magnet—and a good place to pass out surveys. In fact, Kepler's stages twelve to sixteen events each month to entice customers back into the bookstore. Book readings feature celebrity authors along with little-known writers because each draws a different crowd. The less-famous authors often draw Kepler's most passionate customers. Owner Clark Kepler says taking into account such details is one reason his store, which employs seventy-five people, has stayed in business while other local independents have gone under.

Method 6: The Customer Care Team

Who it's good for: Companies big and small that want to create some version of a *customer care team* to give individual attention to customers and make touch base calls

What's involved: Creating a team, which requires a big enough staff to draw from (As a trial, assign customer service and/or sales employees to the team on a part-time basis. Customer care teams are often charged with dealing with customer complaints, but ideally they should also place touch base calls.)

Company examples: The Stanley Martin Companies, Synergy Networks, CCBN, Green Mountain Energy, C.B.&H. Parts Corp.

When Steven Alloy created his customer care team, it meant doing a complete overhaul of how his company had interacted with customers. Alloy is president of the Stanley Martin Companies, a home builder in Virginia and Maryland with 162 employees and about $120 million in sales.

Alloy explains the evolution of his team: "We sell three hundred new homes per year, priced from $300,000 to $900,000. Each customer order results in thousands of parts and specifications being selected. The administration used to be performed by an assistant in sales, then by an assistant in estimating, then by an assistant in construction, and finally by an assistant in warranty service. A year ago we changed the model to eliminate the specialists in each department and created a group of generalists organized around the customer. Each customer now has one *customer coordinator* who handles his or her sales, estimating, construction, and warranty needs during its eighteen-month order-through-warranty completion cycle. This allows for greater connection with the customer and fewer mistakes from passing information down the line."

The company took the concept a step further by designating a high-level manager as director of customer care. This individual has one mission: to achieve a 100 percent satisfaction rating from customers. "The position is senior enough to be empowered to orchestrate change in the organization and to provide solutions to virtually any customer satisfaction issue," says Alloy. "When this position was created ten months ago, our satisfaction rating was down to 84 percent. Today it is over 95 percent and climbing rapidly toward 100 percent."

Synergy Networks designed its customer care team to keep tabs on small clients—those deemed house accounts because these customers' purchases were too small or infrequent to assign to a sales rep. The care team first consisted of four or so in-house customer service and sales support people. Their task was to call the one-time, sometime, and otherwise small customers and simply ask how they're doing. Each person placed telephone calls to a dozen names in the customer database each week, so that after a year the staff made contact with more than a thousand small clients. The most promising of those accounts were called four or five times during the year.

The telephone conversations helped revive the connection with small clients and reacquaint them with Synergy's services; a number of past customers asked the company to come back for another project. CEO Mark Gordon tracked the repeat business over a year and credited the customer care team with $800,000 in incremental sales. "It correlated to more business pretty fast," he says.

Spurred on by the results, Gordon hired a marketing person who will continue the calling regimen, passing on industry news of interest to clients and again, just to say "How are you? Can we do anything for you?" and "Are you happy with our performance?"

Some companies assign a customer care rep to every customer regardless of the size of the account. That's the way it works at CCBN. "In our kind of business, you go in, you pitch a customer on your services, then when the customer decides if he or she wants to buy, he or she gets turned over to a customer service specialist," says CEO Jeff Parker. "We assign one specialist to each account, so that customer care becomes personalized, and clients can call and talk to the same customer service agent every time. In addition, the bigger the account, the more attention and interactivity they get from their specialist. At times we might talk to customers five times a day." At the very least, because corporate earnings announcements come out quarterly, CCBN staff talk to all customers at least once a quarter, sometimes in a conference call. Assigning agents to specific accounts ensures that there's a "quality means for interaction," says Parker.

Green Mountain Energy takes the time to publicize its care team among new customers. Once a new sale is completed, says CEO Dennis Kelly, "we send a welcome kit to our new customer that encourages them to give us their feedback regularly, by e-mail or through our Customer Care Group. The Customer Care Group is attuned to customer needs and tracks our contact with customers. The information in our customer database is reviewed constantly by the management team. To keep track of things, we try to separate information based on region or state. For example, when reviewing the customer database, we try to find trends and problems and separate them by state. We have a customer care team for each state. We also do *semiannual tracking studies*. With these, our customer care teams call customers, ask what they like, what they don't, what they would recommend to us, and then we track those surveys to see how we're doing."

Green Mountain's team performs another important function: gathering customer comments culled by employees in the field and disseminating the information to everyone monthly. "The comments are good and bad, and everybody in the company gets them and reviews them," says Kelly.

C.B.&H., an automotive parts and supply store for vehicles and trucks, also has staff dedicated to resolving individual customer issues. They have several designated customer service people who take repair orders at each location, along with one contact person for each location. "This way, the customer knows exactly who took their order, and who the contact person is if they need to call anyone," says president C. B. Tooley Jr. The customer is also provided with a card after the repairs have been done that lists what repairs were completed along with the contact person's name and other pertinent info regarding the repair, so that he or she will know whom to call if there is a problem. This helps things run more efficiently for both the customer and the business.

Method 7: Exit Polls

Who it's good for: Any company wanting to test the winds immediately after the customer has experienced the company's service or product and is most likely to offer feedback; particularly companies with many customers

What's involved: Physically administering a survey, although exit polls can be taken online if staff is limited and customers are willing; measuring the results of exit polls against later surveys that may not yield the same rosy results

Company examples: Funtown Splashtown USA, Stanley Martin Companies

Keeping the pulse on customers is especially important for Ken Cormier and Funtown Splashtown USA because his amusement park has direct contact with its customers for less than half the year. There's no way the award-winning park in Saco, Maine, could possibly take the pulse of some four hundred thousand guests who come to ride the roller coaster and frolic in the water park. President Ken Cormier does the next best thing by conducting an exit survey (literally) as guests walk through the exit gates. Once or twice a season, over a period of two weeks, Funtown personnel stand at the main entrance/exit, ready to reward guests who answer a short survey. The "gaters" as the people doing the polling are called, ask a few basic questions, check off a preprinted form, and write out any specific suggestions customers make. The gaters don't ask for personal demographic information other than home state. The questions are few and simple like "Did you have a good time at the park today?" "What new attraction would you like to see?"

Annual rider surveys not only measure customer satisfaction, they are especially important for gauging expansion. The overwhelming interest in a free-fall tower led to the recent construction of a ride called Dragon's Descent.

"Surveys are feedback that people give you and if people say to you that we want this and the respondents measure up to 75 percent, you better listen because they're sending you a message. However, if respondents are 15 percent for this, 20 percent for that, then *you* have to make a decision, what do you think is best? We decided to go with Dragon's Descent because it was the right time, we had the right amount of money, and the survey respondents wanted it." (Cormier also keeps in mind that customer feedback can be influenced by nature; there was an incredible heat wave when nearly 50 percent of one exit poll voted for a bigger water park.)

The exit surveys helped Cormier realize that "grandma and grandpa" were not buying season passes because many just came to walk the park with children riders or for other reasons, so Funtown Splashtown recently added a reduced-price walker's season pass, which also includes a day's free admission for a family member. Altogether, the new attractions and ticket options helped boost attendance 25 percent in the 2001 season.

The park's website also features a customer satisfaction survey that asks park attendants to rate their experience with many aspects of the park as well as how they got there, with whom they came, and how long they stayed.

For home builder Stanley Martin Companies, there are scheduled face-to-face meetings with customers throughout the six-month order and delivery process. That's standard in the luxury-home-building industry where orders are too complicated to process without verifying that a customer understands what he or she is buying. "We survey them the day they take delivery, and then we survey them again sixty days later," says CEO Steven Alloy. Beginning this fall, he is also implementing a twelve-month survey as well. Why go the extra step? After-all, Alloy's product does not exactly lend itself to repeat sales—just how many $500,000 dream homes does a family need in its lifetime?

Still, by surveying customers more frequently, the construction company gets a lot in return. "This allows us to target incentives for our sales and construction personnel based on their customer ratings and to find out which mortgage companies perform best and which subcontractors provide the best service," says Alloy. In other words, the company gets an important heads up regarding a variety of factors that affect satisfaction. "It also provides great feedback on our product design and specifications." Not to mention that surveying more often helps prompt more referrals. "Although our product does not lend itself to repeat business from our customers, it is critical that we connect with our customers to generate referrals." Referral sales are now at 14 percent and climbing, he says.

"With respect to the surveys, we ask sixty-four questions," Alloy says. "We ask about the mortgage and title satisfaction because third-party providers can ruin a good customer experience we have created. In fact, we entered these businesses for the sole purpose of ensuring that we could control the quality of the mortgage and closing components of the transaction." By taking the customer pulse more often and more thoroughly—along with other measures like creating the position of customer care director—Alloy says his company has been able to boost its customer satisfaction ratings.

Creating Your Own Economic Indicators

Beyond the methods we've just described, many companies devise their own unique benchmarks—or internal economic indicators—for keeping track of the pulse of customer relationships. One number can say a lot about the health of a relationship—if you're tracking the right number.

Ken Cormier, for instance, focuses on the number of season pass holders of Funtown Splashtown. If the number drops off, he knows he's in trouble. But so far, in the three years he's been following the progress of pass holders, this crowd has grown each season. "Most are coming back, they're bringing their friends," he says. Such evidence of how customers are feeling gives Cormier a boost of confidence when he makes plans and sales projections for the next season. He also feels good when he sees guests convert their day passes to season passes after they spend an afternoon at the park.

In fact, season pass holders are so important to Funtown that they receive a little holiday care package in October or November that includes a newsletter, informing them of new rides and attractions in the works for the following year—"so they can be excited like the rest of us," says Cormier—and an enticement to preorder their season pass.

The incentive varies, but usually includes $10 off the pass for buying before the first of the year, plus a day's free entry for a friend or family member and discounts on store merchandise. All of the bonuses are good chemistry boosters. Preseason sales are another kind of exit poll for Funtown Splashtown. By ordering their season passes in advance, customers are voting with their feet.

Here's another example of a compelling business indicator: in corporate circles one test of customer loyalty is whether you can put your client on contract—and for how much. For instance, Andrea Keating of Crews Control pays a lot of attention to how many of her corporate accounts operate on purchase agreements rather than asking her to submit an invoice for each and every project.

"Most of our clients are Fortune 500 companies and our goal is to have each of them open a blanket purchase agreement (BPA) with Crews Control," says Keating. Each BPA stipulates an annual dollar amount that has been preapproved to be spent with her company. Keating and her staff review the BPAs midyear and contact those clients that have spent more than half of that amount to let them know the balance. (Since Crews Control's customer contacts often work in production, not accounting, they often don't track what they've spent.) For those who are running over, "we encourage them to amend the BPA upwards to make sure that there are enough funds in the account to carry them through the remainder of the year," she says. Since most of Keating's projects involve a very quick turnaround, spending more than a BPA amount could jeopardize Crews Control's chances of being awarded a contract or could draw out payment to ninety days or more until the increase is approved. As most companies work on a "use it or lose it" system for BPAs, this also helps ensure that the BPA amounts will be increased each year and spent in full.

Keating reports that more than half the top clients have a BPA, which is common practice in large purchasing departments because it streamlines the accounting process. While there are no guarantees with any customer, Keating says her BPA levels are a good indication of future business. The ability to make smart projections is a huge advantage for any company builder but it's just one of the many benefits of taking the pulse.

Chemistry Checklist

1. *Conduct a status review of your best customers.* Devise a way to do a quick customer-pulse assessment with your team. Review your list of best customers and rank them using a simple scale of 1 to 5. 1 = We are on top of this customer's needs. 5 = This customer needs intensive care or we risk losing the account.

2. *Divide and conquer.* Take a triage approach. Assign team members specific customer groups or clients to contact with a "How are we doing?" telephone call or meeting. This will allow you to confirm your quick internal status check. Compare your actual results with your gut reactions to your quick status review.

3. *Identify cracks in the foundation.* You have worked on identifying customer touch points, launched communication plans, and mapped buying cycles. However, some customers may still slip though the cracks. Those customers who are not ranked a 1 on the pulse meter may not have responded to any of your efforts. Why? Are there better ways to cement these best relationships?

4. *Silence is not golden.* Lack of communication from a customer can be a signal that something is wrong. Review your activity report for your best customers. When is the date of last contact? If you have not heard from a customer within your company's acceptable timetable guidelines, pick up the phone and place a call.

5. *Create your "Pulse Plan."* Select three of the different pulse-taking ideas presented in this chapter that make the most sense for your customers. Once you have selected your action items, assign a date to each customer conduct for the activity. Meet weekly with your team to assess the results.

6. *Be flexible.* Remember that customer relationships are fluid and always changing. Listen to what your customers say as you reach out to take their pulses. While you may have developed a master customer-chemistry plan for the year, individual customers require customized programs and responses in order to keep and grow their businesses. Be prepared to change course.

CHAPTER 9

CONCLUSIONS, PREDICTIONS, AND CHEMISTRY CHECKUP QUIZ

E ntrepreneurs and business managers are accustomed to setting goals, reaching them, and moving on to the next challenge. We get an adrenaline rush from checking off our to-do lists and from the sense of completion. As I stood on the roof of our first building fourteen years ago, I had a vision of placing a concierge in every office building in Washington, D.C. I also imagined a very large, multimillion-dollar business that would ultimately expand to other metropolitan markets and eventually the world!

My vision didn't unfold exactly as planned. We did grow to serve more than eighty office buildings, and Capitol Concierge is the oldest and largest on-site corporate concierge service in the country. But instead of expanding to hundreds of new buildings across the United States, we stayed close to home and managed a thriving business with a select group of profitable existing customers. Instead of selling franchises, we set up a consulting division that helped other women launch concierge businesses in their own hometowns. Instead of doing a costly physical expansion, I took a leap and opted to develop a "virtual" concierge service accessible through toll-free number, e-mail, chat, palm devices, and Web phones. This last change would prove to be the biggest testing ground of my entrepreneurial career because it involved taking our customer-chemistry lessons that were now working for Capitol Concierge "back to the future." Effectively taking all of our hard-learned personal-touch strategies, we spun off a brand-new Internet company.

Like everything else, the new company didn't happen overnight. It was the summer of '96, shortly after the company celebrated its ninth anniversary—and was well on its ways to taking relationship building to the Web—when we contemplated starting a new company. We wanted to bring a real-time concierge service to a whole new generation of consumers and corporate clients across the nation via the Internet.

Until then the team had often debated the wisdom of trying to bring the concierge concept national. The interest in concierge services had skyrocketed because of numerous articles in the press, so my angel investors and I started to have meetings every Friday to look at possible directions. Where are we going to go? We looked at putting together a centralized order facility for other concierge companies. We considered expanding our sales base across the country by franchising or by forming some sort of concierge consortium. We looked at the Web.

As I looked deeper into Web-based technologies, I realized that this new phenomenon, the Web, could take our business and all of our customer-chemistry plans to a whole new level. We could harness the power of Web-enabled applications to increase the level of personalized service. We could also go beyond the confines of the local office building business.

We had the model for an enticing new business: a virtual concierge service available to be accessed by millions of customers. The name we eventually arrived at for the new venture: VIPdesk.com, Inc. I made one of my longtime managers, Sally Hurley, the first employee of the new division, launching it in May 1996.

Equipped with a call center and the power of the Web, there was finally a way for us to potentially take the business far beyond our home base of Washington, D.C. VIPdesk was our most ambitious attempt to bring the concierge service to a wider market through a variety of channels. MasterCard was one of the first major clients to sign on, using its own website and call center to tap into the concierge service.

In the summer of '99 I made a huge decision: to bring in outside management help for the day-to-day running of Capitol Concierge so I could devote my energy to building the Web-based concierge service.

We hired a seasoned executive to serve as president of Capitol Concierge. One of the toughest challenges an entrepreneur faces is turning over the reins and not interfering. As tough as it was to entrust my venture to someone else, I knew that the only way that I could pursue the Internet dream was to step aside from the day-to-day management of Capitol.

Meanwhile, we were gaining momentum at VIPdesk. The team began private labeling of the VIPdesk website platform for other clients, including Citibank and OnStar. The combination of a virtual Web-based service supported by live concierges was enticing.

While VIPdesk was designed to make good on our Capitol Concierge experience, we were still sailing into uncharted territory. Capitol Concierge was literally homegrown and bootstrapped. To succeed in the fast-paced world of the Internet, VIPdesk needed to develop powerful technology, build an executive team, and be the first to market and execute to perfection. This would require significant money and talent. My original Capitol Concierge investors and I decided to take the plunge into the world of *venture-capital (VC) financing*.

In September 1999, after months of crafting the business plan and new business model, I set out to meet prospective investors. With so much at stake, this was the biggest sales challenge of my entrepreneurial life. After countless meetings, trips to Silicon Valley, and hours of rewriting my scripts, VIPdesk secured its first round of VC following my presentation at a regional venture-funding fair. We ultimately closed on $12 million in funding in December 2000. We also now had a formal board of directors made up of representatives from Women's Growth Capital Fund, Scripps Ventures, and Pennsylvania Early Stage Fund.

I thought I had learned countless lessons from my years of methodically building Capitol Concierge, but nothing compares to the lessons learned from transitioning our old-line company to the wild, wired world. The pace at which we grew and worked was unlike any other. In the first six months of 2000, we took many leaps: VIPdesk grew from nine to sixty employees. At Capitol Concierge it took us four years to reach this size. For VIPdesk I hired executives from the outside, whereas at Capitol Concierge our team grew up with the company.

VIPdesk also launched our Web-based concierge platform. For the first time concierges could work from home: a remote concierge application allows VIPdesk to route customer requests that come online to concierges sitting at home. That was a true breakthrough. While we have faced considerable challenges trying to staff office buildings in a tight job market, our new technology allows us to tap a highly qualified home-based workforce of stay-at-home parents, grad students, and retirees. Last but not least, we rolled out twelve major national clients. That last achievement really astounds me. Technology rollouts at Capitol Concierge sometimes took years, but at VIPdesk, we've already released six new versions of our website and have begun implementing the new platform in the office building market.

With VIPdesk coming into its second full year of operation since receiving funding, we are in the beginning stages of implementing the customer-chemistry techniques that took us years to hone at Capitol Concierge. It takes time and patience to begin to gather the customer histories, transaction patterns, and buying cycles. Today we are implementing a client "scoreboard" that provides us with an up-to-the-minute snapshot of the service elements that our clients have determined are their critical success factors. Client managers conduct weekly conference calls with customers and hold daily reviews of customer e-mail feedback. At VIPdesk I'm at the beginning of a new journey with a new set of clients. I've come full circle.

Susan and I have shared with you dozens of ideas and tools from my experience at Capitol Concierge and from the experiences of more than forty other entrepreneurs. I have also shared my bumps in the road and our "if I could do this over again . . ." missteps. Try out the different ways to rate customers, stay top of mind, and reward your best customers. In other words, find the chemistry mix that works for you. The quest for customer chemistry leads to some interesting places.

The Making of a Marriage

Customer relationships have a clear life cycle and each stage requires different communication styles, tools, and strategies. First, it's making the match—identifying your best customers. There's the courtship phase—pursuing and selling the customer. First comes love, then comes marriage—building and sustaining the relationship.

To help sustain the marriage, you must become adept at recruiting—finding employees that are a good match for your customers. Recruiting moves naturally on to training—demonstrating techniques and tools that enable your team members to create learning dialogues with customers in order to deliver superior service. Bonus systems and recognition programs need to be tied not just to new revenue, but to renewing and expanding current customers. All customer touch points need to ultimately support all of your customer-chemistry building efforts.

The first steps—matchmaking and courtship—are easy and exciting compared to the effort to make the customer relationship a long and profitable one. But if you are committed to creating chemistry, the rewards will become evident over time.

Review of the Rules

The customer chemistry journey is a never-ending one. There are, however, critical success milestones to plot your path and assist your company in the benchmarking process. These milestones have been presented throughout the book as eight sequential relationship-building rules.

1. *Know your customers.* That's the first step to building customer chemistry. Identify customers, interact with them, and use every chance to be personal. As you know your customers, so they will know you.
2. *Rank your customers by being brutally honest.* Not all customers are created equal. This is the starting point that will shed light on which customers are contributing to your company's long-term growth and which customers could potentially stunt your growth. By ranking customers by profitability, you will be able to allocate your customer-chemistry building resources accordingly.
3. *Teach employees to focus on best customers and prospects.* Once you have identified your best customers, your team needs to know who they are. Provide your employees with techniques to uncover customer preferences and make every customer interaction count.

4. *Never stop learning about your customers.* The customer-chemistry building process employs methods to continually understand and stay on top of your customers' needs and expectations. By applying what you learn from the methods, you will always be one step ahead of your customers. The result will be long-lasting customer relationships.

5. *Create top-of-mind marketing campaigns.* Learn to map your customers' buying cycles and timetables. Deploy a communication plan that plants reminders with your customers just in time and captures every potential selling opportunity.

6. *Treat your customers like your best employees: recognize and reward them.* Everyone likes to be appreciated. No one deserves recognition more than the customers that fuel your growth. Relevant rewards that demonstrate your knowledge of your customers will result in unsurpassed levels of loyalty.

7. *Say good-bye to bad business.* Parting is never easy, but smart companies systemically shed customers who are a drain on time, resources, and profits. Plan regular reviews of the quality of your customers and end poor relationships on a positive note. And never burn a bridge. Today's bad customer may be a best customer sometime in the future.

8. *Take the pulse of your relationships.* Your customers' needs are never static. Monitoring the status of your best-customer relationships is a critical step in maintaining relationships. Employ pulse-taking activities to make sure your customers are happy. If any are not, have the insight to change course, make corrections, and keep the chemistry growing.

Beginning the Journey

If you build it, will they come?

Of course, there's no guarantee that because you want to become more "intimate" with customers they will feel the same way about you.

Indeed, in the beginning of its initiative to lavish more attention on its top clients, Custom Research Inc. worried that customers might reject CRI's bid to get closer. But they didn't, and CRI succeeded in growing sales and profits substantially. The strategy of doing more with a highly screened group of clients has served the company well. Despite a brutal time in 1999 when several of CRI's large clients were acquired by other businesses and cut back their market-research budgets, CRI survived—by expanding the definition of its best-customer profile to include smaller and midsize companies. In 2000 the company recorded one of its best years for sales and gross margins.

When you embark on the quest for customer chemistry, you will by turns be exhilarated and exhausted. Certainly the decision to pursue some customers and not others requires you to be tough. Focusing on your best and current customers, however, doesn't mean you stop looking for new clients. You need to find a balance. Spend the bulk of time on current customers—nurturing them, learning all you can about their needs. You won't regret it. At the same time don't be closed off to new opportunities. The only way to keep the balance is to constantly review the customer tiers you've established. Your definition of best customer will no doubt undergo a few revisions as the market changes. Your strategic emphasis will change as you take the pulse of your current customers.

Customer chemistry is also a quest to find what you most love about business. Seek out those clients who stimulate you, make you think, teach you new things. Find the ones who want to help you grow your company and stay true to you past the courtship stage—and you them. Search out those individuals you would want to have as clients wherever they are employed—and follow them when they change employers. Find customers who respect you and treat you as an equal. They are the customers you can build a solid company around.

Farther Down the Road

Where are you after you've completed all the steps in the customer-chemistry building process? No doubt you are a changed manager leading a changed company. Not as frenetic, perhaps, but more intense. You have the strength of your convictions. You have said good-bye to a customer or two (and perhaps a few have said good-bye to you). You might be working with more customers or fewer. You've seen how performing extra services for top customers converts into new sales and valuable referrals. You've survived a downturn or two on the strength of your best relationships. You've learned chemistry is fluid: your best customer for three years was suddenly acquired or changed direction. A new cycle began with a new client. The process of learning about customers never ends. The job of teaching employees to be detectives and goodwill ambassadors starts anew with each person you hire.

The process is not always easy. There are rocks in the road that will make you stumble and fall. At times the journey is downright painful. Throughout, you will question every assumption you've ever had about how to make money and run a business. Remember Claudia Post, the CEO of Diamond Courier who loved to sell, sell, sell? When her company was unprofitable, she recalls thinking, "Here I am with a company that's doing $3 million plus, and I have no money. I'm working a gazillion hours a week. There's something terribly wrong here." There was. So Post not only reorganized her business, she also changed her own priorities. For an entire year she stopped selling. Instead, she threw herself into the task at hand—visiting dozens of customers and writing to hundreds more affected by the changes she was making. Frankly, she found the whole process liberating. Five years after her momentous decision to turn away unprofitable business, Post still sounded liberated. She had survived numerous assaults on her company and come out on top.

As painful as the process can be, it works. Remember Green Hills Farms grocery store? With just one small location, it has survived and even grown sales while competing against superstore competitors; the store is more profitable too—sales per square foot are about twice the industry average. All the results stem from Green Hill's single-minded determination to learn more about all its customers and to reward the very best.

In a completely different but just as competitive world, there is Connect, the I/T staffing firm that in five years nearly tripled the size of its staff from seven to twenty as sales took off. Using a customer-chemistry approach, the business took off despite the brutal state of the I/T staffing market that has seen many smaller players gobbled up by acquisitions or go out of business. To increase its share of customer, Connect dropped unprofitable service lines and created new ones such as adding a permanent-placement service for its largest clients and conducting workforce effectiveness workshops for them as well. At first, the Connect partners say, the amount of work that needed to be done to get closer to key customers was overwhelming. But they also appreciated how many options this new strategy afforded them, and they enjoyed jumping in with both feet. "The whole prepping process was rigorous and good," says Maureen Clarry. "It was good to analyze our product lines and see which clients were which. There was anticipation and excitement."

Today they define customer chemistry as reaching a level where you're not afraid to voice your opinion to the customer. Partner Kelly Gilmore sums it up this way: "There's mutual respect and a healthy dialogue."

Mutual respect and a healthy dialogue—isn't that what everyone wants in a relationship?

Customer Chemistry and the New Economy: Our Predictions

What role will customer chemistry play in the new economy? How much more will personal relationships matter in this age of electronic everything? If handwritten notes still carry special cachet, it's not hard to see the value of personalizing every aspect of your relationship with customers. Entrepreneurs will focus on customer chemistry because it's a business philosophy that doesn't depend on big advertising campaigns to succeed; it's a bootstrapped approach that relies on personal contacts, creativity, enthusiasm, and superior service. Our predictions:

1. *Companies will band together to leverage their relationships with key customers.* "Coalition loyalty programs," as they've been called, will become more common as groups of retailers and other companies

create group reward programs for a common set of customers. This is already being done in downtown shopping districts in Boulder, Salt Lake City, the Hawaiian island of Maui, and Eugene, Oregon.

In Eugene, for example, independent retailers joined forces to reach out to shoppers. A cooperative advertising program, known as "Unique Eugene," aims to persuade citizens that patronizing these local stores is a better shopping experience and better for the community. In addition to print and broadcast advertising, Unique Eugene has created posters, a website, and gift certificates redeemable at any member business.

Maui retailers have also banded together to reward customers and counter the effects of chain stores in the area. A few years ago, twenty-four locally owned businesses launched the "Ohana Savers" loyalty card program (*ohana* means family in Hawaiian). The cards enable customers to accumulate points on purchases and redeem the points at any of the participating businesses. The Ohana Savers card covers a variety of businesses, ranging from a grocery store to an appliance dealer. As of 2001, more than twenty thousand people had signed up. A marketing magazine ranked Ohana Savers as the fastest-growing loyalty card program in the nation.

We predict the trend will become big in service sectors where compelling alliances are now sprouting. For instance, the PRConsultants Group brings together thirty independent owners of public relations firms around the nation. Together they have won some big contracts they could not have gotten alone. PRConsultants Group meets the needs of large clients requiring quality PR coverage across the country. According to the leaders of the PR alliance, clients appreciate having one point of contact that can handle market coordination, billing, and reporting the results.

2. *Marketers will get smarter about asking people to prequalify* themselves as good, better, or best customers. Best customers may be willing to pay more for certain conveniences, extra services, and flexibility. If they're not willing to pay extra, they may at least be willing to pay in advance—like the season pass holders to Funtown Splashtown USA who buy their passes months before the gates open.

3. *Workshops will spring up teaching companies how to fire bad customers.* In an uncertain economy more companies will be hard hit by late-paying customers—and saying good-bye to bad customers will take more than the usual courage. Because companies are more reluctant to fire any customers in a downturn, they will be tempted to become less choosy. In the event of a sustained downturn, the best strategy is to carefully cultivate relationships with current customers and be even more vigilant about extending credit to new customers. Don't hesitate to cut off relations with customers that take longer and longer to pay their bills.

4. *Companies will cultivate alumni networks to offset the effects of customer turnover.* Despite long-standing relationships, customers will continue to be lost to the effects of mergers and acquisitions. Clients that spent a lot with you will suddenly cut back their budgets after being acquired. The M&A factor makes it all the more vital to deepen individual relationships. When you really know the people you're working with (as more than just customers), you're far more likely to get advance warning when a big change is coming that could decimate your sales. Many companies will follow the lead of companies such as Connect, which has created an alumni network and alumni events so that business doesn't end when the customer goes bankrupt or a key contact person moves on to another job.

   Andrea Keating of Crews Control takes the alumni concept a step further; she sends a special care package to the people in her network when they change employers. "If our old contact is moving within the industry, we get their new address and set them up with a Crews Control care package wrapped in cellophane and ribbon at their new office. We have a great duffel bag with our logo and we fill it with our oversized coffee mugs, designer coffees, biscotti, Crews Control note cubes, and a Crews Control polo shirt along with a note of congratulations on the new job. We send the same package to the new person who is taking over the job vacancy at the original client—and our new relationship is on its way."

5. *The hot question in corporate circles will be "Who owns the customer relationship?"* The role of sales support staff will finally be addressed

and compensation plans will be adjusted to give greater rewards to relationship-driven salespeople, customer service reps, and support staff. High-level customer service managers will play an increasingly strategic role in keeping high-level clients. And they will work for companies who see their importance and pay accordingly. At Stanley Martin Companies, a regional home builder in Virginia and Maryland, each of the 162 employees has a bonus riding on the company's customer satisfaction rating. Additionally, customer satisfaction is one of three goals that needs to be hit for every employee to go on excursions such as a Bahamas cruise, says CEO Steven Alloy.

6. *Customer service will be the great equalizer.* Proactive service will become one of the fastest ways to jump-start customer chemistry. No more waiting until the customer comes to you. Smart companies will increasingly reach out to their best customers to anticipate their service needs.

7. *More companies will attempt to do some form of mass customization of products, services, or marketing messages.* As the price of technology continues to go down, customization will become affordable to more companies. E-mail communication will continue to grow more popular as loyalty marketing increases online.

8. *Companies will increasingly work to create an emotional bond with customers* that may include joint participation in a social cause. Social responsibility is a powerful chemistry booster. Leonard Berry, author of *Discovering the Soul of Service*, arrived at seven core values in his book that define the best service organizations. "Social profit," or generosity, is one of the key values Berry associated with sustained service performance.

Liz Claiborne Inc., the hugely successful women's clothing company, presents a vivid example of how cause-related marketing can drive sales to the brand while building goodwill among consumers. In 1991, after researching its consumers, the company launched its Women's Work program focused on educating the public about domestic violence. The program started locally and has since expanded across the country to include handbooks, surveys, campus outreach, and a toll-free hotline for Liz Claiborne associates. Partners include local retailers and community groups.

9. *Relationships with customers will go well beyond prescribed business roles.* For example, a client and supplier go into business together as equal partners to tackle a new market. Such formations will cause a profound shift in the way we think about customer relationships.

   You can find a model of this trend in companies like Operations Associates, a fast-growing business consulting firm with 2000 sales of about $6 million in Greenville, South Carolina. Operations Associates CEO Alan Nager says he teamed up with a client of ten years, Toyota Motor Sales, to enter a whole new marketplace. Together they created a seminar program called Lean Logistics targeted to aerospace and electronics companies. Nager says the joint seminar captures both companies' expertise.

Customer-Chemistry Checkup

Where are you now and where are you going? Here's a quiz to check your status in eight areas crucial to building customer chemistry.

1. List of best customers.
   a. Haven't gotten around to it yet   (0 points)
   b. Made a mental list based on my gut instincts   (5 points)
   c. Compiled a list of historical sales and ranked customers by profitability   (10 points)
2. Best-customer profile. I've used the following information:
   a. Customer name and telephone number   (0 points)
   b. Demographic information—age range, industry, geographic location, etc.   (5 points)
   c. Demographics, plus input from my employees on characteristics of our best customers   (10 points)
3. Employee training now includes
   a. the basic requirements of the job   (0 points)
   b. sharing our best-customer profile   (5 points)
   c. detective training—how to continually learn about our customers   (10 points)

4. Customer touch points to capture customer data.
   a. What are touch points again?　(0 points)
   b. I include a fact-finding question during each customer interaction.　(5 points)
   c. I've incorporated a master data-capture profile into our customer database system.　(10 points)

5. Customer buying cycles. I'm gleaning new insights by
   a. writing up the sale after it takes place　(0 points)
   b. mapping customers' historical purchases　(5 points)
   c. proactively identifying cycles through a budget-planner tool (10 points)

6. Customer-recognition program now includes
   a. saying thank you after a sale　(0 points)
   b. delivering a value-added perk at the time of purchase (5 points)
   c. tailoring a reward to the customers' unique preferences (10 points)

7. Bad customer relationships. I know "when to fold" because
   a. customers stop buying　(0 points)
   b. we created relationship "red flags" to identify trouble signals　(5 points)
   c. recovery resolutions have not worked and we and the customer have amicably agreed it is time to part (10 points)

8. Taking the pulse. I check in on my customers by
   a. take the pulse? I'm not a doctor.　(0 points)
   b. conducting surveys at regular intervals　(5 points)
   c. directly interfacing with my customers to ask, "How are we doing?" and to listen to the answer　(10 points)

Scoring

- *0–20 points:* Go back to school and study your chemistry lessons. You and your company are at risk of being severely out of touch with your customers. Out of touch can mean out of business. Reread the Chemistry Checklists at the end of each chapter to have an understanding of your path to moving to the front of the customer-chemistry class.

- *25–40 points:* You are a high roller. While you are playing the game, you are rolling the dice with your customer relationships. You know the rules but are counting too much on luck to win at customer chemistry. Stick to the basics of your plan, practice them consistently, and increase your odds of hitting the customer jackpot.
- *45–60 points:* Your glass is half full. You are on the right track. With a little more concentrated focus, your customer-chemistry cup will runneth over.
- *65–80 points:* Congrats! You are a customer-chemistry champion! Your grasp of customer chemistry and new practices will carry you across the finish line. Your company is outpacing the competition and the gold medal is in reach. Remember, however, that true winners dedicate most of their time to an ongoing training regimen.

REFERENCES

All interviews for this book were conducted by Susan Greco and the researchers named in the Acknowledgments. Individuals who are quoted without an accompanying citation provided material expressly for use in this book. Some individuals and companies in this book have appeared in *Inc* magazine stories by Greco in a different context or form; those stories are referenced here for further reading. Readers can access *Inc* stories online at www.inc.com.

Preface

Capitol Concierge: see Greco, "The Road to One to One Marketing," *Inc*, October 1995.

One to One Marketing: see Don Peppers and Martha Rogers, *The One to One Future: Building Relationships One Customer at a Time* (New York: Currency, 1993).

Chapter 1

The Mackay 66: to get the list of questions, go to www.mackay.com /howhelp/Mac66.html.

Chris Zane: see Don Peppers, "How CRM Pumped Up This Bike Shop," *Inside 1to1*, an online publication of the Peppers+Rogers Group, August 17, 2000.

Norm Brodsky, "Forget Spreadsheets," *Inc*, November 1997.

Al Ries, *Focus: The Future of Your Company Depends on It* (New York: HarperCollins, 1997).

Research on falling in love: See Patricia Wen, "In Science, *Love* Now Has A Reality Check," *The Boston Globe*, February 14, 2001.

Chapter 2

TelStrat International: see Greco, "Making Goliath Pay," *Inc*, October 2000 (*Inc* 500 special issue).

Ranier: Greco interviewed the company in 1997.

Adjacency: Greco interviewed in 1998. The company was purchased by Sapient Corp. of Cambridge, MA, in March 1999.

Schecter: see Greco, "When Small Isn't Beautiful," *Inc*, March 1997.

Activity-based costing: see Srikumar S. Rao, "ABCs of Cost Control," *Inc Technology* 1997, issue number 2.

Custom Research Inc., see Greco, "Choose or Lose," *Inc*, December 1998.

Fallon McElligott: corporate information provided by Julie Thompson, communications director.

The phrase "raving fans": see Kenneth Blanchard et al., *Raving Fans: A Revolutionary Approach to Customer Service* (New York: William Morrow & Co., 1993).

Magda expressed her fears at an online message board for women entrepreneurs.

Michele Gerbrandt sold her company, Satellite Press, to F&W Publications in July 2001. At this writing she remains editorial director of *Memory Makers*.

RightNow Technologies: information on its "Inner Circle" club was obtained from RightNow's website.

Chapter 3

Beverly Hall Furniture: see David Schreiber, "Superior Service: How to Create Memorable Service Experiences," *Atlanta Business Chronicle*, Nov. 29, 1999.

SoftAd Group: Greco received information from Elizabeth Cundiff, director of communications, by e-mail.

Parental Stressline: Greco gained firsthand experience on the training as a year-long volunteer for the hotline.

ProFlowers: Greco exchanged e-mails with CEO Bill Strauss.

SRC: see Jack Stack and Bo Burlingham, *The Great Game of Business* (New York: Currency, 1992), p. 89.

Grand Circle Corp.: Greco spoke with Sherry Walker, then a PR representative for the company.

Fallon McElligott: see note for Chapter 2.

The screen for qualifying cold leads was adapted from a list of questions that CRI asks potential customers who contact the market-research firm.

Script Save: see Greco, "Phonetics," *Inc*, April 2000. CRI: see note for Chapter 2.

Chapter 4

See Jan Carlzon, Tom Peters, *Moments of Truth* (New York: Harper-Collins, 1989).

USAA's "ECHO" System: See Leonard Berry, *Discovering the Soul of Service* (New York: The Free Press, 1999).

Stew Leonard Jr. was interviewed by Greco in December 2000 by phone.

Tuxedo rental company: see Leslie Williams Johnson, "How to Measure Customer Pleasure," *Atlanta Business Chronicle*, May 24, 1999.

Grand Circle: see note for Chapter 3.

IRIS was sold in July 2000 to HomeSeekers. Maggie Etheridge left IRIS in 2001 but, as of this writing, remains a shareholder. The sample chat box is used with her permission.

Advanced Micro Devices: information on AMD's customer satisfaction survey was provided at the website of CustomerSat.com.

Pros and cons of survey methods were culled and summarized from several sources including the websites of CustomerSat.com, the Council of American Survey Research Organizations, and Response Design.

Green Hills Farms: see Greco, "The Best Little Grocery Store in America," *Inc*, June 2001.

Chapter 5

Road Runner Sports: interview with Jeff Rohling, vice president of marketing and company catalogs.

Giorgenti: information about the company was gleaned from its website and from the website of SalesLogix, and in an interview with CEO Janine Giorgenti.

British Airways: see Bob Mueller, "Making Online Marketing Part of Your Plan," *Beyond Computing*, October 2000.

See Peggy Post and Peter Post, *The Etiquette Advantage in Business: Personal Skills for Professional Success* (New York: Harper Resource, 1999).

Frontline Group: Greco interviewed CEO Sullee in October 2000.

Timbuk2: e-mail message from customer provided by Timbuk2's Jordan Reiss.

Little Nell Hotel: Greco interviewed the hotel's assistant general manager in 2001.

Figure 5.2, The Marketing Budget: we based our percentages for conventional mass marketing on rough estimates of how much more it costs to do mass marketing via TV commercials, newspaper inserts, and the like than it costs to send direct mail to a limited universe of targeted customers. The percentages are not presented as an exact representation of the spending habits of mass marketers.

Chapter 6

Road Runner Sports: see note for Chapter 5.

Green Hills Farms: see note for Chapter 4. Also see Gary Hawkins, *Building the Customer Specific Retail Enterprise* (Skaneateles, NY: Breezy Heights Publishing, 1999).

Leonard Berry: Greco interviewed him by phone in December 2000.

Roth Staffing: see Edward O. Welles, "The People Business," *Inc*, October 1999.

Dan Miller: see Greco,"CEO's Notebook," *Inc*, August 1998.

Chapter 7

Diamond Courier: see Greco, "Are We Making Money Yet?" *Inc*, July 1996.

Chapter 8

Zagat Survey: information was gleaned from a press release issued by Zagat and Insight Express.

The *Inc* 500: see *Inc*, October 2001 (special issue).

Chapter 9

Custom Research Inc.: the company was sold in 2000. As of this writing, Judy Corson was CEO and Jeff Pope was retired from CRI.

Diamond Courier: see note for Chapter 7.

"Unique Eugene" and other examples of local alliances: see Stacy Mitchell, "The Hometown Advantage Bulletin" (The Institute for Local Self-Reliance, 2000 and 2001, Minneapolis) at www.newrules.org. Mitchell has been tracking such efforts for several years.

PR Consultants Group: see Greco, "Declaration of Independents," *Inc*, September 2001.

Liz Claiborne: information on its cause-related marketing program was received by its PR agency. The company measures the success of "Women's Work" in part by the awards it has received from the PR community, as well as letters from local agencies and the advertising value of the media impressions generated by newspaper and magazine stories.

SUGGESTED READINGS AND RESOURCES

Suggested Reading

Here is a list of some of our favorite relationship-marketing books.

Aftermarketing: How to Keep Customers for Life Through Relationship Marketing by Terry G. Vavra, 1995. This book covers database development, customer satisfaction research, customer service, and direct marketing, showing how to use them together to maximize their power in strengthening relationships with customers. *Aftermarketing* tells how to construct a customer database, manage it, and establish information dialogues with customers by actively answering their complaints and compliments.

The Customer Marketing Method: How to Implement and Profit from Customer Relationship Management by Jay Curry and Adam Curry, 2000. Price $25.00. A step-by-step guide for implementing CRM for small to medium-sized companies. Jay Curry explains how CRM can help managers boost profits by implementing a customer-focused strategy. Using easy-to-understand graphics, he introduces the customer pyramid—segmented as "Top," "Big," "Medium," and "Small"—to help the reader visualize, analyze, and improve customer profitability. Success comes to those who follow this three-step Customer Marketing Strategy: (1) get new customers into your pyramid; (2) move customers higher into your pyramid; (3) keep the customers in the pyramid.

The Customer Relationship Management Survival Guide by Dick Lee, 2000. Price $29.00. Lee offers a comprehensive view into the world of CRM (customer relationship management). A great guide to considerations for pursuing a CRM solution and implementation.

Enterprise One to One: Tools for Competing in the Interactive Age by Don Peppers and Martha Rogers, Ph.D, 1999. Price $15.95. Peppers and Rogers expand on their marketing classic, *The One to One Future*. By treating customers differently and engaging in learning relationships, you can transform the profitability of your current customers one at a time. The book is full of case studies and instruction on how to leverage technology to realize mass customization.

Loyalty.com: Customer Relationship Management in the New Era of Internet Marketing by Frederick Newell, 2000. Price $29.95. Updating his 1997 book *The New Rules of Marketing*, *Loyalty.com* makes the case that standard loyalty programs produce the least loyal customers. Instead of piling enticements and incentives on customers, leverage technology to offer relevant and specific offers based on the knowledge of an individual customer.

Mastering Data Mining: The Art and Science of Customer Relationship Management by Michael J. A. Berry and Gordon Linoff, 1999. Price $44.99. Using numerous case studies, this book outlines how to use data-mining strategies to improve your marketing plans and increase sales. In addition, the authors use illustrations from numerous industries and review the use of popular tools. This is a great book for business managers beginning to explore data mining.

The One to One Future: Building Relationships One Customer at a Time by Don Peppers and Martha Rogers, Ph.D., 1997. Price $17.95. From the pioneers of relationship marketing, this is the book that launched the one-to-one movement. *One to One* focuses on share of customer vs. the traditional share of marketing. By learning to engage in dialogue with customers, one at a time, you can build loyalty that results in long-term opportunities for highly profitable relationships.

The One to One Manager: Real-World Lessons in Customer Relationship Management by Don Peppers and Martha Rogers, Ph.D., 1999. Price $21.95. In *The One to One Manager*, Peppers and Rogers walk you through how to specifically implement their principles of relationship management. Using real-world examples, "take-home" value that can be acted upon is revealed through interviews with executives and the people on the front lines that deliver the service.

Permission Marketing: Turning Strangers into Friends, and Friends into Customers by Seth Godin and Don Peppers, 1999. Price $24.00. Seth Godin, one of the foremost online promoters, argues that businesses can no longer rely solely on traditional forms of "interruption advertising" in magazines and mailings or radio and television commercials. A long-term relationship can result when a customer volunteers his or her time. "By talking only to volunteers, Permission Marketing guarantees that consumers pay more attention to the marketing message," he writes.

Relationship Marketing: New Strategies, Techniques and Technologies to Win the Customers You Want and Keep Them Forever by Ian H. Gordon, 1998. Price $34.95. This book provides a step-by-step guide for implementing a relationship-marketing program in your organization; supplies tools for measuring results; and explores the practical role of technology as a key enabler in successful relationship marketing. And just as importantly, it discusses the hottest new spin on relationship marketing—relationship management, or the forging of relationships with investors, suppliers, and employees, as well as customers.

Relationship Marketing: Successful Strategies for the Age of the Customer by Regis McKenna, 1993. Price $17.00. McKenna elaborates on the concept of relationship "infrastructure" marketing. This book is geared for those in the technology field as it describes the steps in bringing technology products to the marketplace. This book is relevant in today's high-tech market.

Strategic Customer Care: An Evolutionary Approach to Increasing Customer Value and Profitability by Stanley A. Brown, 1999. Price $34.95. This book fully explains the three stages in the evolution of customer care. Readers will be guided through the process of acquiring customers, retaining them through segmentation and management of the relationship, and targeting their most significant marketing efforts to the most profitable segments.

Streetwise Relationship Marketing on the Internet by Roger C. Parker, 2000. Price $17.95. This book explains why many one-to-one efforts fail: complexity of the relationship marketing plans. As an alternative to complex personalization schemes, in *Streetwise Relationship Marketing on the Internet* Parker proposes a simple, easily implemented five-stage Customer Development Cycle. The stages include: (1) Awareness, (2) Comparison, (3) Transaction, (4) Reinforcement, and (5) Advocacy. The goal is to provide different information to customers at each of the five stages.

Welcome Back e-Loyalty: How to Keep Customers Coming Back to Your Website by Ellen Reid Smith, 2000. Price $26.00. A comprehensive guide for creating a successful website that delivers repeat customers.

Websites

There are several websites that provide additional support and ideas for creative ways to build customer chemistry.

- www.customerchemistry.net. This site provides sample tools and forms used by various companies referenced in *Customer Chemistry*. In addition, companies can share their chemistry-building strategies with the authors and other companies.
- www.peppersrogers.com. The ultimate authority on relationship marketing, this site provides a complimentary one-to-one newsletter, resources, and schedules for upcoming relationship marketing events.
- www.inc.com. *Inc* magazine's award-winning website provides online business building articles, advice, free tools, and complimentary guides on dozens of marketing topics.

Data Mining

Creating customer chemistry is a customer-focused approach to increasing sales and profitability by concentrating on creating unique relationships with individual customers. Instead of selling a single product to as many customers as possible, the development of chemistry means selling a single customer many products or services over a long period of time and across product and service lines.

The key is to know all of your customers so that you can strategically plan your chemistry-creation efforts. This starts with data capture. Capitol Concierge started with pen and paper, migrated to a DOS system, and now is unleashing the power of the Web.

Companies are turning to data warehousing, automated call centers, websites, and integrated applications. Now small- to medium-size companies can harness the power of the Web by mining pieces of data—surveying customers and gathering information about them—in order to prompt customers to buy more and to tailor services that will keep them coming back. When Capitol Concierge started its data-capture journey, powerful software tools were out of the company's reach due to large price tags. Over the past few years, countless new affordable, Internet-based tools have been developed. Currently, no single product or solution can address all of our personalization goals. However, all the components are out there. The challenge is to understand what each of the tools can do and then integrates them correctly.

Securing Customer Feedback

Good chemistry starts with listening. The only way that you can ever truly learn about your customers is to give them the opportunity to tell you what they want, listen, and then apply what you learn. Several technology companies have developed tools to help you listen to your customers—from conducting surveys and online questionnaires to tracking customer click stream.

WebTrends

If you have a high-traffic website, WebTrends offers complex website analytics. WebTrends provides solutions that enable its customers to manage and enhance the success of e-business initiatives, including Internet infrastructure, e-commerce strategies, and e-marketing activities. Today, companies invest a lot of time and money in building Internet sites and there is a high expectation for significant returns on that investment. WebTrends products help companies manage an array of areas including eBusiness intelligence, eBusiness systems management, and eBusiness security. Most of its customers are Fortune 500 companies and their products are used by executives as well as marketing and sales managers. WebTrends products address all four key e-business management needs in addition to addressing hardware issues relating to software such as proxy servers, firewalls, e-mail servers, and database systems.

- eBusiness Intelligence products analyze users' activities including how much time they are spending on websites and what they are viewing through unique reporting methods. The information gathered is then used by content managers, marketing departments, and business managers to help them streamline the online processes.
- eBusiness Systems Management from WebTrends helps you check items on your site such as broken links, HTML syntax problems, and download times. This product is an application that monitors servers, routers, etc.
- eBusiness Security applications focus on security issues such as firewalls and security vulnerabilities.

In addition, WebTrends offers training and technical support. Some of its clients include Dell Computers, DoubleClick, Microsoft, Netscape, Xerox, and several other Fortune 500 companies.

WebTrends Headquarters
851 SW 6th Avenue, Suite 1200
Portland, OR 97204
Phone: 503-294-7025
Fax: 503-294-7130
www.webtrends.com

NetGenesis

NetGenesis is a provider of e-customer intelligence through its software and consulting services. The main product is NetGenesis 5, a suite of software products that determines and analyzes customer behavior. Companies using NetGenesis 5 can predict and anticipate visitor usage patterns. Currently, more than 450 customers use the product. Netgenesis's products include:

- e-Customer Relationship Management (eCRM) service and solutions enable the logical analysis of data collected to better understand customer interactions.
- InfraLens, a reporting system
- NetGenesis Developer's Kit (NDK), a kit to allow for the integration of a third-party platform
- CartSmarts, for interactive reporting
- E-Metrics Vision Engine, a data-mining module
- Activator, an extension module

NetGenesis's customers include Bear, Stearns & Co.; 3Com; Delta Airlines; Lotus; and Visa International.

NetGenesis Headquarters
One Alewife Center
Cambridge, MA 02140
Phone: 617-665-9200
Toll free: 800-982-6351
Fax: 617-665-9299
www.netgen.com

Accrue
Accrue is a provider of eBusiness analytic solutions for visitor response to websites. Its products help companies build long-term customers by providing a description of customer behavior patterns. Currently, Accrue has over 550 customers including Federal Express, WebVan, Knight-Ridder, Wal-Mart and Deutsche Telekom. All products can be customized to meet a company's requirements.

- Accrue Insight 5 Datasheet is a comprehensive analytic solution for optimizing visitor response. It analyzes Internet marketing campaigns, content effectiveness, e-commerce merchandising, and affiliate programs. It is a flexible solution and its four modules can be tailored for the client. The software licensing for Insight begins at $425,000 and the total price varies depending on the client's needs.

- Accrue Hit List is an enterprise solution that provides an analysis of both online and legacy data. Hit List generates custom reports and is fully flexible. The licensing costs for Hit List are $15,000.
- Accrue Decision Series determines the behavior, tastes, and preferences of the visitors from a distance.
- Accrue Neovista Suite of products is for retail clients.
- Accrue Pilot Suite is a platform for defining and deploying business intelligence applications for corporate networks.

Accrue Software, Inc. Headquarters
48634 Milmont Drive
Fremont, CA 94538
Phone: 510-580-4500
Toll free: 888-4-ACCRUE
Fax: 617-374-1110
www.accrue.com

Managing Customer Contacts

Software programs exist that can pull together a wide range of customer information based on how they interact with the company—through meetings, online, telephone inquires, sales and/or buying services, and products.

Kana

Kana is a provider of enterprise relationship management (eRM) solutions. Its products provide comprehensive applications for managing relationships between customers, management, and partners. Kana integrates three components of relationship management—marketing, sales, and service—activities across multiple channels. Kana seamlessly combines all channels of communication on the Web, including e-mail, chat, instant messaging, and voice either on the phone or over the Internet. Kana currently has more than 700 customers including Cicso, Chase Manhattan Bank, Yahoo!, and Northwest Airlines.

Kana's solution gives its clients control over how they learn about their customers. Through personalized Internet portals, its software provides information about every interaction in a customer's life cycle. In terms or eBusiness Applications, Kana Service helps the entire company manage the customer activities throughout the company and Kana Commerce, a personalized shopping helper. Its eBusiness Platform includes Kana Conduits, a system whereby CRM applications can be linked with Kana's communication applications, and Kana Studio, software that helps you develop new applications easily to meet demands. The following products are part of the communications applications.

- eBusiness Platform, a Web-based technology that seamlessly integrates with legacy applications
- Kana Connect, direct marketing software that helps users personalize communications to customers
- Kana Advisor, a quasi-virtual assistant that helps you with customer transactions and helps you provide the best options to the customer
- Kana Realtime Communication Channels, software that allows for live interaction with online customers through instant messaging, voice, or chat
- Kana Response, an e-mail response–management tool that can help you manage the tons of incoming e-mails
- Kana Classify, software that helps with efficiency

Kana Headquarters
181 Constitution Drive
Menlo Park, CA 94025
Phone: 650-614-8300
Fax: 650-614-8301
www.kana.com

Siebel

Ranked by *Fortune* magazine as third among the "100 Fastest Growing Companies," Siebel is a leading provider of eBusiness applications and tools. Siebel has a wide range of products and services for all of your

Internet and marketing needs. Its dot-com applications enable its clients to leverage the Internet in obtaining new customers and maintaining quality relationships. Siebel's products identify, develop, and customize program service offerings to meet clients' needs. In addition, Siebel has a call center application that has state-of-the-art technology that meets the highest demands of today's customer service world. The call center applications are automated and easy to use and include comprehensive Web-based architecture.

Siebel Systems, Inc. Headquarters
2207 Bridgepointe Parkway
San Mateo, CA 94404
Phone: 650-295-5000
Toll free: 800-647-4300
Fax: 650-295-5111
www.siebel.com

PeopleSoft (formerly Vantive)

PeopleSoft acquired Vantive and through its relationship offers applications that help companies with back-end applications as well as products that help manage customer relationships. Currently more than 900 companies all over the world are using Vantive applications. Some CRM customers are GTE, CyberCash Inc., and Novell, Inc., who use the applications for a wide range of activities from managing entire customer support processes to reducing call times.

- PeopleSoft CRM 8 is a solution that helps companies maximize acquisition efforts. The PeopleSoft CRM 8 achieves quality goals, streamlines processes, and increases sales and productivity, all through a closed-loop system.
- Vantive eBusiness applications provide customer relationship management that automates companies' sales forces and reduces costs.
- Vantive 8.5, a CRM architecture system designed with Java integration, is very versatile and supports pure-browsers and other clients. Vantive's product is offered as part of PeopleSoft's suite of end-to-end eBusiness solutions.

PeopleSoft, Inc. Headquarters
4460 Hacienda Drive
Pleasanton, California, 94588-8618
Phone: 925-225-3000
Toll free: 800-380-SOFT (7638)
Fax: 925-694-4444
www.peoplesoft.com

Personalized Ad Targeting

Services that serve up and track advertising across a network of sites. The companies below monitor who is clicking on the ads, how often, and whether the ads convert to sales. Profiles can also be developed that include information on demographics, tastes, or e-mail addresses to improve targeting and response.

Engage

Engage helps its customers with personalized ad targeting through new media techniques, analytical tools, ad management, and a knowledge database.

- Engage Media, customization of the right media and the Web to deliver the online objectives
- Engage Business Media, a business-to-business advertising solution that includes targeted e-mails and advertising
- Engage AdKnowledge, a profile database
- Engage Enabling Technologies
- Engage Software, closed-loop permission-based marketing solutions

Engage Inc. Headquarters
100 Brickstone Square, 3rd Floor
Andover, MA 01810
Phone: 978-684-3884
Toll free: 877-U-ENGAGE
Fax: 978-684-3636
www.engage.com

Customer Service

This software enables those with e-commerce and content sites to automatically reply, route, and segment e-mails so companies can more accurately respond to customers.

NewChannel

NewChannel is a hosted service that allows salespeople to proactively contact the hottest prospects on their website. NewChannel analyzes the behavior of visitors on corporate websites, determines how that visitor is behaving, alerts the sales staff to the presence of a new prospect, and engages the sales team with the prospect while he or she is on the site. Users benefit through shorter sales cycles, increased revenue, higher conversion rates, and lower customer acquisition costs. Some of NewChannel's clients include GE and Cable & Wireless.

NewChannel Headquarters
370 Convention Way
Redwood City, CA 94063
Phone: 650-261-9500
Fax: 650-261-0473
www.newchannel.com

Avaya

Avaya helps companies increase customer loyalty through communications systems and software for enterprises. Its main products include voice, converged voice and data, customer relationship management, messaging, multiservice networking, and structured cabling products and services.

It provides multimedia customer care and computer telephone applications, customer relationship management software, predictive dialing solutions and interactive voice response products. Its products include CRM Central 2000 intelligent work management software; CentreVu routing, reporting, and Interactive Voice Response solutions for the front office contact center; ViewStar workflow management software; and the Mosaix Predictive Dialing System.

Avaya Headquarters
211 Mt. Airy Road
Basking Ridge, NJ 07920
Phone: 866-462-8292
www.avaya.com

Chordiant

Chordiant offers a unified CRM solution for companies that creates a single view for the customer including all of their transactions, integrates multichannel customer interactions, and delivers consistent business processes. Its CRM application enables e-mail, fax, and telephone interactions with ease. The Chordiant CCS is architecture that's set up to support multichannel customer interactions through telephone, e-mail, fax, Internet, and branch office activities. Like Synchrony, Chordiant's software provides a one-screen view and the history of the customer, which allows you to create long-term customer relationships. Some of Chordiant's customers include General Motors, MetLife, First USA Bank, and Lloyds TSB.

- ChorServices, software that links to legacy systems
- ChorObjects, a work-flow engine
- ChorApps, a real-time application to answer calls from multiple channels

Chordiant Software, Inc. Headquarters
20400 Stevens Creek Boulevard
Suite 400
Cupertino, CA 95014
Phone: 408-517-6100
Fax: 408-517-0270
www.chordiant.com

Data Analysis

Once data is captured, the learning begins by mining interaction data for hidden trends. These systems can be pricey. They enable the user to analyze information from legacy systems that companies already have in place.

E.piphany

E.piphany serves more than 300 companies in e-commerce, financial services, communications, consumer packaged goods, and technology through its intelligent customer interaction software. E.piphany delivers an integrated platform that provides Web-based analytics and CRM applications. Its applications are all Web-based, easy to use, and highly scalable. Most of its clients are Fortune 1000 companies and include Charles Schwab, Hewlett-Packard, and Nissan.

- E.5 System, a Web-based intelligent CRM solution that coordinates and unites in real time all inbound and outbound interactions with customers
- The Campaign Management product helps companies plan, execute, and analyze data from multichannel marketing campaigns. It's very flexible and has an opt-in and opt-out option built into the system for permission-based marketing ideas. This product allows you to create targeted and powerful campaigns.
- E.piphany has a campaign management for e-commerce that easily integrates with e-commerce servers such as ATG, Microsoft, and Vignette. In addition, E.piphany has campaign management for e-mail so that you can gain insight into users' preferences and respond immediately.
- Connected Sales offers sales teams a single view of the customer and his or her history through a Web-based application. All information is stored and then assigned to the appropriate team member(s).

E.piphany Headquarters
1900 South Norfolk Street
Suite 310
San Mateo, CA 94403
Phone: 650-356-3800
Fax: 650-356-3801
www.epiphany.com

Blue Martini

Blue Martini is a software company that provides enterprise-wide e-business applications to target, retain, understand, and interact with customers. The software can be used on the Web, in call centers, in stores, over wireless devices, or on trading exchanges. It provides both business-to-business and business-to-consumer software. Some of its clients include Levi Strauss & Co., Polaroid, Gymboree, Virgin Atlantic, and the Men's Warehouse.

Customer Interaction System that provides enterprise-wide applications to companies in retail, manufacturing, financial services, telecommunications, and distribution industries. This system consists of thirteen modules that can either be implemented together or individually to target products and content to customers.

Blue Martini offers a training program, 24/7-technical support, and consulting services.

Blue Martini Software Headquarters
2600 Campus Drive
San Mateo, CA 94403
Phone: 650-356-4000
Toll free: 800-BLUE MARTINI
Fax: 650-356-4001
www.bluemartini.com

MicroStrategy

MicroStrategy is a provider of a scalable architecture that offers a full range of e-business, business intelligence, and CRM requirements. Some of MicroStrategy's customers include eToys, Snap.com, Arthur Andersen, Ernst & Young, and Net Perceptions.

- MicroStrategy 7 is a platform that allows organizations to analyze large amounts of data and find answers to critical business questions. This platform analyzes raw data and creates solid information for the company so that it can become more efficient. It is an all-HTML solution with an XML-based architecture suitable for enterprise-wide solutions.

- The eCRM 7, eCRM 6, and the MicroStrategy Web Business Analyzer are applications for one-to-one marketing. They leverage large amounts of online and offline data, analyze it, and provide the company with valuable customer data to be used for customer retention.
- Business Analyzer is an application to generate sales and repeat visits.
- In addition to these products, MicroStrategy provides consulting, training, and support services.

MicroStrategy Headquarters
1861 International Drive
McLean, VA 22102
Phone: 703-848-8600
Toll free: 800-927-1868
Fax: 703-848-8610
www.microstrategy.com

E-Mail Direct Marketing

These services enable companies to rapidly deploy direct-response campaigns that would typically take weeks using traditional mail.

Responsys

Given the complicated nature of e-commerce infrastructure, Responsys has developed a fully integrated e-commerce platform for online direct marketing. The Responsys platform allows marketers to create and deploy online marketing campaigns that result in higher response rates and customer retention.

Responsys Interact for permission-based marketing and Responsys Jumpstart for template modules for marketing campaigns. Interact is a Web-hosted application that enables businesses to create, launch, and manage permission-based marketing campaigns. One unique feature of Responsys is the automatic one-click response whereby the customer clicks once to purchase, submit, or accept. Based on the response from the customer, Interact automatically generates a personalized response.

All of its products are easy to install and flexible so that companies of any size can use them.

Responsys Headquarters
2225 East Bayshore Road, Suite 100
Palo Alto, CA 94303
Phone: 650-858-7400
Toll free: 888-219-7150
Fax: 650-858-7401
www.responsys.com

Digital Impact

Digital Impact is the provider of other e-marketing solutions that help with customer acquisition, customer retention, and analysis. Its Customer Acquisition Solutions include Media Planning, Cooperative Marketing Solutions, and Viral Marketing Solutions. Digital Impact's Media Planning solution combines proven technology and expertise to effectively create customer-acquisition campaigns. Digital Impact's client roster includes Bloomingdale's, Citibank, Discover Card, Hewlett-Packard, Marriott, Travelocity, and Publishers Clearinghouse to name a few.

- In the Cooperative Marketing Solutions, Digital Impact allows you to intermingle with top-tier companies in the Email Exchange Network, a network of 43 companies that represent 73 million online shoppers. By using the Email Exchange Network, companies can decrease their customer-acquisition costs.
- Forward-to-a-Friend (FTAF) technology helps user to leverage best customers. User can even track usage and determine the most active customer recruiters. In addition to customer acquisition tools, Digital Impact offers customer retention tools to keep those customers in this competitive landscape. By using Digital Impact's customer retention tools, companies can up-sell, send targeted e-mail messages, create newsletters to inform customers of new products and services, and mine data.

- Analysis Solutions provides companies with research on individual clients that allows for determining the return on investment and effectiveness of marketing strategies.

Digital Impact Headquarters
177 Bovet Road
San Mateo, CA 94402
Phone: 650-356-3400
Toll free: 800-491-9320
Fax: 650-356-3410
www.digitalimpact.com

Annuncio

Annuncio provides an e-marketing platform to help its customers leverage the Internet and build long-term relationships. Annuncio's products allow you to manage customer interactions through e-mail, website, and traditional marketing channels through which you can maximize your customer relationships. In addition, you can build in-depth customer profiles and personalize all interactions. Its products are for consumers as well as those companies that are doing business-to-business sales. Some of Annuncio's clients include eBay, Netscape, Lucent, Ariba, Intuit, Dell Computers, and iVillage. Annuncio has offices throughout the country and in Germany.

- Annuncio Live, software to help customers automate their marketing campaigns
- Annuncio Bright, software to help clients with customer retention though e-merchandising and Web customization
- Annuncio GoTo, a hosting solution

Annuncio
2440 West El Camino Real, Suite 300
Mountain View, CA 94040
Phone: 650-314-6000
Toll free: 877-933-6060
Fax: 650-314-6100
www.annuncio.com

INDEX

Page numbers in *italics* refer to illustrations.

A-team approach, for ranking
customers, 31–32
Accrue, 211–12
Acquisitions, customer lists
and, 59
Active listening, training for,
49–50
Activity-based accounting
(ABC), 31
Adjacency, 28
Advanced Micro Devices
(AMD), 96
Advisory groups, customer,
168–69
Aims Logistics, 49
Akridge, John, 161
Alloy, Steven, 174–75, 178–79,
194
Alumni networks, 193
Anniversary circles, 85
Annuncio, 222
Artis & Associates, 105
Ascher, Susan, 20
Avaya, 216–17

BabyCenter, 116–17
Bad clients. *See* Dysfunctional
clients
Berry, Leonard, 139, 194
Best-customer profiles, 33–35
Best practices, Capitol
Concierge
for employees, 63–69
for rewarding customers,
139–41
for top-of-mind marketing,
113–15
Beverly Hall Furniture
Galleries, 46
Birthday clubs, 85
Bizrate.com, 91
Blanket purchase agreements
(BPAs), 180
Blue Martini, 219
Blue Mercury, 137
Boxtree Communications,
141–42, 144
Bright Horizons Family
Solutions, 120

British Airways, 116

Brusger, John, 117

B2B (business-to-business)
world, customers in,
25–27

Budget planners, 108

Buksbaum, Lisa, 141–42, 144

Business-to-business (B2B)
world, customers in,
25–27

Buzz, value of, 28–29

Call centers, 89

Capitol Concierge. *See also*
VIPdesk.com
best practices of, 63–69,
113–15
building relationships and,
159–62
customer contacts and,
75–77
customer rating and, 23–24
customer recognition at,
127–28, 139–41
dysfunctional clients and,
147–49, 158
employee training at, 43–45
inner circle of, 37
mass marketing at, 107–9
orientation and training
program at, *64–65*
putting out fires and, 17
recruiting at, 48
start-up of, 11–12
top-of-mind marketing at,
112, 113–15

Carbonell, Bob, 20, 48

Carroll, Bob, 27

Cash-flow approach, for
ranking customers, 27

Cause-related marketing, 194

Cavanaugh, 112

Cavanaugh, Pat, 120–21

C.B.&H. Parts Corporation,
165, 176–77

Centurione, Janene, 52, 100,
132

Chat, online
for customer contact, 78, 91
IRIS and, 91–93, 94

Checklists
for customer chemistry, 21
for customer contact, 105–6
for customer databases,
102–3
for dysfunctional clients,
158
for employees, 72–73
for ranking customers,
40–41
for reviewing relationships,
181
for rewarding customers,
145–46
for top-of-mind marketing,
124–25

Chordiant, 217

Chung, Luke, 15, 150

Cieri, Wanda, 139

Clarry, Maureen, 59–60,
100–101, 143, 155, 191

Client Service Cards, 75, 76

Clients. *See* Customers;
    Dysfunctional clients
Coalition loyalty programs,
    191–92
Communication plans, for
    customer chemistry,
    80–81
Concierge services, 184
Connect: The Knowledge
    Network, 59–60,
    100–101, 143, 155,
    190–91
Contribution margins, 40, *41*
Cormier, Ken, 15, 177–78,
    179–80
Corporate Communications
    Broadcast Network
    (CCBN), 79–80, 144,
    169, 175–76
Corporate Concierge Service
    Planner form, 67, *70–71*
Corson, Judy, 32
Creative Communications
    Consultants, 46–47
Crews Control, 136, 145, 164,
    173, 180, 193
Custom Research Inc. (CRI),
    32–33, 59, 136, 188–89
Customer advisory groups,
    168–69
Customer Care Institute, 93,
    99, 100
Customer care teams, 174–77
Customer chemistry. *See also*
    Relationship marketing
    checklist for, 21, 72–73

checkup quiz for, 195–97
communication plans for,
    80–81
contact checklist for,
    105–6
definition of, 1–3
embarking on, 188–91
knowing customers and,
    12–13
new economy and, 191–95
quest for, 19–21
rules for, 187–88
rules for building, 3–5
stumbling blocks to,
    16–19
as team effort, 62–63
training employees for,
    43–45
Customer contact. *See also*
    Touch points
    at Capitol Concierge,
    75–77
    checklist for, 105–6
    cost of, 93
    e-mail for, 78
    focus groups for, 82–84
    importance of each, 77–81
    managing, 212–15
    opportunities for, 82–88
    technology and, 88–91
Customer databases, 99–103
    questions to ask before
        investing in, 102–3
    Web-enabled, 104–5
Customer feedback, securing,
    209–12

Customer loyalty ladder,
35–36
Customer service
customer appreciation and,
138–39
software for, 216–17
Customer-specific employee
training, 50–51
Customers. *See also*
Dysfunctional clients;
Relationships
broadcasting top customers
to employees, 51–52
in B2B world, 25
encouraging compassion
for, 50
Five Ws of staying in touch
with, 163–66
getting to know, 13–16
life cycle of, 157–58
listening to, 49–50
personal preferences profile,
65, 66–67
profile forms for, 54–55
profiling, 33–35, 52–53
questions for would-be, 61
quizzes for, 5–9
ranking, 24–27
rewarding, 129–31, 137–39,
145–46. *See also*
Loyalty programs
sharing best-profiles of, with
employees, 52–53
special events for, 141–45
stumbling blocks to
knowing, 16–19

Data analysis, software for,
217–20
Data mining, 208–9
Databases
customer, 99–104
web-enabled customer,
104–5
D'Avanzo, Claudia Brooks,
46–47
Day-Timers Inc., 112
Detectives, teaching employees
to be, 56–60
Diamond Courier, 151–52, 191
Digital Impact, 221–22
Dominguez, Frank, 14–15, 168
Dreese, Mike, 117
Dysfunctional clients. *See also*
Customers; Relationships
at Capitol Concierge,
147–49, 158
checklist for, 158
circumstances for saying
good-bye to, 152–56
dealing with, 149–52
right ways to break up with,
156–57

E-mail, 15–16, 194
for checking relationships,
165
for customer contact, 78
direct marketing services for,
220–22
etiquette guidelines for,
119–21
event-based, 116–18

opt-in, 15–16
vs. snail mail, 119–21
E-mail clubs, 118–20
E-mail newsletters, 90
E-mail surveys, 98
ECHO (every contact has
    opportunity), 80
800 numbers, 79
80-20 rule, 23
Employee road trips, for
    checking relationships,
    173–74
Employee training. *See*
    Training, employee
Employees
    broadcasting top customers
        to, 51–52
    creating customer chemistry
        culture for, 45
    as detectives, 56–60
    finding caring, 46–48
    pillars for relationships
        with, 46
Engage, 215
E.piphany, 218
Etheridge, Maggie, 91–93, 94
Etiquette, e-mail, 119–21
Event-based e-mail, 116–18
Every contact has opportunity
    (ECHO), 80
Exit polls, 177–79

Face-to-face surveys, 97
Fallon McElligott, 34–35,
    60–61
Farley, Brian, 110–11

Fax surveys, 97
Feghali, Charles, 164
Fish Mart, 166, 172
5/5 rule, 99
Five Ws of staying in touch
    with customers, 163–66
FMS Inc., 15, 142, 149–50
Focus groups, for customer
    contact, 82–84
Focusing
    companies and, 18
    employees and, 60–62
Foot Nurse, 100
Forms. *See also* Reports
    best-customer profile,
        54–55
    client profile, 65
    Client Service Cards, 75, *76*
    Corporate Concierge Service
        Planner, 67–68, *71–73*
    Personal Preferences Profile,
        65, *66–67*
    Property Management
        Budget Planner, 65–67,
        68–69
Frequent-buyer clubs,
    84–85, 90
Frey, Joshua, 113, 142
Frontline Group, 120
Fulton Street.com, 89–90
Funtown Splashtown USA, 15,
    177–78, 179–80, 192

Gerbrandt, Michele, 36–39
Gilmore, Kelly, 59–60,
    100–101, 143, 155, 191

Giorgenti, Janine, 115–16
Glick, Patti, 100
Gordon, Mark, 166–67, 175
Grand Circle Corporation (GCC), 51, 81
Granny's Goodies, 91, 113, 142
Great American Marketing and Events (GAME), 28–29
Great Harvest Bread Company, 52, 100, 115, 132
Green Hills Farms, 101, 119, 132, 133–34, 144, 190
Green Mountain Energy, 169–70, 176

Harris, Wade, 80, 95, 139
Hawkins, Gary, 119, 133
Hurley, Sally, 184
Hux, Jerry, 46

Imperial Construction Group, 14, 168
Interstate Resources Group, 164
IRIS, 91–93, 94

Jensen, Joe, 156
John Akridge Company, 161
Johnson, Brian, 165

Kana, 212–13
Kane, Trish, 118–19
Keating, Andrea, 15, 136, 144–45, 164–65, 173, 180, 193

Kelly, Dennis, 169–70, 176
Kepler, Clark, 143, 164, 174
Kepler's Books, 143–44, 164, 173–74

Lambert, Art, 102
Leegin Creative Leather Products, 29
Leonard, Stew, Jr., 79, 89
Leveen, Steve, 119
Levenger, 119, 139
LexJet, 101–2
Lifetime value (LTV) approach, for ranking customers, 30–31
Listening to customers, 49–50
Little Nell Hotel, 122
Liz Claiborne Inc., 194
Loyalty programs. *See also* Customers
coalition, 191–92
for customers, 129–35, 146
legal issues for, 135
for service firms, 135–37
LTV (lifetime value) approach, for ranking customers, 30–31
Luker, Mike, 87

Mackay, Harvey, 13
Mackay 66 list of questions, 13
Mail Boxes Etc., 138
Mail surveys, 97

Marketing. *See also* Customer
   chemistry; Relationship
   marketing; Top-of-mind
   marketing
cause-related, 194
permission, 15–16
traditional vs. top-of-mind,
   122
Memory Makers magazine,
   36–39
Mergers, customer lists
   and, 59
MicroStrategy, 219–20
Miller, Dan, 135–36
Mission approach, for ranking
   customers, 29
Morfogen, Stratis, 90
Motoring Services Auto Repair,
   165

Nager, Alan, 195
Nelson, Dave, 49
Nelson, Ned, 49
NetGenesis, 210–11
New economy, customer
   chemistry and, 191–95
Newbury Comics, 117–19
NewChannel, 216
Newsletters, e-mail, 90
Next Monet, 87, 95
Nickelsen, Myrna, 87, 95
Nunley, Roger, 93, 100

Ohana Savers loyalty card
   program, 192

Online chat
   for customer contact, 78, 91
   IRIS and, 91–93, 94
Online customer feedback
   groups, 169–70
Online surveys, 96
Online top-of-mind marketing,
   115–19
Operations Associates, 195
Opt-in e-mail programs,
   15–16

Pain In The Ass (PITA)
   principle, 156
Parental Stressline, 49
Parker, Jeff, 79–80, 144, 169,
   175–76
PeopleSoft (Vantive), 214–15
Peppers, Don, 30
Permission marketing, 15–16
Personal Preferences Profile
   form, 65, *66–67*
Personalized Ad Targeting,
   215
Phase II, 80, 139
PITA (Pain In The Ass)
   principle, 156
Pope, Jeff, 32
Post, Claudia, 151–52, 191
Post, Peggy, 120
Post, Peter, 120
Postcard surveys, 85–86
PRConsultants Group, 192
Pride Mortgage Co., 110–11
Proactive service, 194

ProDriver Leasing Systems, 47,
172–73
Profiles, best-customer, 33–35
employees and, 52–53
forms for, *54–55*
ProFlowers, 50
Project-management programs,
28
Property Management Budget
Planner, 65–67, *68–69*
Public relations, customer
appreciation and, 138

Questions, asking critical,
166–68
Quizzes
for customer chemistry,
195–97
for customers, 5–9

Rainier, 28
Ranking, of customers, 24–27
A-team approach, 31–32
big-spender approach, 29
buzz-value approach, 28–29
cash-flow approach, 27
gross-margin approach,
29–30
lifetime-value approach,
30–31
mission approach, 29
payoffs from, 39–40
venture-capital approach,
27–28
References, 86
Reid, Laura, 172

Relationship marketing, reading
list for, 205–8. *See also*
Customer chemistry
Relationships
asking critical question for,
166–69
building, at Capitol
Concierge, 159–62
in changing economy,
162–63
checklist for, 181
creating own economic
indicators for, 179–80
customer advisory groups
for, 168–69
customer care teams for,
174–77
employee road trips for,
173–74
exit polls for, 177–79
methods for monitoring,
160–61
online customer feedback
groups for, 169–70
stages of, 186–87
taking pulse of, 163–66
touch base calls for, 170–73
using e-mail for checking,
165
Relocation Management
Resources (RMR), 20, 48
Reports. *See also* Forms
customer activity, 57
share of customer, 57, *58*
Responsys, 220–21
Ries, Al, 18

RightNow Technologies, 37, 136

Road Runner Sports, 132, 137

Road trips, for checking relationships, 173–74

Rockford Construction, 62, 86

Rogers, Martha, 30

Roth, Ben, 143

Roth Staffing, 143

St. Paul Saints, 51, 82, 132

Sallee, Marguerite, 120

Sam Whitmore's Media Survey, 170–72

Sather, Andrew, 28

Satisfaction surveys, 95

Schecter, Eric, 28–29

Schmus, Christopher, 47, 173

Scope-of-work overlay, 149

Scrapbooks, customer, 63

ScriptSave, 50–51

Semiannual tracking studies, 176

Siebel, 213–14

Signal of silence, 160

Simpkins, Ron, 102

Skyline Displays, 84

Smed International, 51, 142–43

Smith, Kimball, 112

Snail mail, vs. e-mail, 119–21

SoftAdGroup, 47–48

Special events, for customers, 141–45

Springfield Remanufacturing Corp., 51, 142

Stanley Martin Companies, 174–75, 178–79, 194

Starbucks, 18

Status quo mode, stuck in, 18–19

Stew Leonard's, 79

Strauss, Bill, 50

Sunny Fresh Foods, 87

Surveys
    for customer contact, 82
    methods for, 96–98
    postcard, 85–86, 90
    role of customer satisfaction, 95
    use of professionals for conducting, 95–96

Synergy Networks, 166–67, 175

Technology, customer contact and, 88–91

Telephone surveys, 97, 99

TelStrat International, 27

Teltronix Information Systems, 156

10/30/60 formula, 123–24

Thank-you notes, 85

Timbuk2, 120

Toll-free phone numbers, 79

Tompkins, Paula George, 48

Tooley, C. B., Jr., 176

Top-of-mind marketing, 108.
    See also Marketing
    budgeting for, 123–24
    at Capitol Concierge, 112, 113–15
    checklist for, 124–25

customer-chemistry
 approach to, 109–10
event-based e-mail for,
 116–18
online, 115–19
personal approach to,
 110–11
timing and, 111–13
vs. traditional marketing,
 122
value-added services and,
 121–22
Touch base calls, 170–73
Touch points, 79. *See also*
 Customer contact
Training, employee
 for active listening, 49–50
 at Capitol Concierge, 43–45,
 64–65
 customer-specific, 50–51
 to "get it," 48–51
 for role of detective, 56–60

Unique Eugene program, 192
USAA, 80

Value-adding, top-of-mind
 marketing and, 121–22
Vantive (PeopleSoft), 214–15
Venture-capital approach, for
 ranking customers, 27–28
VIP programs, 85
VIPdesk.com, 184–86. *See also*
 Capitol Concierge

Web-enabled customer
 databases, 104–5
Websites
 for building customer
 chemistry, 208
 for obtaining customer
 feedback, 90
 surveys, 98
WebTrends, 209–10
Wheeler, John, 62
Whitmore, Sam, 170–72

Zagat Survey, 170
Zane, Chris, 13
Zane's Cycles, 13
Zimmerman, Mark, 13–14, 115

ABOUT THE AUTHORS

Mary Naylor, CEO and Founder, Capitol Concierge, Inc. and VIPdesk, Inc.

Mary Naylor is founder and chief executive officer of VIPdesk, Inc. and Capitol Concierge, Inc., companies that help busy people get things done through on-site concierge staffing and real-time Web-based coordination of personal and convenience services.

Through Naylor's business instincts and perpetual drive, VIPdesk has grown since 1997 to be the leading personal concierge service with more than ten million users. Naylor has raised $11.8 million in venture-capital funding and is rapidly expanding the business.

Prior to developing VIPdesk, Naylor created and grew Capitol Concierge Inc., the nation's first and largest corporate concierge service with tailored programs for more than eighty commercial office buildings, from an idea and $2,000 to annual revenues of more than $5 million in annual sales. The company's phenomenal success and vision were recognized by *Inc* magazine's cover story in October 1995.

She has received numerous awards for her work including *Inc* 500, 1997 Entrepreneur of the Year Finalist, and 1997 *Inc* National Marketing Masters Award for Business Services. VIPdesk was ranked twenty-ninth out of the Fast 50 by *Washington Techway Magazine*, and Naylor was awarded the 2001 Entrepreneurial Excellence Award from *Working-Woman* magazine for Original Product and Service.

Susan Greco, Senior Writer, *Inc* Magazine

Susan Greco has spent twelve years at *Inc* magazine in Boston, where she began as an intern and worked her way up to senior writer. A number of her stories on sales and marketing and other topics have made the cover of *Inc*. In addition, several of her pieces have been featured on the website of the *Wall Street Journal*. Susan is a native of Miami, graduated from Boston University, and now lives with her husband, Doug, and sons Christopher and Casey in North Andover, Massachusetts. She is a proud aunt to Christine, Anthony, Ben, Kelly, Amy, Elizabeth, Alex, Anna, Sophia, Jake, and Samuel.